REMINISCENCE

I'm a well, travelled horse

But, now I feel old!

It's about a horse, his right to life, the friend's he made, and, how he met them. The hardships, he endured and overcame. The air he breathes, and the life, he's learned to love. This is his story, this, is Faustino.

FXXV11

For the Preservation of World Wildlife

'A friend, is a fine thing.'

INTRODUCTION

Birth is beautiful, it's what happens afterwards that shapes us.

The Andalusian, foal is fascinated by the spider. The speed of his legs, the sheen on his spine, and the web of string, he can so quickly climb. The foal snuggles and sighs, into his mother, sleep arrives. But, the silence is broken by shouting and banging. Breakfast is brought in for mother. The man is bored and wipes cob webs from the Wall. Web tissue torn in two, the spider falls to the floor. He scurries away and reaches a corner, for now, he is safe.

A field of fashion, immoral transaction

An inbuilt clock, four matching socks

Presence and pressure, pain and leisure

tracking and training, shooting and aiming

Winter glory, what's the story

A bib or brace, blanket and trace

Spurs and boots, nose and twitch

Carrots or apples, my lucky dip

Feathers and whiskers, bucket and whip

Auctions and dealers, lorries without grain

Oh, for some peace, just no more pain

Some seasonal class, but, will it last.

Faustino

Oxygen engulfed my throat, where there it loitered, like a half sunken boat. Then as if by magic, into my lungs it did float. The sight of a spider, strands of straw, these, were the first things, that I saw. I shivered in the early morning cold, instinctively, searched for a sister or brother. Instead, I consumed, the sweet smell of mother, all white hair and legs, she swayed over the water bucket, like a buoyant peg. Steadily, she shuffled closer, laid back down, cradled and cleaned my head. An angel without wings, oh, how my heart did sing.

"Jet black, Ophelia did well!" I was only hours old when my door clanged open. There it was, that human smell that brought fear to mother, but bravery as well. I felt tensions grow, and into my nostrils, sweat and leather did flow. The man crouched before us on his calves. Spurs spinning, they echoed into my ears. Fascinated, his piggy eyes, button fastened to mine.

"C'mon, little fella, stand up." Nicotine breath numbed my nose.

The man slapped mother, and though exhausted, up she got. Back on his feet, the tip of his boot tapped my hooves. Awaiting activity, he stared into space. Web spotted, he tore it down, and like paper in two. Twice the legs I had, my spider fell and escaped across the floor. Sightless, towards the man, mother had only me in mind. I felt a second prompt. Endeavouring to unhinge my legs, I jelly rocked onto my knees. Another kick, and I shot like a tortoise, back into my shell. Hooves tucked under my chest, I stumbled, like a half-filled sack onto my side. Animals all done, the other man arrived.

"Right on the count of three..." He had a real gruff accent.

Together, they hoisted me onto my hooves. Ears envelope flat, mother urged me to stay upright. Heeding her warning, I skated, like Bambi on ice, out of the barn, and into the baking heat. Squinting and shaking eye flies, I finally found my feet and fumbled after mother. The paddock, I say paddock, the baron enclosure, offered only an olive shrub for shelter. A better option, I, took cover underneath mother's front legs. There, her belly, shielded me from the sun. A parched pancake, the surrounding land was vast. Dotted in the distance, rooted like face freckles, horses shied from the sun.

"Pass me the spanner."

The men fixed a leaking tap beside the house. New valve fitted, they disappeared back into the barn. The sound of clips, buckles and bolts echoed. Then, out of the doors, a black stallion shunt shuffled forward. Tied up like a turkey, the horse was covered in adjustable aids. Behind him, clasping two strips of sun burnt leather, one of the men ordered him onwards.

"Get up Monty!" A whip tightly tucked between his finger and thumb, the man, fly flicked the horses back. a leather cord hitting water, the clack was loud. Head restricted, the horse jerked gingerly forward. "Shame, the foal won't stay this velvet black." Unable, to point, the man thrust his head, towards the hop scotching hind of the stallion.

"Different breeds that's all...!" The man, beside him tightened his bandana. "Andalucía's have an antidote to darkness!" He laughed.

"Hard to imagine, Monty, was once snow white." The trainer motioned his burnt leather reigns towards the rump of the horse.

"Or that the little runt, will one day become swan white like his mum." The referral to me, was rude. "Bit of magic aye!" Laughing, the man helping straightened his bent roll up, ran ahead of the horse, and kicked the schooling gate next to us open.

Camouflaged against the ground, two tan dogs leapt up. Almost as big as me, the barking made the stallion start stalling.

"Get back!" One boot showering them in sand, the hands-free man ditched his fag and rushed the dogs.

Doing one, they both retreated behind a rickety fence, from there, they sat attentively. The black stallion went up on two legs, fronts pawing the air, retaliation was resumed. The whip at work, it came down. Clack…Left reign, tighter than the other it tore his mouth. Another clout, and I saw the stallions flesh swell like yeast. A surge forward, and both men yanked on the silver bit. Elbows drawn, knees bent, they forced the horse to sit. While one, held the reins, the other opened a satchel. Sides heaving, the uncomfortable horse, was stock still. Improvising, the satchel man, put a contraption over the bridle and tightened something to its head piece. Cups clipped either side of his eyes, the horse may as well of been wearing binoculars.

"Try him now, Jake."

Ahhh, a name at last... Reins loosened, the horse lumbered to his feet. Jake ruffled the tatty leather, and like a hunter pointing two rifles, made the horse implement his tools.

"Long reigns..."

I glanced up to find fire in her face.

"Sorry you had to see such things, so soon." Mother, Knew, we didn't have long. Not wanting to spoil my freedom, she quietly closed her eyes. Her energy was edgy, her sorrows, crystal clear. I didn't probe or delve, for it would only cause her more anguish. Aggravated, by the metal band, biting his nose, the stallion gave in. Pressure points, speered, I cringed at such cruelty. After two hours of army tight training. Congealed blood on his muzzle, blinkers lopsided like broken glasses, Monty, ground to a sweaty halt. Hounds on his heels, the horse was led back to the house. Buckles undone, his naked body glistened abuse. The shower washed many things away. Dignity, blood and foam, just a few of the liquids that lacquered the ground. The soaked and broken horse was then taken back into the barn.

"Damn their medieval tactics!" Unable to contain herself, mother, was furious.

Hungry, and in need of comfort, I suckled on milk. Mother's lunch however, came over the fence in the form of straw. A pitiful offering, it wasn't worth her rushing. Not wanting to breach, my belly shade, I duck waddled to keep up. Steps quickening, my legs fox trotted, beneath my canopy. Mission achieved, her sides heaved from the heat. Grinding and munching, I heard her stomach rumble, a few seconds later waves, bubble and ripple. Stood like two tin soldiers, swirling inside the trough appeared to amuse the men. Inquisitive, I tottered over and stood before it. Thumb over its end, one of the two men, pointed a plastic nozzle at my nose. Aiming, he released his finger and pelted my face. A minute later the hose was directed downwards. Traumatized, I watched foggy waves, reach the waterline. Straw finished, mother came closer. Respect shown, the men removed the hose. Thirsty, she bent her beautiful neck, and drank from clean settled clouds.

"You did well, old girl, just swell!"

In the ripples, mother observed their reflections. The beard stubble and shirt stains that fitted them and their attitudes, like gloves. They nodded to her, then laughed at me. From his satchel, Jake, retrieved a pair of hand cuff hoops. A reaction in mind, he raised them up. Ears collapsed, mouth dripping water like something from the depths of Lock Ness, mother, was mad. Intimidated, she bit and snapped at the air. Evading her teeth, the two men increased the water pressure and pelted her face. There was barking, and loud neighing from inside the barn. Several more supporting sounds from the corral behind the house. Mother made off towards the far fence. Tottering after her, I went back beneath her belly. There, I shied, into my shoulders.

"What was that about?"

Mother flicked a forelock of flies to one side, and if I'm not mistaken, a tear too. She fell silent, but her brain, I could hear beat. Evasive, her eyes scanned the land, and all that was out there. She took a big sigh, before glancing back down at me.

"Nothing you need be concerned with. Yet..." She whispered.

The temperature dropped, and we were taken back into the barn. Unlike the others, chained to the wall, we were privileged, and put in our stable. Door made of bars, I was able to watch them from behind it. Going under their necks, and weaving around the horses, one of them spilt grain into a feed sink they shared. Rations to small, the horses stamped their feet for more. But, the men shouted for law and order, and as hungry as they were, the horses ate, amicably. On the end, stood Monty, the stallion from earlier. Pride prickled, mouth hurting, he didn't eat. Counting those tied beside him, I made it fifteen in total. Mother was given a bucket, once I'd examined the oats, she busied herself eating them. Only a small wall either side of us, a goat appeared on my left and made me jump. Hooves hooked tightly to its top, she balanced on her back legs.

"I thought they'd have given you some straw," she said to mother, "if, only, for his sake."

"Straw is food," over-heard, the goat attracted the attention of a mare. Neck twisting as far as the chain would allow, she rolled the white of her eyes.

"It's about time," another added, "that they brought the tractors in too." Legs buried in stone cold muck, it squelched.

"It doesn't look nice." I sounded meek, "not one bit."

7

"Think yourself lucky you can lie down!" The goat disappeared down her side of the wall.

Indeed, those chained, had no alternative but to stand side by side. And I could neither imagine, or want to know, how that felt. Evening entered my bones. Chilly, I collapsed on the ground. I didn't have to wait long for mother to join me. Like a big woollen blanket, I suddenly felt safe and warm within her wraps. I looked up, and saw for the first time that the roof, had squares of Perspex in it. A cheap form of lighting, it also made an exceedingly grand theatre, from which the stars thrashed the sky. Fascinated, I fell asleep counting them. It was the cold floor that woke me. Mother no longer close, I squinted about for her. The moon offered me her silhouette. Stood before the water bucket, it sounded as though she was drinking through a broken straw. She, gurgle, gulped. Tick tock, her brain heaved, harder than a clock. I think it is correct to say, that I was witnessing stress, for the first time. From opposite, I heard splashing, shifty feet and unsettled horses rattling their chains. Mother returned, but I couldn't settle. I wanted questions answered, but, equally, I didn't want to upset her. As if reading my mind, she sang soothed.

"Twinkle, twinkle, little star, how I wonder how you are, up above the stars so bright..."

One eye on the fading stars, the other on her, I slipped back to sleep, for a bit anyway.

The sound of an engine grumbled outside the barn. Frozen, to their sloppy spots, apprehension arrived all around the horses. Doors pulled open and the lorry was backed in. With it, came a deathly energy that made the whole place stand grave yard still.

"Who's going...?" Nameless, entered and swung a rope in the air. A stupid look on his face, he examined mother and me.

"Ophelia's not old enough." Jake mused, "maybe, on the next load aye. Bring Bronte," he scratched the stubble on his chin while batting his eyes back and forth over the line up, "the old bay, that chestnut too."

Closing his obedient mouth, nameless undid wall clips. Every link, an ice cube breaking, the chosen chains whacked the wall. Ropes fastened to head collars, the first of three mares, was backed up, and stood before the lorry. The chestnut dug her hooves in, but a third human came to help. Impatient, the driver tore a whip from the wall and pelted it across her spine. Two more clacks and she reluctantly, clambered up the ramp. Out of sight, mother expressed despair. She was about to speak, when a beautiful bay paused outside our door. Emotions, engrained in her face, the horse was ocean deep. A whack, and she too, was on the transport faster than Jake could click his lighter. My eyes pleaded for an answer.

"As bad as barn life might seem," Mother sounded bleak, "Lorries, mean unknown routes and under hand men…" She bit her muzzle shut.

Last in line slow and struggling, the anguish of the ageing horse saddened me. A scuffle of hooves and the ramp was slammed shut. Private prisoners in a dark box. Journey unknown, there was no undoing destiny's knot. Their departing brought silence and pity. But mother was on the next load. The gaps in the line-up concerned me. The pit of my stomach became weak and watery. An unset blancmange, wobbling without the support of sprinkles, I glared up in search of the goat. And just like that, there she was.

"If any are in luck," she sighed, "replacements, will come off the flatlands."

I frowned, but not wanting to say anymore, she shrugged, unhitched her hooves and let go of the wall again. From inside the lorry, hooves stumbled and voices, whined. Stars only just fading, dawn, was waiting to take over the night shift. An envelope exchanged, the men shook the drivers hand and bid him goodbye. A mechanical cough, dust pools of diesel, and the lorry danced into day. Jake unravelled the money and counted it. Unable to control my bladder, I felt urine on my fur and the stench of our stable suddenly hit me. I stood, I stared, I examined everyone, but there was only distress. The lorry had gone, but oh goodness, to where?

"Valencia...!" The dogs came in and made things clear.

"How do you know?" I could tell, mother didn't trust the dogs.

"We hear everything from outside the house."

"But where..." The goat ribbed the dogs, "where in Valencia?"

"Bull ring is what we heard."

Agonising muffles filled the air. Enveloped in equine questions, my head was a spinning top.

Cheesy

Sun up, both the men started turning out horses, beginning with Monty, the black stallion. Only, when the place was empty, did Jake open our door. A dirty roll up in his mouth, he waved us out. Prickled in protest, mother barged past him and through the big doors. I was right on her tail, when, 'nameless,' got hold of my neck. Wrestled, to the ground, he gave me a playful punch. Legs going like soft spaghetti, my heart trying to leave my chest, Jake checked my hooves and legs while I was down. Once done, I scuffled onto all fours and fled outside. It was smoky, and the smell, was just foul. Cheesy fried feet that had been left to fester for too long. Something, like that anyway. On the other side of the smoke, I saw, and ran to mother.

"It's the farrier." she flicked a thicket of hair out of her eyes, "better known as the foot trimmer." Fringe free, she focused on me!

Opening our gate, nameless, shooed us inside. The foot trimmer must have arrived quickly after the theft truck. Well, in my eyes, it was theft. Theft of stability, friendship, and their home. Visions of those poor horses travelling in the heat, hurt me deeply. Pleased to escape foot persecution, I wandered over to my trough. The heat was stifling and with every gulp, I felt guilt. For even at my age, I knew, there would be no drink agenda, along their route. Smoke subsided, and I could see Monty. The hammer made me cringe. Each time it hit his foot, my head made a half circle jolt. Job done, Monty was put in the paddock beside us.

"Did it hurt?" Mounted on four silver slippers, I could do nothing but stare.

"Sore, aren't they?" Mother moved closer to the post and rails separating us.

"When, cut this short, yes!" Monty flexed his fetlocks.

"Idiots!" Mother was furious. "And they will expect you to pull. Want their monies worth without a doubt!"

Before I could quiz either party, something arrived from around the back of the house. Dogs barking at the wheels, the men dragged it onto the front drive. Plonked down, it tilted forward. Wow, it was pretty. Maybe, they were going to sunbath in it? I didn't know. I only knew that when it was upright, it was a beautifully made wheel chair. Spines leant upon its seat, the men rested, they laughed. Addressing a smelly old roll up between them, it went back and forth.

"What's a bull ring?" There, I had said it.

"Better than a slaughter house!" Monty, barked, shooting mother a shifty stare at the same time.

"Slaughter house? Bull ring!" I sat like a dog. I didn't know what either was, wasn't sure, I wanted to.

Just then a jeep came tearing through our gates. Jam packed with green cubes, it skidded to a halt before the house. Frightened, I shot under my belly shade. While I suckled milk, mother and Monty, watched them shake hands, and unload it, into the barn. Slightly bent, one of the bales escaped its string and scattered upon the ground. Scooped up, some was thrown to mother, the other bit to Monty. As if someone had just given mother a diamond, delight entered her eyes. Palatable, it smelt like summer candy floss. I went to take a mouthful, but mother said I was too little to digest it. For now, I was only allowed milk and soft substances. Mother was elegant beyond explanation, and like the sunshine, had an awesome aura. Beneath her fringe, outlined in charcoal, her blue eyes observed everything. Stocky but slim, the darker flecks on her neck opened into a fan of fetching dapples. Cobalt eyes and lashes, black hooves and legs to die for, she was stunning. I moved closer to the rustic posts and peeked in more detail at the chair. It had padded man seats and metallic wheels. A jack

Russell appeared and jumped into it. A minute later, a woman and child arrived to greet the driver. They stroked the dog, then with diligence, turned to me.

"Ooh, he's gorgeous." The lady closed her distance and reached out to me. Cautious of her touch, I teetered backwards. An orange object in her hand, I extended my neck. "It's for you little fellow!"

I don't know if I should have, but it smelt so sweet. Courageous, I took a tiny snap nibble. I chew blended, and carrot juice dribbled down my face. Consoled by the child, and consumed by her smile, I realised the features of a human are subject to the contents of their hearts. The child entered. Intrigued by his innocence, I didn't move.

"All done..." The men approached. I didn't like them. Even less on seeing Jake, put his arm around the lady. "There's alfalfa, for at least a month Liz."

"Well, I best go get some lunch ready for when you return." Like a flower in winter, her pretty head, bowed, Liz kissed him on the cheek. Still beside me, the boy appeared somewhat bewildered. He pinged a pair of braces. Leaping from my skin, I skated back to mother, which made them all laugh.

"C'mon, lad," Jake hooked his head left. "Let's do the land checks jeep style!"

"Does that mean I get to ride the bumper before he heads off?"

Roof rolled back, the jeep beeped at the boy. The driver then drove a finger into the air and pointed ahead.

"Of course," Jake was boisterous, "but give us five to get in the saddle!"

Slapping my shoulder, the lad leapt through the posts and ran towards the bumper. From there, he watched the men race into the barn and re-appear on horseback. Spurs spinning, sun hats tilted like the pretty chair, they rode towards the boy.

"Right, ya ready?" Reins in one hand, Jake, punched the air with the other. Horses almost spinning on their back hocks, energies live as the engine, it was engaging. Balanced on the bumper, the lad used the little side windows to hold on. Hands set, and semi-safe, the jeep burned off.

"Yee ha!" Charging after it, the hooves merged with wheel dust. Slowing, at the main gates, nameless reached for the boy, hitched him up, and told him to hold on. The boy hugged his waist. Sat behind the saddle, they slowed their pace. A steady canter, they courted the jeep onto the dry lands.

"How those poor horses cope, is a mystery." Mother choked slightly on the last of her alfalfa.

The distance was too great to see details, but the horses looked drought dry and didn't move much.

"What are they doing?" I gazed mysteriously to mother, then Monty. But, both pulled pained faces. A wretchedness about them, neither uttered a word.

"Okay," I pressed, "if you won't tell me about it, how about that, over there?" I turned my attention back to the wheel chair.

"It's a carriage..." Mother confirmed.

"Hence the shoes...." Monty rest his foot on one of the post rails for me to make a more in-depth analysis of them. I examined the metal and its bent back hooks.

"Are they sharp?" I couldn't believe four, silver shoes, had been nailed to his feet.

"Only if they go too high." Monty made a brave snuffle. "They don't hurt today he lied. You'll get acclimatized."

"To what?"

"Hot shoeing," he half laughed, "and, Andalusia!"

Monty put his hoof down delicately. "You'll also have to push the throne one day."

Mother shot Monty a shower of ill looks. protecting me from man, seemed her only priority. Then, talk of the devil, they returned. The boy slid like a rug, from behind Jake and into the house for his lunch. Horses tied either side of the tap, the men showered them. Treading foam into the floor, they were then led around the house and out of sight. An hour later, the men returned and rested. Lunch done, long reigns in hand, they came for Monty and loaded him up. Blinkers and nose blade in place, the horse was made to pace around the paddock. Like a propeller, my head spun after him. They had him go strong for over an hour, before stopping to harness him. Then, backing him up, bars either side, Monty was inside the throne. I watched in wonder, as buckles and belts held the bars to him. Then, getting into the high chair, the boy sat between the men who cracked a whip. Jolting a few steps forward, Monty, abruptly stopped. I couldn't see his expression, but his legs looked delicate. There was unease, in his hooves, but again, a whip was raised. Slowly, like Cinderella gone wrong, the carriage cruised through the gates and gathered momentum. Disappearing, the contraption intrigued, and irritated me all at once.

"They will be gone awhile." Mother didn't say much, but her body language spoke in volumes. Without even knowing it, she was educating and sharpening my senses. Thirsty, I moved towards the trough. Half full, I sipped warm water. I was in a world of my own, when it crawled from underneath. Spotty, I sniffed its slimy back, but the frog leapt into the air and skimmed past my nose. The dogs didn't miss a trick. On their feet, they hurtled into the paddock after it. Ping ponging across the ground, its escape technique, was fantastic. I felt elated as it went unharmed, into what undergrowth we had. The big dogs backed off, but like a pig sniffing for truffles, the Jack Russell, ball bounced, before giving in and backing up. The return of the carriage brought a broken horse and bad banter. Undone, and caked in creamy foam, Monty was led towards the house hose. A brave horse, he'd done his best to balance, on the outside of his hoofs. Feet to short, nails to high, his weight had injured the inside of his hoofs. Jake led the half lame horse into the paddock, then, without so much as a pat, let him go. Concentrating hard, Monty, tried to conceal his pain.

"Diego, commeeerrr!"

So, that was the name of the other man. Sat at a small fold up table, Jake ate a bread roll. Fear of missing out, Diego, paced towards the cold beer and tapas. For his completion of the towns circuit, Monty, received nothing but mouldy bread. Mother, wasn't impressed. Clouds of anger, clear as day, she struggled to hide them. During my first month, I learnt, that animals are only work tools and that human hands, depending, on who they belong to, can bring, nice or nasty things. So far, Liz, was the only being, I didn't consider human. Not that I knew lots of them, not that I wanted to. I just liked Liz, and her abundance of light energy. Each day she came with a carrot. To make it last, I quickly learned to liquidize and boil sweet, suck it. This made her laugh. I was two months old, when she, left for the market. It was also by pure, coincidence, that the tractor was put to work too.

Muck mounds on the move, the barn was stripped back to its concrete face. Going one step further, the men decided to clear the paddock divots too. Taken to the corral on the other side of the house, we joined the barn horses. And so, into the land of legs, I did mingle. Scars, they had a few, jeez, some were so bad, they could have been Andalusian maps. One mare even had odd shoes, one older than the other, it was rusty and flat. At last, the digger was put to bed. Back from the market, Liz brought a box over to us. Rummaging in it, she threw some fruit over the fence. Manners previously beaten into them, the horses dare not fight. There was carrots, cabbage, bananas and leaks, even a melon that fell amongst us. I saw it land, but, picked at the post, Anglo, got there first. It was some hours later, back in the barn, that he got ill. Continuously, he kicked at his belly. Ears glued to his head, his stomach gave way to a faint groaning. Restricted by the wall chain, his neck fell into a painful pose. Barking mad, the Jack Russell alerted the house. Jake and Diego arrived. Like a pair of rabbits in blinkers, they parted the horses. The appalling situation apparent, they moved those either side of him to make space. One, of which went in with the goat next door to us. The other, they let loose. Anglo's weight, now on the chain, it had tightened into a thick metal twist. Unable to unclip it, the men used a hack saw to get through it. Bolts broken, the horse fell to the floor. Sides heaving, he rolled to his right. Jake took hold of his head piece and pulled.

"Up with you...!" Diego removed his belt and lashed at the horse.

Mother, for the first time ever, was acceptant, of the punishment. Her usual hate, replaced with hope, she projected positivity. Strangled in pain, Anglo's legs began to quiver, ground grapple and quake. Like a badger, fighting a soil filled set, the horse painfully progressed to his knees. In a dizzy state, he rocked, before forcing his body onto all fours. Another belt and he was push pulled, out of the barn. A painful pageant, the commotion sounded critical. Shouting and banging, hooves of hardship, moved, awkwardly, into the night.

"Some have died," mother finally pasted, "but I think it will pass."

I pulled a stubborn face.

"Colic..." She clarified. "Belly ache, to put it in more simplistic terms."

"From...?" My voice was but a probing whisper.

"The melon..." The mare moved in the commotion, poked her face over the separation wall with the goat. "It was the only new thing in the box. He was the only one who ate it." I frowned for more. "Horses can't be sick," she continued, "it's death, or the painful upright, until it passes."

"There are medicines," mother intervened, "but, the men are to mean to pay." She coughed, "I saw a racehorse pass once." Anguish all over her face, mother sounded sad. "Unable to get up, his gut twisted." She, lip, chewed, "it was hard to bare such severity!"

"A very uncomfortable way to go...!" The mare tossed her mane as though it were something in a frying pan, "you take care young one! You hear me!"

Eyes as wide as my ears, I listened for the marching feet outside. Beating, like a slow drum, they were somewhere in the distance.

The mare stretched her neck and yawned. "I could lie down right here and now, but as soon as they're done, they will chain me back up."

Like two lumbering lions, the moon enhanced the oncoming dogs who stopped before the loose mare.

"How's it going out there?" Poised, she interacted with them.

"He'll live." It was the first time, I'd found any decency in the dogs.

Just then a lamp lit the barn, and Anglo, was led back in. His stomach may have settled, but his features were depleted and muddled. Oval eyes troubled, his feet trundled after the men towards us. Lantern flame bobbing, it lit the way. Wiping his brow, Diego paused.

Too weak to create, Anglo heaved before my bars. His face was sweat stained, panic and pain imminent, perseverance present, the horse was wiped out. Stepping left, Anglo was steered away and made to stand in his usual spot. Spasms, still stinging, I don't think, even his own mess, bothered him. Mares back beside him, the men swapped the lamp for a torch and left. Still looming, the moon reined streaks of silver foil that allowed us to shadow glimpse the goings on. Supposedly out of danger, Anglo, was still in a state. No longer hungry, my stomach crumple cringed into morning. Up before mother, I reared onto my hinds, reached for the partitioning goat wall, and gazed over it.

"Yuk, I thought we had it hard..." Head partially poked over it, my legs held their position.

Curled up like a dog, the poor goat had little clean space. Desperate to sleep dry, she'd managed to keep one tiny corner clean. Like a wicker basket made of straw, her body had moulded a little bed in it. Surrounded by a moat of muck, she looked china doll sweet. I dropped down, dozing, mother was in a restful world. So much so, that she didn't notice, the creepy quiet, grain hunting mouse. Ignoring it, I gazed through the bars. They were all there, all fifteen hinds, including, poor Anglo. As the moon clocked out, and the sun climbed in, so, the breakfast buckets arrived. A small scoop pecking at the grain, the men dished it out. A dash of panache, an appetizer for life, Anglo ate.

Spirit and Soul

Suet pudding, on Perspex, the sun, hot rose and drenched us. Not all the horses were always turned out, but today, for unknown reasons, we all got lucky. We'd been out there less than half an hour, when a lorry pulled up. Mother stopped eating her straw. Misty muddled, by the behaviour, fear of her being the next gone, I felt my throat go dry. There, was hoof hammering, neighing and tail gate slamming. Movement inside was chaotic, bouncing in accordance to the aggravation, the unpleasantness, got louder. On his hind legs, a colt I called Spirit, sauntered out of it. I named him this, for obvious reasons. Still upright, he ambled a further few inches, before collapsing onto all fours. The men restricted his head, but Spirit went up again and stood on his back stilts. He blind punched the air. Three ropes, three men, and a clueless child with a whip, created an unsightly situation.

"On his back legs...!" Diego screeched at the boy.

Running at the horse, the boy hit his hocks. Clack, a shuffle and side shunt, he lashed out. The rope tore through the drivers, hands, leaving him a nasty rope burn reminder. Diego snatched the boy's whip, he broke it clean across spirit's nose. The brown eyes of the bay turned white with fear temper. He reared up, lashed out and accidentally clipped the head of Jake.

"You're going to pay for that." Teeth barred, Diego looked sadistic. The rein was loosened, and the demented horse allowed to stand down and gain some air. Diego ordered the boy to fetch a satchel from the house. Returning, the lad threw it at his feet. Diego rummaged, he threw a bottle of betadine to Jake. Head wound, squirted orange, the cut was fly free.

"Over there..." Diego pointed to the dry lands beyond my post and rails. Nerves twitching, my eyes busily followed. Seemingly unconcerned, mother was splitting with invisible apprehensions. Keeping spirit at a distance they managed to manoeuvre him to the spot. There, they lassoed him from behind and forced him to the floor. Quickly they tied his backs together and drove a rope around his fronts. Incarcerated in his own body, the horse was bound and destined for bad things. Mother tried to shadow my view, but, like the boy awaiting instructions, I did too. The driver planted himself on Spirits neck, Jake his back. Circling the horse, barking frantically, the Jack Russell made a nuisance of itself. Nearing his private parts, Diego dug a silver scalpel from out of the satchel. Like me, the boy shuddered in horror. Time stood still, and the behaviour that followed was unprecedented. Without anaesthetic or one shred of a heart, the incision was instrumental. Trees bled, nature shrank, and the earth tremored. Like a screaming hot kettle, the sound scarred us all. His eyes spilling inside out, my hatred of man was affirmed with army force.

"He could haemorrhage and die!" It was Monty.

"He's already dead." Mother mourned straight into the eyes of Spirit. Pain unleashed, he was in unknown territory. Diego removed his neck scarf, tying tatters of flesh together, a fierce struggle took place. One final whine, and there was nothing. Nothing but the shell of a bottled soul. And so, into me the price of retaliation was printed. Diego cut the leg ropes. The horse didn't move, and his blood eventually congealed in a haze of heated flies. The boy ran crying into the house and a low flying bird turned away from the scene.

"Monsters!" Mothers fury quickly became a flurry of tears, and from her body a deep sorrow emerged. One that wished, I'd never been born.

Upright, the gelded, Spirit trembled. Discomfort immense, he didn't resist the tugging. Forced to stagger into the barn, blood trailed after him, then, without any pain relief, he was put in the spare stable next to me on the right. Furious, Liz left the house. Thunderous she frog-marched into the barn. The voices were loud, but going up several octaves, she extinguished the men. A storm of opinions emerged, that according to the dogs, left the three men open mouthed. Seething, Liz stormed into the house and slammed the door with cyclone force. Verbally beaten, the men emerged quietly. Gingerly, they opened a beer and in silence shared it. The driver handed Jake a bandana. Taking it, Jake wrapped it over the cut and tightened a knot near his ear. I didn't drink much that night. Mother picked at her grain, but I think we all felt the same. Potent with pain, I could sense Spirit, in the spare stable. Gritting my teeth, I protectively paced up and down.

"Your legs might be better for the walking," Spirit spoke, "but my sleep pattern won't be!"

Going up, I gazed into the right stable. A pool of blood, back legs still shaking, Spirit was writhe with pain. The, moon cringed, and the light grew incredibly dull. I twitched, I sympathised, I sneer snuffled. I got down, hit the deck and closed my heart. At three months, I knew hate, love and retribution.

"Unless you have a wand," mother bit, "there's nothing you can do for such a horrible act. Even less for humiliation..." As if her throat was full of sand, she couldn't spit or swallow, mother sounded croaky. "Leave him his privacy. It's all you can do." Mother heaved a sorrow that soaked our surroundings. "The pain will pass, time, is a great healer." She shut her eyes. Silence settled throughout the barn.

Three horses brought in off the flatlands, the morning didn't meet its usual routine, apart from me and mother, the old and new horses were left inside. Outside, the men got out a largish tin and stood it over a gas bottle and grill. Intricate, its top opened like a flower. But instead of pollen, it contained coals. A gas bottle burning full throttle, they tossed some dry straw into the flower. I watched it flare up. Unfolding a flatpack of fence, they staked it down. Opening the barn and undoing chains, horses were sent down a makeshift tunnel. Directly behind one another a queue was formed. A separation compartment, and the front mare was imprisoned in it. Diego rammed a metal rod in and out of the flower. Removing it, I saw its circular end glow red towards the mare. Mortified, I mirrored her horror. It sank her rear, with singeing persecution. Flesh, fleeing into every crevice, her body became liquid play do. Taunt, her hair stood up like matchsticks and had it not been attached to its roots, for sure, would have fallen out. Exit raised, a symbol upon her hind, she sprinted, into the side paddock. Forlorn in face, she absorbed the nags of ripping heat stroke, and shied into its corner.

"Branding...!" Mother nearly broke a tooth on the word.

"But why...?" I was quiet, as a lamb.

"Ownership, identification...!"

"Do you...?" I ran around to where her rump was. There, clear as paper, was a circle. Inside it some pedigree lettering.

"Yes, and it hurt like hell!"

"Haven't you given him a name yet?"

Anglo arrived in the paddock usually used for Monty. Bearing a brave face, he conveniently changed the subject for mother, who nodded a no. Not wanting to humiliate Anglo further, I searched for anything other than fried flesh. A rabbit poked her head between the ferns, beside our trough. Eyes saucer wide, the rabbit skipped before me, and out onto the open lands. But the dogs got a whiff, and my excitement ended. Eager to kill it, they, shuttle launched after it. My heart raced, it sank, and as the dust cloud lifted, the rabbit dropped like a lift into the ground. I felt sick from caring so much, but a victory for the poor thing too. Tattoos in place, cage empty, the men packed up their stuff and called to the house. Still furious over Spirit, Liz took her time responding. Eventually, she brought out a tray of refreshments, put them down with some plonk and disappeared. Feeling flippant, the men drank the liquor. Drunk, they threw the empty wine bottle across the land. It rolled into our paddock. On the label was a stylish man. Frilly collar and waist coat, he was rather posh. Written boldly above him, Faustino.

"Now that's a name worth having!" Anglo furrow frowned, for mother's approval.

"Fuutino, foootino." I couldn't pronounce, or even sing it, to save my life. Anglo and mother laughed.

"Faustino," mother corrected, "fauuu, not foo!"

A bird on the fence cooed encouragement. Tied in tight expectations, I tried again. Slowly, the foo, turned into three teetering syllables, fau, sti, no. It sounded encouraging. I lit up.

"Then Faustino it is!" Anglo, sounded happy, not wanting to rob him of this, mother went with it.

It was Liz, who came and scooped up the bottle. And as destiny would have it, she too came to the same conclusion. "A Faustino, if ever I saw one."

Holding the bottle up, in an unlady like gesture, Liz blew her glass trumpet towards the men and verbally, christened me. Peacock proud, she then climbed between the posts and waded towards the table. Once there, she slammed the bottle hard down. So much so, that it broke. Leaving them in shattered silence, she traipsed towards the house.

Out there

Six months in age, my family threads were about to be broken. Callous and cold heartedly, the men came. Hooves protesting, the goat bleated, dogs barked, and the birds pecking ground grain, took off. I don't know if it was the shackles, or the separation that did mother the most damage. But, I'll never forget the desolation hankering in the hollows of her eyes. Mother put up a fight, but the big stick sent her to the ground where the men demanded she stay. I clambered to the back of the box, but clumsy as they were, the men caught me. Grabbed around the neck, a halter was fitted to my face. My heart beat bells and palpitations blistered my chest. As they pulled me towards them, mother scuttled back on her feet, the floor was wet, and her knees gave way. Again, she righted herself and lunged for Diego. I wriggled like a worm, but the slippery floor was hard to sustain. Mother opened her mouth, and in full glory, her jaw was revealed. Jagged and stained, her broken teeth soared towards Jake. But again, brandishing his stick across her face and back, Diego, did damage. The door slammed, and my tiny hooves were torn dragged towards a truck. I could hear mother, calling, screaming like a tortured tornado. Tied to the toe-bar, dogs heal barking, they drag drove me towards the flat lands. I didn't want to run, I didn't want to breathe, equally, I didn't want to be towed to death.

"That's it," Diego, scorned over his shoulder, "get used to some discipline you little runt."

They were both as bad as each other, but I hated Diego, much more than Jake. As my legs tired into led, so the rope grew tighter. I felt a million miles away but could still hear mother. A faint whine, dissolving into a mouth drying death, I felt comatose for the first time. Lungs tighter than burnt logs, they matched the clouds of mist in my eyes. Heaving, huffing, crying and cringing, I was in a terrible state, when we stopped. Sweating like a steamed pudding, I suddenly noticed the nearest horse. Another nightmare answered, I saw why their movement was restricted. I also realised why the cuffs they had teased her with had set mother off. They didn't untie me, nor did they offer me water. Painfully, I watched Diego pull out a tin dish. Filling it, he let the dogs wet their whistles. It didn't take much to toss me over. Allowing myself to fall into a living dead land, I was putty in their hands. While Jake held my fronts together, Diego cuffed my hinds. They felt tight, hurt me they did, panic waves flowing, I was an unwilling prisoner.

"Funs over little guy, welcome to the real world."

They let me loose. Lethargic, I lay very still. And when enough pain had stream rushed through me, I rolled over. A lone ranger, my only comfort was whispering winds and sand grains. I tried to stand. But was struck down by my new disability. Back legs, now non-existent, they were metal bound. Doing a painful doggy paddle with my fronts, I managed to drag them up from behind me. My hips twisted under the strain. I felt tenderness tighten in my hamstrings, I wobbled, I went down again. As if someone was wringing out my ankles, both, reality and suffocation set in. The men laughed, and a strange energy invited me to look east. There, like an angel on the horizon, was the silhouette of my mother. The smell of fully fleshed men polluting my nostrils, I turned my tied feet, into a new, singular, tool. Pushing my evil walking stick into the sand, this time, I stood more easily. Through cyber space, I smiled at her, was pleased to know she was free. Hope would keep my soul alive and run beside her, again, I would. Ignoring the dogs and laughter, I moved about two inches, any more and it invited incredible shots that splintered somewhere in my hips and spine. I wanted to pound their heads in, bat the yapping dogs towards the nearest cactus bush and panic all at once. But, panic would only provoke pain. I progressed the best I could towards a brown mare. Though her hooves were chipped, her fur ratty and poor, her flea-bitten eyes, furrowed slits of what she once was.

"It's hot out here son, you're going to burn."

There was no shelter, trees or troughs, just buckets that were neither emptied or cleaned. Removing, water containers from the vehicle, Diego, topped them up.

"It's survival of the fittest out here." The mare shunted my way and a shadow of her shaded me. "I can help you for a bit." Her voice was soothing, "But you'll eventually have to harden to the elements."

I watched the dogs tear after the truck. Stopping before each bucket, the men topped up the algae and sludge lurking in their bottoms.

"Why?" Eyes expanding, I shook my shackles and burst into strangled tears.

"It's cheaper than fencing..." The mare shuffled for the bucket and filled her gut with gungy water glue.

Just as the men and truck had gone, so was mother. I missed her thinking patterns, her precious, cute and cuddly touch. I fought the cuffs, sawing my feet until my flesh undid itself. Cutting, the pain fused my faculties into a new sense of submission. A lost one.

"Hate will get you nowhere."

Older and wiser, the mare openly shared her opinion. I hurt. Submerged in pain, I swayed to the rhythm of buzzing flies and in depth, stress. It turned cold, and I longed for the comfort of my four walls, cold floor and spider. Giving in to it, my soul and body collapsed to the floor. Crumpled, my mind drifted in and out of my mental confines. Giving in to the shallow breathing, I straddled a few hours, sleep. In my dream, I saw wet and shiny stepping stones. Reaching out, I hop, straddled across them. I woke at six to the sound of low key snoring. The outline of the mare was all bone, but had her body matched her face, she'd have been a fine sight. Horse humps dotted about, the horizon was a pitiful sight. Caught in one of life's tangles, I watched an old veteran moved towards his water bucket. One two three, his legs went. One two three. My nose hit the ground, I missed my paddock, stable and olive shrub. Awake, the mare held my gaze. Her thoughts of being alone, greater than the pain of moving, I realised, how much, I must adjust.

The men arrived. Aggravated by their presence, I pigeon stepped towards my bucket. Liquid on coal, the water went down a treat. Hitting my stomach in delight, I desperately needed it. A slice of alfalfa dropped before each horse, the truck weaved our way. Throwing it over board, the alfalfa, opened into a fan of green shades. Framed in soil, the sight was a fine one. Sucking one of the strands up, I tried my new spaghetti. Unlike the smooth silkiness of mother's milk, it was rough and tough. I took two mouthfuls before giving it up to the mare. Munching hard, my first day had arrived and her routine quickly became apparent. Scarce, the few grasses about tried to sprout over night, but, shuffling towards them, the horses topped their tips before they could reach any further. By midday, my back was being cooked. Bubbling along my spine, I felt small blisters rise. It got so awful, that I lay awkwardly down. In a bid to stop them expanding, I rotated my body every half hour. Flies feasting and fluttering, I was being tortured in my own skin.

My eyes hurt from the bites and brightness, blinkers sprang to mind, I sneered. Sunglasses, made by man, for the inflictions of tunnel vision. As the temperatures dropped, I felt the emptiness of fear and the first signs of infection. But with the dark, came the wash away stars. I say wash away, because they had the ability to mesmerise, and make me forget. Punched, into the sky like ebony pearls, their fluorescent souls flickered upon me like secret shepherds. I'd done my best not to think of mother, but now like the cold, she was seeping into the marrow of my bones. Holding the tears back, I turned to the mare. Inviting me under her invisible wing, she stood, but a few feet away. Snorting was heard, and a wild boar arrived. Young at her side, they scratched and dug for roots. I envied the mum and so wanted to meet them. But by the time I'd dragged my pus ridden heals up, they'd scampered away. Insecure, I searched for the neighbouring horses. Distant and sleepy, they reminded me of camel humps dotted in the dark. I must have drifted off, because I woke, with wet skin. It was only a shower, but quickly became bullets of water. Big, they burst my blisters. Vulnerable and isolated, the mare moved closer, clamping herself like a magnet to me. Compared to the barn floor, it was a different kind of cold. Not just the sort that soaks and rolls off, but one, that insists, on getting under the skin. Legs swollen from mud fever, flesh forced over and around the cuffs it rose like yeast. Harden me through suffering, that's what the men wanted. My soul was a sponge, and they were ringing it out. I had to be careful not to let them win. Born again, the morning truck brought the usual alfalfa and water slop. A bottle of something in his hand, Jake approached. Brain dead, I didn't resist.

"Hmm just as I thought." Jake pressed upon my metal cuffs, pus, became visible.

"Usual, under the circumstances!" Taking a tube from Jake, Diego, squirted yellow liquid inside both shackles.

"He'll live." With that they left.

Brutal, the winter brought rain scold, and on the odd occasions the truck didn't start, starvation too. But I taught myself to embrace pain and switch off to rain. I knew what hunger, thirst and sunburn was. But worse of all, what it was to feel lonely. I hummed, made private poetry and counted clouds. Within one I wrote...

My mind is a hurricane,

my heart a touch insane

my body can't sleep to dream

my eyes are about to scream

my mouth is a thin street line

I struggle to pass the time

But the morning will soon come

And with it the blazing sun

Until again, another day is done.

Another day,
another way

I was eighteen months old when they came for me. Slowly, they undid my shackles, but they'd become embedded in my heels. Instead of falling off, they hung like two strips of tin foil from my fetlocks. For the first time ever, Diego patted me, eased his way towards the cuffs, and leant over to reach them. Catches clipped to them both, he handed the leashes to Jake.

Stood a few feet away, Diego, reverted to his usual harshness. "On, the count of three!" His voice was pure venom.

Afraid, I lunged forward. There was a tear and tingle, a ripping scratch, then something hot flowed from my feet. Jake held my iron heel cuffs up. Upon them, I saw a thick skin attached. It mattered not. Free of my foot cage, I could fly like a bird, leap like a lamb and run like a leopard. I galloped several feet before the training line tightened. Neck jarred, I jolted still.

"Not so fast Faustino!"

Hare style, I stamped my feet. How dare they still be playing power games. The mare shunted towards me, caught my eye and made me focus. In, order to get on, I had to obey. Head collar embedded in my poll, they changed it for something bigger. Again, I was tied to the truck. Only this time, instead of wailing, I was walking. As we grew closer to the paddocks, I searched for signs of mother. Instead, healed and half happy, Spirit was there. Despite his scars, he'd filled out, muscled up and become obedient. He made a point of acknowledging me, and though I'd had it hard, it could never be compared to his atrocity. Admiration in abundance, I offered only respect to him. The truck stopped before the house and beside the barn. Diego undid my rope. A new arch ahead, it cut off the usual walk around the house. Everything had been moved and more added. There was a brick BBQ, a double dog kennel on breeze blocks and a carriage garage, to protect the newly purchased and polished vehicles. Beside the Mitsubishi stood a Barouche and buggy. They'd obviously been busy making money and a much better life, for themselves anyway. The back paddock, however, was still the same, and amongst the heavenly stock, stood new and old faces. Amongst them, I spotted one I knew. With him, memories of the melon colic returned. Gosh, it all seemed so long ago. Had my brains been glue fried in the sun? Before I had a chance to speak with Anglo, he was taken away. I felt somewhat embarrassed as the mare approached. I didn't know her, but she knew my shackle story.

"Not everyone endures it," she was undressing my mind, "and not all equines get through it!"

I didn't want to discuss it. I had mother in mind, but, if honest, was almost afraid to ask after her. Digesting, her words, I watched the men harness and attach Anglo to a yellow training Gig.

"He's getting good now!" She continued. Hitched up, Anglo pushed the throne, and man pigs up the drive.

"Faustino! you've grown some." The barn horse pushed through the new stock and past the mare to greet me. "And by the looks of it, the suns bleached you a bit."

Feeling rude that I couldn't put a name to the face, I faltered. "I, actually feel as if I've shrunk." I stared at the new arch and outlined the grout between the granite.

"Not the nicest brickwork is it?" I didn't answer the barn horse, instead, I turned back to face the mare.

"is mother...?" There, I had said it, felt relieved and hopeful all at once, but the fleeting shadow in her eyes indicated otherwise. She was gone. but gone where? Please, tell me...

"After..." the tune, in her tone turned sour, "you were taken, they tried her in the carriage. Protesting, she rolled it, hurt herself in the process she did.

Unfortunately, one of the dogs was underneath and died."

"So, they sent her to the auctions." fast off the mark, the barn horse interrupted and answered for her.

"Auction!" My voice went up an octave.

"Sellers, showroom." The mare so tried to soothe the real blow.

"Gosh, is there no end to this equine stuff!" I was hot, furious and flustered at these findings. "So," I tremble nudged the mare, "she could be anywhere?"

Conformation came through her face. Yapping at the returning carriage, the dogs made me jump. All hot and sticky, the horse looked like a large toffee. Dunked in glazed sugar it mirrored the sun. While the Jack Russel continued to yap, the bigger dog approached and gave me a dirty look. Under the heat and tightness of the harness, Anglo heaved. His training finished, he emptied the water trough. Unharnessed, hosed and returned, his eyes dazzled me.

"Is it true and if so, where?" Older and wiser, I considered him something of an oracle.

"Bull ring!" I knew he'd get right to the point. "Pulling a dead carcass, was punishment for the carriage collision!"

Now he was too informative. Not wanting to add guilt to the emotions in my gut, "Thanks," was all I said. The men were deplorable. Did I really expect a decent answer? And what of Monty, unaware who my father was, he was the closest to one I had. I didn't dare ask anymore.

Stable days deported, I was chained next to Anglo, on the end wall. The goat was gone. In my old stable stood a mule and her youngster. Mixed memories of my youth, I didn't sleep well. The morning grain was scarce, but manners we had, and share, equally we did. The muck was mounting and when they came to let us out, it squidged and swirled, around my scars. Though I'd never seen them, they felt like two big band aids held in place by an invisible apparatus. I was taken to the front of the house and tied to a ring there. The saddle landed with a furious clump. Distaste, in my mouth, I descended upon Jake and tore his shirt. Diffusion in the pipe line, Liz appeared with an apple for me. Cheeks flushed like almond blossoms, body perfect inside a peach pant suit, she was beautiful inside and out. Her touch shamed humanity, and again, my thoughts raced around my brain tracks. How could a couple be so different? Diego returned with a dirty bridle. Hanging like a pendulum, a silver moon ticked from its middle. Held in place by unoiled leather, the gag was forced into my apple eating mouth. Sand paper, on my skin, the bit hit my teeth with a lot less comfort than the apple. I chomp panicked, and the bar of steel sent twinges of tin, over my teeth. I grinded, I grated, I wanted to swill and spit. Diego pulled tightly on the girth. Ouch! It pinched my skin. I bit hard into the air and pulled a face that got me a slap. How I hated him! Without warning or permission, a foot in the stirrup, Diego pulled his body towards the saddle. He hadn't swung his leg over the seat, when I went up, accidently sending Liz, sideways. Diego hung on, but I bucked faster than a rabbit burrows and he hit the deck. Triumphantly, my stony eyes, stared through him. Jake removed me from the front of the house and into the school. Calmly, he hoisted his weight into the saddle. A leg either side of me, I was ok until his heels tapped my ribs. Rearing until vertical, he too, was thrown. Hurtled, like a dart across the school, he skidded past the dogs and hit the post and rails. Not content cuffing, chaining and hitting me, they now wanted a ride too. Well, I wasn't having it. The mounting went on for hours and the days were soon woven into weeks. Eventually, tired of the food rations, I was forced to give in, and let them ride. Diego took great delight in turning his spurs into a tattoo gun. Flicking them from left to right, until my broken skin mastered the side walk. Good, too, I was. In fact, I was so natural, that there was talk of selling me for decent dollar. I was trained every day until persuaded into perfection, then one day a new face turned up. I had no idea he'd come to purchase me. Me being me, I did the dance well, and Diego, for the first time ever praised me. They quibbled over paper work and pesetas, shook hands, and handed me to the man. Jake removed his saddle, slapped me on the back, and sent me on my way. I was barely three years old when the ramp came down. Stood before it, I gazed across the flat lands. The mare was still there, and something told me that she always would be. I put one foot in front of the other and entered the smelly tin can. Truly alone, I felt secluded. The back of the ramp made a loud bang. Pitch black, my only comfort was the engine hum. As we sped across the flat lands, I left a piece of my heart with the shackled, mare.

Ferals and fincas

White washed, the new stable block was vain bright. Stable bars, polished to perfection, I viewed those in my aisle. Far too fat, to just be full of food, opposite me was occupied by a majestic dam. And by the way the mare was gazing at the stallion four down, he must have been the sire. Observant a few geldings occupied the far end. On the ground, cats played and prowled. Dominating the place to a high degree, I never saw a single mouse. Unlike the last place clean water was no problem. Automatic fillers, I sipped, from a silver soap dish protruding from the wall. Mother would have loved this place. I couldn't help myself, I missed her so much. Still unsure of exactly what one entailed, thoughts of the bull ring, made me mad. Oats, ingested for the first time, the food was a major improvement. For over a week I stood in my stable. Bored, I searched for a spider, but it was so clean, not one was seen. When they'd finished fattening me up, I was put in one of the many paddocks. The white post and rails complimented the horses and defined the magnolia mansion. A patio extension in place, Terracotta tiles decorated the porch and part of the circular road. Upon it, parked outside the main entrance, stood a golden coach. Captivated, I couldn't believe its handsome appearance. From the door, a woman holding up a pretty umbrella arrived. Taking her hand, the men helped her into it. A flick of the reins, and the big bay pulled away. For every horse hanging about, there seemed to be a groom, to man handle it. Amongst them, if my eyes didn't deceive me, was Monty. Before I could gain his attention, men, put blinkers on him and pushed a rather large Landau, towards his hind. I paced in anticipation for over an hour, but when he returned, they whisked him off to another part of the property.

"What's your name son?" Two bright eyes holding him together, the grey muzzle, gave me an indication of his age.

"Faustino, sir..." The old stallion, overlooking my fence, offered friendship.

Your mother taught you manners." He tossed, a tangle of mane aside, "that's important."

"What's a bull ring?" I blurted, hopeful, that he would divulge me the details.

47

"Is that, where they sent her?" His muzzle made a nasty knot.

"So, I was told." I sounded like a sheep now.

"The good thing about gossip," he gave in to tact, "is, it's usually just that. Without facts, chit, is chat, idle gossip, that will interrogate your imagination." The old stallion snatched a mouthful of alfalfa from the floor, "Facts, is all that matter son. But," passionate, he spoke with his mouth full, "finding some, is rare."

I digested his words, and later in the stable, was thankful to the lid of hope, he'd have me believe. The morning men arrived, poking and prodding every equine, they bounced about the place like peas, leaving pods.

"Come on you." Unsure if it was for me or the new neighbouring, mare, I turned towards the voice. "Yes, Faustino, you..."

A man, I quickly named 'Ugly Arrogance,' entered the stable. Hat tilted upwards, his leathery lips chewed a liquorice stick. He smirked, and the craters in his skin became a mass of creases. An open shirt, the medallion, made his neck appear shorter than it should be. From under his chaps, peeked two silver ankle clamps, wheels with darts, the spur tips terrified me. A tatty worn hand took hold of my headcollar. Hooked to a rope, he slung it over his shoulder. Out of the block, he reeled me into a busy school. There, reaching to another of the ranchers, he snatched up a second head piece and put it over the first. There was no care or thought, into its positioning, it was just slammed across my nasal bone. Hungry, the metal teeth on it, tightened and tucked in. For Pete's sake, it was like having someone plug up your nostrils, while at the same time prodding them with a pitch fork. Out came the long reigns. Fitted to the clips either side of the teeth, I felt trapped. But, 'Ugly,' urged me onwards. Confused in pain, I plain sailing hated humans. Each time I went forward, I was tugged back. This went on until my nose bled and my legs buckled. Through pain alone, I was under uglies command, only moving a muscle when instructed to. That night I had a terrible headache, a horse migraine I suppose. But worse. There was no pain relief and as a run of the mill punishment, I was put on food rations for not learning fast enough. In the morning, I heard them coming. Nervous, belly ache and loose bowels, made me shy to the back of the stable. But, there was nowhere to hide. Ugly, Arrogance, took me outside and hosed my back legs down. Hugely inconvenient, he wasn't happy with me. My nose hadn't even scabbed over when it came. Crashing down on raw sensitive skin, I went through the roof of rearing.

"Ahh, he's getting it now, "arrogance added to my hurt and hate.

Ugly, yanked me down until I embraced all four legs and stood easy. Retaliation too much to contemplate, I caved in. I wanted to stay still for movement only invoked the unbearable, but a crack of the reigns and obey, I did. In a bid to avoid the sharpness, my neck arched, and my head hung like a bluebell. Like a distorted swan on ice, I conveyed my movements with delicate accuracy. After half an hour they loosened the teeth, but instead of bringing relief, the evil head collar slid down an inch onto fresh flesh. Oh, how it hurt to start again. By the end of the day, I had razor marks all over my nose. A zebra crossing dripping red sauce, I must have looked ridiculous. Painfully I drifted in and out of nasty nightmares. In one, I cringed. Diggers didn't have teeth, but this one did. Driving it, Ugly, undisputable, aimed it straight for me.

"Take it easy lad." The mare opposite spoke in a disturbing tone, to which I woke to. Shaking scared, and in traumatized tatters, the nightmare, took time to shed. But the prospect of another arrived at dawn with the men. They studied the rawness across my nose, with x-ray eyes. Angry it had swollen, they shrugged disapprovingly at the scars spreading across my face.

"Sod it!" Angry, aggression, turned to face the mare and new filly opposite. Only hours old, I was inspired by her innocence. Uncontaminated, she was exquisite. A breath of fresh air, that for now brought clarity to the block. Already indoctrinated, mum knew what kind of inflictions her offspring, had to come. Shying away from them, the mare was uninviting. The men turned back to me, Aggression, didn't agree with me being left in. But, the others insisted that working the war wounds, would only lead to infection. Angry, Aggression stormed down the block, and snatched, the end gelding instead. Fears defrosting, I was more than happy to stand in my own muck all day. Even the sea of urine swimming about my feet, was a better fate than another minute with Aggression. Opposite, the pretty filly peeked me a hello. Perfectly proportioned on four white socks, she was a real stunner. Inquisitive, I watched her sniff the air, floor and mother's face, leap over poop piles and pivot, towards cleaner spots. Full of lively beans, she brought stability, to my empty soul. A wheelbarrow appeared. The stable hand tied the mare up, before beginning his daily sweep and shovel. Not enough new shavings for a hamster, it didn't take long for the damp floors to get messy again. But, this was life, and the least of our worries. Fortunately, our straw feeders hung from the walls, but as always, remained empty until lunchtime. I was nose, nibbling at it, when an exquisite, lady entered the block. Figure hug tight, her corset sat like a flute on a balloon. Covered in corrugated cotton, the gowns bottom, was laced in frills. A matching ribbon wrapped around her ringlets, she was remarkable. Hair bouncing about, she stopped at stable three.

"The stallion isn't up to standard," Aggression ran up beside her, "He's too dangerous!" He panted.

Lady, shot him an angry look, belt her gloves over the back of her hand and turned to face him.

"You were supposed to inform me of his progress and potential! Why, is it, you won't listen?"

Unhappy, at being worded by a woman, Aggression, was agitated and under pressure.

"The show is next month!" her tone was mildly sarcastic, "what, do you suppose we do then?"

Leaving him, she floated my way. I felt relief as she passed. But, afraid, as she slowly, backtracked. Stifled, I shuffled backwards until the wall stopped me dead.

"And who is this young man?" Teetering on her tap shoes, her pretty made up face filled my doorway with perfume.

"Faustino has..."

"By the looks of it," she, snap, snarled, "been worked over good and proper by you!" She put her gloves away and pulled on my latch.

"I don't think that's a good idea."

"Indeed," she belted back, stepping into my stable at the same time, "nothing, you do is."

Hoisting the bottom of her dress up, she clipped it to her belt, where it bounced upon bloomers. I glanced down. Flawless legs, they were like two ivory pegs. Her touch was soft, and my face fell, victim to the souls of her hands. Like a feral cat, I could almost hear myself purr in her palms.

"He's never done a day's work, let alone a dance," Aggravation didn't like her amby pamby, ways, "there isn't time to teach..."

Leaving my face in mid-air, her hands ran down my ribs. As if reading brail, she felt for spur dots. Finally, her fingers returned to comfort my face.

"He's out of work today." Aggravation was determined to win.

"Thanks to your impatience, yes." She spun like a wheel, "bring him, and a soft bridle set, to me!"

Outside, the men lowered the leather nose band, but the lady raged at them.

"He needs to be free, able to breathe!" She raised it above the zebra crossing, pain entered my eyes. Tearing it from the head piece, she removed it altogether. Pelham and brow band, I think, I could manage. In her private school, I not only stood like a lemon, but could smell them from the surrounding trees. I knew, nothing of song, show was a new word, and flamenco dancing, totally taboo. Aggression hit a button, and music reigned. Soul soothing, I was, fixed fast to the spot. The lady entered. Like a bullet leaving a gun, her heels hit one another with stunning authority. Then, with angel grace, she floated around me. Mesmerised, my eyes enveloped her every move. Pain prized away, it was put on hold. Dress swaying, she circled me, was the wind, sun, sea and sand, all in one. Hypnotised, I could have watched her forever. Arms, graceful as silk, hair like a string of beads, she reached out, and over her head. There, her arms and hands swayed like river reeds. Indeed, it was a five-star performance. Music cut, she took hold of my face. Brown eyes penetrating mine, I suddenly felt penalised.

"Hurt him didn't you!" She snapped to the men stood behind the fence. "Saddle him."

"You're not serious?" One of them gulped.

Evasive, her eyes shot past the men and towards the tack room. Not wanting her invitation to Iceland, a saddle was supplied. Emotionally assured, I didn't move a muscle. Tack in place, girth tightened, she again danced. Only half way through, she put her foot in one of my stirrups, gazed at me, and paused. Our, energies engaged and there was none of the normal rage. Swaying softly in our imaginary breeze, she got on and unclipped her hem. Decorating my back, it draped over my hind. And though, I was hot, retaliate, I did not. A small kick, and my defiance walked with dignity. My every breath, at one with hers, I'd found my pain relief. A little more leg pressure, a gentle kick and I became a prince. Pride my new name, I cantered the perimeter and counted the paces. Around we went with my neck all bent, the gentle transition, the perfected position, at last, I was receiving real recognition. By the end of the dance, I was rewarded real hay, a handful of treats a cuddle and play. Oh yes, my lady, please stay. We practised every day, and for the first time in my life, I was living. By the end of the month, My, neck arched a bridge and my legs rose higher than sunshine. Side walk sharpened, I was set. The lorry, Persian purred, and meadow hay made my day. The only thing I didn't like, was that Aggression, attended too. Whether she really needed him, or just wanted to prove a point. I don't know.

Nervous

Alive, like a busy hive, the show ground hissed. Occupied with breeds I'd never seen, they were openly tied everywhere. Plaited necks and painted hooves, they were truly tarted. Make-up and hair clips, castanets and fans, never, had I seen so many fancy females. I drank heartily, and due to the spectacular scene, even let Aggression, tighten my girth, without barring my teeth. Side saddle set, he helped hoist my lady into her seat. We passed the people of its province, and went in. Pausing centre ring, she bowed before the big bowler hats. Braced in salty air, I felt the sea and wind, whip lap, our skins. The bell and guitar, both struck the same chord. I pointed my glass slipper to one side. Apprehensive of how soft the air was, I began by sponge dabbing it. Gingerly, my rears reached their fronts, and with frosted tips, began to ice it. Flawless fondants, the time between foot and floor, became a flurry of quick steps. Passion pushing my performance, it flowed into pedantic air prances. Scrumptious sprinkles, they landed spot on. A figure of eight, it pink polished, our cake. Sweeping the sand, the sugar came too late, but we pulled it back, with presence and gait. A collective canter circled the cake, then straight down its middle, a breath, I did take. Soothed beneath the slower strings, I bunny hopped, an inch at a time. Bouncing hooves, bobbing lace, oh how, did she manage to sit with such grace. Pushing elegance to the end, we engaged the euphoria. Doubts cleared by the claps, our best we had done. No idea of place or position, I felt enriched by the people. Even allowed Aggression, to enjoy his anchovies and olives in peace. An elegant eater, my lady used a knife and fork, and refusing to drink from a can, she used a cup. I was sunning my skin, when she Leapt to her heels.

"Were in, Faustino, were in!" She entered the lorries living quarters. And champion change, she did.

"You not content with your hay boy!" I shied away from Aggression. I didn't like him and wasn't about to pretend, I did. He made me tense, undoubtedly, he took away my feel-good factor.

Hair undone, a scented flower in it, I initialised myself for the next step. Comforted in the happiness of her soul, she offered sanctuary from the harsh horse world. A bell called, and numbers were dished out. We were seven. We were next. Like a long-haired butterfly, up she went. Polka dot green, upon silk, she spread them over my back. And as we neared the entrance the spots became stars. And oh, how I did reach for them...

Sharp witted, and keen, I waltzed into the ring, and half way down its middle, I stopped dead. Up I went.

Perfectly positioned, I bolted my legs to the bottom of the sea. Meringue stiff, I managed to stay put, punched the air and unhinged my hocks. Sugar and spice, it was everything nice. A lamb, I was light, a bird in mid-flight, I gave it my all, every bit a fight. Disciplined muscles, they made good moves. Tip toes and treasure, my circles, I did measure. Precision excelled, my steps did fasten, a compact gallop, my gears were composed. Until, finally, I, halted with fatigued pleasure. Jousting jingle bells, the crowd did roar. Utterly joyous and with Jaybird breaths, we left the ring. Outside, not even Arrogance, could overturn my opulence. With open arms, he caught her. Cheeks tweaking in anticipation, he tied me up and went with my lady, to watch the last contender. Anticipation alarming, my eyes rolled after them. Then, over the tanoy, and in reverse order, it arrived. In third, was the Lipizzaner filly, I fancied. Sleek and stunning she was a real catch. Water dribbling through my lips, I watched a Mustang take second prize. It was her shrieking that unsettled me. Air lifted into his arms, Aggression threw my lady at me. Ecstatic, hay still hanging from my mouth, she galloped me in. Skidding to a halt, I could feel her heartbeat. A sash around my neck, I, was high as a kite. Tied up in tinsel, we left the ring in soothing guitar tones. A Rioja region, Aggression had been to a local bodega. Oaked, the 1969, Faustino, was opened. Flavoursome, gulp it my lady did. Apples in abundance, I was applauded again and again. After that, ranch life got easier. When I wasn't in a dance class, I was used to clear cattle from the land. I enjoyed the freedom, but not the sight of calves being lassoed. Worse still, was the wailing of mothers tearing after their tangled calves, I tried to slow my canters. I didn't share man's way of separation, his disrespect or vulgar views. Unlike us, when put into pens, and depending on destinations, cattle were prone to a number of nasties. Hooves often cut to short, tattoos, ear piercings, injections or the slaughterhouse. Bruised and breathless, the calf called out, but the drovers had long driven its mother back. Mocking the calf, the men waved a u, shape under its nose. Pupils, now vulnerable white, their, insensitivity was incredible. I halted before the half-filled pen. My rider booted me on but my legs, like my eyes, refused to budge.

"Hey, I think Faustino wants to make a statement!"

"Or steak…" The u shape hit the calf with singeing persecution. Wrestling him to the ground, two of the drovers ditched him on his back. Bawling and wriggling, the calf looked directly up at me. Humble under the hissing, the sight disturbed me. Staggering into the transfer pen, the reek of roast beef followed him. A kick in the ribs and I was heading out for more. A stench of sweat, tobacco and tears, it stayed with me all day. Evidently, my nightmares were branded too. In them, was the whiff of steak, mutton and mule. A slaughter house and tools, the isolation, bolt gun and brawls. The sound of a barn owl woke me.

"They took her!" the mare opposite was frantic and finished all at the same time, "sent her away somewhere..." Prize possession gone her heart poured emptiness.

"Surely not!" My voice was calm, but, inside was brittle still."

Shaken from my own nightmare, I searched the darkness, she, had to be there. For sure, the filly was hiding. A flip of fate, a flood of tears. I couldn't find words. But, words alone, would never be enough. Evacuating her heartache, I sipped water from my dispenser. Despair in the air, I lay down, and into dawn did drift. Back biting, the drovers entered...

"But, she said no!" There was a glimmer of human goodness in the voice.

"Yeah, she did turn ten thousand down!" Loud, and clear, it was Aggression.

My bolt slid aside, but stationery, I stayed. Arms crossed like their faces, him, and two others blundered in, and stood over me.

"She categorically confirmed, he would be staying here?" Attempting to talk sense, one of the two men tackled Aggression.

"Aye, that she did!" Aggression featured greed, "but they came back and offered fifteen!"

My soul sank into the overspill pipe. Ignoring what I considered to be the good guy, Aggression knelt to put a halter on me.

"So, you're just gonna fleece her instead of utilising his flair?"

I give him his due," Aggression dusted my main, "he's talented."

"Then why waste it...?" the decent guy persisted, but greed was now set in stone.

"To put it in simpler terms," Aggression clunked a clip to me, "I want my commission. However, he has no 'Pura, Raza, Espanola, papers." Pushing me upright, he waved for the men to get out of his way, "if we wait for the idiots he came from to fill in the form, we'll lose the deal!"

"You are joking?" The man of morals pulled a painful face.

"Am I laughing!" Aggression gave me a tug and out we went.

I refused to go near the cattle cage, but a whip on my hock scars, sent me sailing into it. In agitation, I watched them unscrew the u, and replace it with a circle. In it, was a prominent, Andalusian symbol like the one mother had had. A wet leaf in winter, my muscles recoiled like snakes shedding skin. I searched for lady liberation, surely, she wouldn't allow this. I felt it sink me and was air born within seconds. I blushed a fever, burst a blood vessel and felt the confines of my mind cascade cruelty. One two, one two, it was intimate. Felt like a million mosquitos all scratching me at once. I yearned for the hose pipe, an ice cube, anything cooling. The lack of humanity was lethal. Mental pain, my only companion, I dismissed creative dance and crawled inside myself. Melting like my skin, our winning performance dissolved into a pool of naïve and foolish vanity. Never, had I felt so demoralised. Then, as if that wasn't enough they inflicted more. In all my five years of hell, I'd only felt the odd rasp. Feet trimmed to a more suitable size, band aids torn clean away, I felt blood collect, in the canyons of my heels. The sound of gas was heard, shockingly, I saw four silver moons BBQ until red. Hot tonged towards me, the first of four, smoke sizzled into my foot. A strange sensation, it was a bit like having the tips of your nails soldered with several matches. Removed and hammer hit, it was then bent into shape. Potent, but not poison, it was a strong pong. The nails went high, Monty sprung to mind. I never did get to see him. But, now knew, what he'd hidden in the golden days. Twinkle twinging, I prayed the nails didn't bite my inner flesh. A twist, and the ends were snapped clean off. Four fittings later, I stood half an inch taller. So, I was wearing high heels and had a horrible tattoo, but why? And where was my lady? It had literally been weeks, since I'd last seen her. Strutting musical airs had kept me going, and if I'm honest, alive. I could salsa, tap dance and flamenco. A shammy leather corrected my coat. There was a clack, the shake of hands and the horrible introduction of Tom. I didn't take to him at all. His energy was bad, and the look in his eye was all business. Documents forged, they were ready to sign.

"The only thing he doesn't do is drive." Aggression never failed, to irritate me.

Dancing dragons, what did man, expect from one animal alone?

"He will..." Tom took my rope and scrutinised my nose scars. He wasn't going to be easy. Frantic, I looked for her. The blue-sky bond gone, not a cloud of my lady was in sight. Her absence made me both mad, and sad. Silly me, silly Faustino, onto the ramp you go. Shut in, I gave humans some more thought. They had little regard for anything other than food or money, and even that, had implications if scarce. A microwave on wheels, the lorry was a stuffy inferno. Heaving hard I reached for its one window. Not big enough for a cat, I struggled hard to extract oxygen. Evening eventually arrived, clammy, cool, I needed a drink. We stopped for fuel, and for all my hours of standing only half a pail was put before me. I drank the bucket dry, was desperate for more, when I saw the garage sign. Hundreds of miles from home, I was now in the province of Marbella. The door shut. Hang on, is there no more water? But the wheels turned and so did the lorry. Heading left, the highway seemed to drag its heels. An hour later we stopped for good. Both, the air and lingo, was very different to anything of past. But on a positive note, I was put in an outdoor stable block that overlooked everything. Entertainment, Bodega, house, bar, the lot. The biggest yet, the schooling ring was surrounded by a decorative wall. Intricate flowers and symbols upon it, it must have taken the artist hours to paint. A foreigner to these parts, pronounce them, I couldn't. Swivelling between the house and my block, the bar linked it all up. Plate sized seats on broom handles, they swept along its front. A dozen tapa tables, the place was very accommodating. I saw the sunset people arrive. Adopting stools, they sipped cool beer and tapas while they waited. But waited for what? From my stable, I saw a baby bull brought into the ring. I didn't get it. One minute they were meat, the next a major part in a play. Even in my tired state of mind, I couldn't figure out why the bull was in the ring.

Oh, bull ring. Was I about to get an insight into something… In a silly hat and silk neck scarf, a man entered. Attracting the attention of the bull, he waved his arms around and shouted at it. Eventually tired of his teasing, the bull charged him. Running for his spine, the man leapt onto the gate and threw himself over it. Clunk! The bull hit his horns against the wrought iron entrance. Pleased, the people cheered and bought more beer. Bowing my head, I was bothered by the pulling. It had been mentioned that mother would be hauling a carcass! Confused about the bull ring, I closed my mind. But, the man didn't close his bar until midnight. A night of noise, I felt nostalgic. Morning brought a mosaic of movement. Dogs, cats, men and carriages all about the place, it had woken up. I'd been long reined before, but never backed into a carriage. For goodness sake, I was a dancer. Despondent, I went with it. Blinkers on, I was blind pushed back between two narrow bars, I was nearly in position when I panicked. A whip was waved in my face, cowering, I gave in. Loops fastened, buckles tightened, I managed to stay focused. That was until they flicked the blinkers over my eyes and eliminated, my enthusiasm. claustrophobic possessed, carriage cramping my sides, I shot off. The men missed the reigns and screamed obscenities after me. Unable to catch up, engines were cranked. Two trucks on my tail, they overtook. Then, from one open top to the other, a line was thrown. Lowered, my fronts tripped and took it all down. Carriage, collapsing onto its side, I heard a wheel crunch. My back hurt, I could only see out of one eye. Buried beneath the other blinker, sedated in shock, I was downcast. I bit my bottom lip, and with frightened ears, listened for the outcome. A lunge line exercised its end across my back. I cringe grappled to my knees. But the gravel hurt, grazed them with its intricate sides. There was a lot of commotion, concern for the carriage greater than me, I felt my neck twist. Free of buckles and brass, I collaborated with life. Muscles twitching, my feet coordinated onto all four.

'Come!' Discouraged, I followed Tom.

In my stable, I was deprived of supper. Pride persecuted. I took to the back wall, where there, I rooted myself in a gloom of glue. They called my lady to take me back. It was a no, she didn't want me. I felt so depressed and down, I probably matched the mare, mourning her filly in the last place. Would of have happily been a slave to the slaughterhouse. The cockerel liberated me back to life. What life? Men left the outhouse. Armed with pitchforks and shovels, they began their duties. Dogs unclipped, bulls fed, they began with the furthest stables and worked towards one another.

"The people need a new show." One of the nearest men chatted to his neighbour.

"I hear, he can dance." Another of them plonked his wheelbarrow before my stable.

"What, on air?" There was a lot of laughter.

"He might do our tourist treks down the beach." A groom shouted from two stables along.

"I don't trust the bugger!" Sat at the bar enjoying his morning café, Tom, gave me a dirty look.

Instead, they put tassels over my face. Irritating, I shied away. But was held until acceptant of them. Bells on my back, I didn't want them either. Equally, I didn't want a beating. Though my fur was whitening, the skin beneath, was still black. Facial scars, unfit for theatre, they made a chalk paste. Spread over my nose, it blended a blue bottle grey. A gruelling disguise, I was tied to the wall of my stable. From there, out of my right eye, I watched the bar fill. Finally led out, I stood like a lemon before a made-up Marbella. Not a patch on my lady, I struggled to appease the woman. Opening and closing her castanets like a Venus fly trap, her arms teetered ahead of her. I wiggled slightly, looked over her high collars, and down at the ground. I wanted to switch her off like a TV show you don't want to watch. But, one of the men reached into his boot. A whip removed, I side walked. Circled her, bowed my head and flicked my main a few times. The music slowed. I jogged on the spot. Left right, left right, I was in the army. The more control shown, the more her audience clapped. The faster I worked, the more the bells rang. Heavy little jugs, they hurt too. Spooked by them, I made an idiot of myself towards the end. Effectively, ruining the show. Furious with my overall performance, I was put up for sale.

Luck of the draw

A middle-class family on the other side of Marbella, I was one, of three horses now housed there.

"Decent, they are…" Taffeta, was the first to speak.

"Bit of driving," Crimson the other mare confirmed, "Oh, and weekend riding when 'she,' comes home."

I didn't ask, who,' she, was, and just as the mares expressed, the family were nice enough. Carlos, especially. The sight, of the Gig, frightened me. But, Carlos was patient. Spoke kindly and encouraged me in all areas. Too good to be true, it took me a few weeks to trust, but trust him and his Gig, I did. Evenly distributed, the workloads were shared, and we were all treated the same. Diligent, I finally hit the road. Enormous, I was enlightened by the city. Enthusiastic, I pranced about, collecting folks, and dropping them at their desired destinations. Unlike, other horse owners, lunch was important to Carlos, and when he ate, so did I. Providing me with a hay bag, my respect for him grew.

"Sorry Sir," he said to the couple contemplating before us, "my horse will need at least half an hour to digest his dinner."

Hallelujah! I'd arrived. Avenging all the others, I, ignored the sun and thirst. Shoes wearing thin, I kept up my speed. A little kindness, and my strength shone. I slept soundly at night and on my days off, rejuvenated, my energies. Even better, I had the company of whichever mare wasn't working. And then something magical happened. 'She,' came home. Pig tails and dimples, patient and daring, she was awesome.

"He's gorgeous papa. Can I ride him?"

Disappearing, she didn't wait for an answer. Returning with a Spanish saddle, she put it on my back.

"I want to show you the beach, Faustino."

"Marina, you don't even know him." Carlos dived after his daughter, "You've just broken up, at least let me see you ride him first."

Marina did up my girth, turned to her father, and wrinkled her nose. Freckles all over her face, she was cute. I liked her energy. Recognising this, Carlos gave me a stroke.

"You look after her, you hear me!"

"He will pa." Marina flicked my fringe aside and did up my throat latch. "Hey, Pa, how big do you think he is?"

"Well, there's only one way to find out." Carlos took down a long stick from a shelf. Snatching the reins from Marina, I pressed myself against the beams.

"You've scared him!" Marina hurried towards me. Fair minded, I felt warm strokes upon my muzzle.

"Sorry son." Carlos lowered the contraption. "I only want to see how many hands high you are.

Reassurance in his voice, I relaxed. Gently, the stick sat snug upon my shoulders and the wriggly bit of wood hit my withers.

"14.3, but he looks much bigger."

"A pony, horse." Marina beamed.

Outside of the stable, Carlos cupped his hand for Marina to step in. Then, with all the grace of a ballerina, threw his darling daughter into the air. Landing like a feather, and impartial to further interference, she kicked me towards a sand track.

"I'm at university Faustino." She had gentle hands, "But I come home every month." She paused, "You'll stay with us, won't you?"

Young and unpolluted, her mind was pure magic. Feeling blessed, I broke into canter and as much as I wanted it to be true, I knew that hope, was all I had. But hope I did, all the way along the beach. Marina steered me towards a rock formation. Passing through an arch, I was over whelmed. A half sun burnt moon before me, it framed the bay and sea. Blue as the sky, I delicately stepped towards it. Not a human in sight. It wasn't just a bay, it was a shooting star that had fallen and unfolded into an oasis.

Upon it, star fish, did sit, crab catching, there were gulls too. I embraced the sea with excitement. Tossing its surf like a thousand footballs, I made Marina laugh and chuckle, until her sides hurt. Gently coaxing me further in, the ground gave way. Her arms clapped around my neck, I bounced over oncoming waves. Legs going like propellers, I confronted the currents until the strength of the ocean outweighed mine. Sensing this, Marina turned me around, flat upon my neck, she surfed me back to shore. Soaked in happiness, I galloped upon golden grains, until breeze blown dry. Pig tails protruding from her head, ribbons flowing like the rosette, I'd once won, her smile liberated me. Yes, love and light, that's exactly what she brought into my life. Apart from the odd human who shared its values, the vastness of our oasis, was all ours. And when

Marina left, she took a piece of me with her. Volunteering to work extra runs, it helped pass the days and pave the time towards her return. And time, with Marina, was always worth the wait. And like a ray of light, there, she was. Saddle ditched, legs clinging to me like a little red Indian, into the surf we rode. Afterwards, we flumped onto a new dune of sand. Rucksack undone, Marina munched on her toasted bread. Olive oil and tomato sauce, I spat out the tomato. This made her laugh. An apple at hand, she quickly removed the taste. After, she would put her head upon my stomach. Sometimes, she woke before me. Legs vanishing upon vanilla sands, I would chase her bronzed shadow. Committed to her baby brother, I didn't really know her mother. But, as the time disappeared, so he did grow. I was into my third year when the toddler first appeared. A feather duster in hand, he tottered onto the porch and began beating the cat. Hmm, I didn't like it. My only hope for him, was that he would grow up, to be like his sister. Monday was an early start, and apart from throwing day hay at the mares, we left without preparing the evening meals. By nine o-clock Carlos and I were exhausted. At a steady pace we exited the tourists and headed home. Out, of hay, Carlos carried a ladder into the barn and leant it against the hay loft. I watched his feet disappear up the rungs. The yell knocked me for six, the thud, my nerves. I leant over the door until my neck hurt, but see Carlos, I couldn't. The mumbles grew, they mounted, before slipping silently away. The ambulance came, and his wife and child disappeared with Carlos inside it. Frantic, I forgot my hunger. Carlos didn't come back, but his wife, Tia, did. She put the child down, took a deep breath and poured milk for the cat. Curiously, she didn't stop until it spilt onto her sandals. Tia spoke to the cat, stroked its head and scooped up the boy. Disappearing, she went inside the house.

"Spinal!" The cat told us what she knew. "According to the doctors, it will need operating on."

A deathly silence followed, we all hung our heads. In between her hospital visits and housework, Tia, fed and watered us. Undeniably, the problem was painful, and Tia, unsure of anything. The toddler followed her everywhere, and like the red rims of her eyes, was sore in foot and face. Mucking out was quick, hay thrown over the door and hens constantly locked up, she was a mess. I wanted to see Marina, but due to her studies, Tia, had temporarily spared her the news.

"I sense, we'll be sold." Crimson spoke for the first time since the accident.

"Please, don't..." A portrait of her parents, the Iberian Peninsula of her past, ever present in those sad, but pretty eyes. Taffeta was distraught.

I didn't breathe a word. Would have begged to work. The situation spiralling, a mist of depression hovered. Unpaid hospital bills and Marina's fee's mounting, money was scarce. I knew our time was running out. Evidently, things got so bad, that Marina, had to come home early. Taking a double harness, she drove both me and Crimson into central Marbella. It was busy... Going the extra mile, we pulled for our lives, fetching and ferrying to fill the pot and pay for our keep. It had been three months of operations and open surgery on his spine, but when the results returned, it was abundantly clear, he'd never walk again. The wheelchair brought back memories of my shackles, my foot infections too. The scars were at least two inches wide and half that in height. I know so, because Marina told me. Slowly, Marina pushed the wheelchair towards the paddock. Pleased to see Carlo's we simply stood and stared. Bidding him hello, both the mares bowed their heads. He reached out, and I sniffed his skin.

"I'm so sorry." Carlos sobbed.

Had it come from anyone else, it would have been meaningless.

"If only you were miniature, I could take you indoors," he sobbed, "instead, it must be my mind." I'd never seen a man so upset.

Marina put on the foot break and climbed in with us. Throwing her arms around me, I felt floods of tears tamp my neck. My guts turned into a sieve. Floating above it, I held my emotions in for as long as possible. But as she let me go, I lost control and they began to pour. The first to go was, Crimson. Sold to a lorry driver, who'd lost his licence, her taxi days would never end. Driving for a drunk, my heart went with her. Putting their bills first, and against all of Marina's pleading, Taffeta, and I, were sent to auction.

"I love you, Faustino..." Doors up, Marina disappeared, and the lorry departed.

A pound or two

Tight as two tourniquets, we arrived tense and tearful. Pushed further and further into pony pens the reality was harsh. Cramped and hot, until impossible to move or turn at all. A choir of neighs, bundles of nerves, it was no surprise when I felt the kick. Ouch, my shin hurt. A moment later a man waving a whip entered. Spooked into pony nut clusters, the perpetrator, hauled the horse out. Tied to the nearest tree, my heart sank. Clack, the whip cut. Skin torn, it split like an overripe orange. Frightened, and in a frenzy, the horse swivelled left, then right.

"I'll not have injuries in the pen." The man threw down the stick.

On his knees the horse was hollow. Horrid, I felt responsible. Regretted ever being born. Broken and bruised the horse was left without water or dignity all night. I didn't sleep, eyes upon the victim, the hurt in my leg didn't match my hate for man. They came back at seven. Tugging at the horse tied to the tree first, they led him towards two sheets of sliding metal. Inside them, I heard lots of chanting and bickering, the crashing of a hammer, and as expected the horse didn't return. Tight lipped and terrified, Taffeta, was caught next. My head shot up, capturing her dread, the breeze too. Pony perfume, sweet as spring, she was a darling. Certainly, didn't deserve this. Saturated in sadness, I could only soak up her despair. Too far away to console her, I heaved dejection. Upset, my undercarriage erupted, and had I been able to be sick, would have. I drew determination, I straddled a few steps. Horror amongst the ponies they panic pranced about any small part of the paddock they could. Strangled in terror, and still staring at me, Taffeta, turned in. Pitched in mid pen, surrounded by a harassed heard, the smell of doom dispersed. Process, repeated, one by one, they nipped down the numbers until only a dozen remained. Rosy cheeks, brown teeth and a dirty head of hair, he man handled me. Uninterested in my shin, I was trawled towards the tin doors. To slow, he raised a hand to my head. I shy quivered to one side. Three good legs taking the fall, I dragged the fourth into a bidding ring. Stood before an auctioneer, he ogled my overall appearance. I was then turned to face the music.

77

"Nine, year old Andalusian stallion," loud, the butch voice cut the air, "who will start me? I'm told he drives, dances, too."

"What on three legs." One bidder bragged.

And, so the speculative spill began.

"What's he doing the hop scotch!" another chanted.

The men waved their money about and the bidding began at 1,000. There was lots of shouting, conversing and challenging. Closed to the ordeal, my mind clammed up. Wavering on three legs, my eyes shut too. Poked and prodded, I found, man more offensive than any other being.

"Looks broken to me...!"

"It's only a graze!" The auctioneer, authenticated, "I'm not giving him away."

Fifteen thousand gone behind the lines, I fetched a feeble five. I hobbled through a different door and into an outdoor maze. Made up of purchase pens, each, housed equine upset. Absorbing their feelings, it was like walking the plank, and oh, how I'd have happily jumped. Cuts and bruises all over the place, not one of us hadn't been hurt. A flap of flesh hung from the hip of one mare. Bone exposed, her level of pain alarmed me. I searched on the off chance for Crimson. I was out of luck. Taffeta, on the other hand, now occupied the end pen. Engrossed in fine features, her angelic face kept me from going mad. Paperwork signed, men came to collect their stock. Forced into lorries, trailers, and in some cases, the back of trucks, they dispersed in different directions. I felt a fly and itched my shoulder. A diluted, dapple grey, it was as if thinners had been thrown over me. Dark auction over, the days had to get brighter. Didn't they?

The new owners arrived. "A day or two and he'll be right as rain."

They gassed, smoked and planned. I was lousy, wanted pain relief for my shin, but like fences, medicines cost money. And like fences, pain wasn't something men put right. Not, when they could buy a pint of beer, or gallon of petrol. So, suffer I did, all the way to Torrevieja. Trying to stand on four legs, isn't easy when your shin feels fractured. Weight bearing on it, into my hip the ache did surge. I tried to sit down, but the rope didn't reach and snapped. Onto my bottom I went, then, like a broken Jack in the box, back up. Unbalanced, I stumbled to stand, occasionally putting all my weight on the bad leg. A thousand swords cut into its flesh. Ignoring the possibility of permanent damage, I found staring at the same spot a decent diversion. But, the road grew dilapidated and rickety. knocking the slim partition, I, over-reached several times. Ouch, it hurt, anxious and angry, I chewed on my bottom lip until it bled. Focused, I taught myself to embrace, and ignore pain. I did well, until we came off the main road and into the town.

Leaning requires balance, and steadiness, requires four stable feet. I withstood the first two turns, but, went down on the third. Squashed on the floor, partition straining against my weight, the position flattened one lung. Air planted in the pipe it wouldn't flow. Hyperventilating, the right, functioned for both. What I'd have given for lubrication, a lozenger or lung pump. Panic, for sure would have suffocated me. Immersed in my own calm, I convinced myself there was something worth waiting for. Palpitations, prickling my senses, fears stirring my wind pipe, I was weakening, when, finally, the door flew open.

"Mudra, Mia!" The men rushed in.

Unable to unbolt the partition, I felt an arm under my neck, another, pulled at my head collar. A few slaps and a lot of tugging, I was up. Overwhelmed, oxygen flowed like water into my lungs. Set back from one of the streets. I didn't take to the yard. Run down and ragged, it was poky, smelly and eerie. Hung on the wall, I saw the harness. Baking beneath the sun, its crusty leather should have come with a health, hazard label for horses.

"Yes, it will cut into your skin!" Observant, I glanced around for the voice.

Hot and exhausted, clumped in a wire enclosure, several horses shared a manger of manky straw. The cheapest form of equine food, I knew I was in for a trashy time. Taken into a stable, I was chained to a loop in the recently plastered wall.

"That will keep him from twisting himself again!"

A few minutes later, one of the men returned and filled the manger with the same straw the others had. In my feed sink, a kilo of grain.

"Eat well. Soon, we work!"

Despondent, I nibbled on mouldy spores. Upright and uncomfortable, sleep was minimal. I was comfort, consuming my breakfast, when, crispy leather covered me. I hadn't finished my last mouthful, when over it came. Collar to tight, it pinched my neck, burnt bacon reigns, either side, they rubbed before I'd began. The old cart was large, but the whip left no time for contemplations of any kind. Harness, carving me up, I pushed the damned thing into the streets and joined a queue, of horse drawn vehicles. I was on my third trip across town, when, my shoe came loose. Awkward, it clanged against my frog and foot. Antagonising me, it hindered my already lame leg. The driver hauled me to a standstill.

"Excuse me!" Passengers put in the picture, he took a tool box and jumped down.

He lifted my leg, a wrench in hand, he pulled back the shoe. Nails bending in all the wrong places, my outer hoof ripped as if teeth had torn it off. The metal moon hit the floor. No time to lose, the driver scooped it up, and sent me scooting ahead. Clomping on three shoes, I struggled till ten. A quick break, and work was resumed. Tourists have a thing about travelling under the stars, and as much as I believe in dreams, my only wish, was to feel well. Limp hopping, I dragged the last customer towards a cruise ship, finally, we turned for home. Abrasive on my flesh, I was pleased when the harness finally fell to the floor. Fumbling towards a bucket, the gulps, I took were enormous. Stomach now moist, I managed to lay down without further damaging my skin. Nose nesting on my foot, not even my shin lesion bothered me. In fact, I'd never felt, more, sorry for myself. Morning was a struggle, but for my troubles, I got two straw slices. The word vet was mentioned, but, never, did I see one. Instead, I was left to rest the sole of my foot. Wise enough, to know my life depended on work, I embraced my energy and put my head down. An ache surged through me, lashing upwards, it joined my shoulder sores. The farrier came. And against the will of nature, nailed the shoe back on my foot. Pins and needles, hammers and bats, bed knobs and broomsticks, how can they do that? Tongue tight between my teeth, it shrank. An unwilling slave being slaughtered, I felt crushed. Cursing coal mines, my muddled brain tried to summon protective powers. Soothed by a flock of birds, I went with them to cushion clouded skies. Overshadowed by three men, I'd never felt more vulnerable.

"You have until tomorrow!" Removing a twenty from his pocket, my owner paid the foot butcher.

To try and dry up my sores, I was tied between two trees in the heat. In my place, a mare was taken from the paddock. Attached to a Gig, she sped into the light of the day. A second one in motion, and the men were gone. Achy, and as if, I'd had too many salted peanuts, a thirst replaced the pain. I looked for water. Though I had slack, there wasn't so much as a cup of the stuff in sight. By lunch time, the sun had cooked my sores and my throat was on fire. In fact, I remember feeling a bit delirious. There was a thud. I was ecstatic, but, was the estuary, real? In abundance, water rolled towards me. But, what's this. Parched, the ground consumption slowed its waves. I reached out, dragged on my neck muscles, and drank before it dissolved. Indeed, the ground got more than me, but quench my mouth, it did.

"It's all we had." The paddock ponies looked over in pity. Beside them, their empty water butt wobbled back and forth.

Astonished at such selflessness and feeling like long John Silver, without a crutch, I was speechless. Still thirsty, but by no means ungrateful, a smile gate crashed my face. Through watery black pools, I watched the steeds move towards a shelter. Several hours, I stood out there. Dry as a funeral drum, I swayed between heat stroke and dizziness. Hallucinogenic hot, I saw them return through a misty haze. Tight as tape, my belly beat a strange sound. I felt a tug and like colliding marbles, my teeth clacked.

Mixed up, motions moving, I clip clopped into the stable. Sniffing the air, I followed my nose arrow. Jaw lowered, I ate at the water. The trees didn't rustle, the mice didn't march. In fact, the quench, was so fantastic, that I began to fade into a desert. Drifting without a name, I dragged myself over a hundred dunes. Each one different from the last, my unorganised feet stumbled and fell. Creepy quiet, I didn't notice the storm coming. It rolled like pastry, pushing me back until my face was paper thin. Swept away, I woke unconcerned by the dream. Instead, my wispy feathers, felt a tightness. Sweat and blood and all things bad, they were crusty, damned right dirty. My heart was sick from pain, when the cat came in. Purring, she was a great comfort until the cock crowed and the men rose. There was a creek, and I was pull, pushed into the paddock. As rough as I felt, I knew I had to prepare to pull. Raise my spirits and switch off to the terrible tightness. Building blocks of resistance aside, I bit my lip, and took off. Putting one foot softly in front of the other, I wandered into town. Joining the carriage cue, I was grateful of a tree that temporarily shielded me. Today, tourists were few. For this, I was truly grateful. It was over an hour before our services were sought. Using, my focus, I managed until two. It was the three o'clock that undid everything. Late, they needed to get to a booking. I hadn't planned on trotting, had only programmed my pain to a walking pace. Sugar, it hurt. Throwing my weight into a sideward stance, I tried trotting on half a hoof. It was awkward. But working. I halted outside the restaurant. The woman got down and came around to see me.

"He looks sad." She ran her hand over my face and kissed my flaring nostrils. "I'd take him home if only I could." She cancelled the evening collection, then leaving me entered the restaurant.

Done, I could do no more. Trundling home, my owner was angry and left me in my harness overnight. While I embraced the throbbing in my feet, my driver threw a set of blinkers at me.

"That will stop the poor me, see if they can see you in them!"

Tied in knots, it was one of my worst nightmares, only this time I wasn't asleep. The harness and morning upon me, strung up like a piece of Sunday ham, I prayed a predator would come and eat me. With breakfast, came the blinkers. I threw my head about, but, was hit, until I heeded. As if someone had stolen half an eye from each side, the patches, scratched and suffocated me. And so, with a sore foot and hardened soul, we went. I don't know, what I'd ate, only, that I suddenly had fallacious feet. Spellbound and parallel, I trotted beside a busy beach. Enjoyed the sea gulls and flecks of foam gathering upon potential tides. Speckled blue sheets, some rolled into the shore. In sync, my imagination ran upon ballerina hooves, danced delight, and counted shells. I didn't know, I was drugged, until it wore off. Only then, did the rusty realisation hit me. Hobbling, and hungry, we stopped. I didn't refuse the nose bag. Nibbling on alfalfa, I ate the lot. A second dose of drugs, and the lameness didn't return, till ten that night. Dragging my feet and wheels, I was done for. Pleased to see my dingy stable, I staggered inside. There were no sleeping pills or nice dreams, just hammering hurt and trauma. Work continued in the same numb way, until, immunity shot, injuries visible, I was no longer of any use. It was time. Shoes removed and double drugged, I arrived in Alicante.

The Lady

Sold to a Lady Abbot, who I nicknamed, LA. I stepped into the grounds, of her private villa. Out back, it opened into thirty thousand square metres of land. Fruit bearing branches and olive bushes, there was even bees buzzing from a row of pastel hives. Indeed, the place had a healthy heart. Without questioning anything, LA allowed the lorry to leave, she then asked her groom to run me up. Pain relief all absorbed, I could only, hop hobble. Furious, LA punched a portable phone in several places. Pantaloons flapping, she unbuttoned her shirt and seethed into the mouthpiece. Please, I thought, don't send me back there. I can heel, I just need to rest.

"She won't." I felt fur wrap around my leg. Glancing down, I saw a Persian cat. "She likes a challenge. Once she calms, you'll be ok." Observant, the cat examined my leg scars. "We race here."

"So," I felt stupid, "What does she want with me?" My nose flapped with anxiety.

"According to ancient history, Andalusian's are amazing on flat ground."

I laughed, lifted my back leg and shook it. Thickly scarred and scraggly, it was too injured for speed. Clunk, the phone clicked off.

"Liar...!" LA knelt, one by one she felt my legs. Lifting the injured shin, she examined my torn hoof too. "It will grow," she tutted. LA leaned into my face. "scars make you strong! There's life, in you yet."

She undid my halter, "go, rest and play, work will come later. Overwhelmed with fruit and freedom, I stood rigid like a reed without wind. I heard, LA, laugh. She took a broom and ushered me towards the trees. There, I sniffed the air and snatched at an apple. Amongst the trees I saw stables and outbuildings. Not ready to integrate, I grazed rich grounds instead. That night it was a pleasure to put my head down. Warm Mediterranean air and the scent of olives, I found some eternal peace beneath the universe. The cat arrived just as the star fell. A glint of silver it shot across the sky. I made a wish, and with a hopeful heart, took it to sleep. Seaweed in my supper, not only energized me, but helped my body heal from years of turmoil and hard graft, finally I felt, I had a new purpose. Those first few weeks, brought clarity to my mind, quickly extending itself into my limbs. Walking with ease through the food lanes, I filled myself with fruit, and various vegetation. Slowly but surely, my next venture, like my health, began to take shape. Communication and confidence coming back, I acknowledged, the Arab block on the opposite side of the orchard.

"We wondered when you would show." Though, petite and stealthy, the mare had an air of arrogance about her.

"Your perseverance is commendable." Steady and sleek, a second neck extended its status.

"Your legs are strong," a third frowned, "but are they speed built?" Like steam searching for outlets, their necks synchronized forward.

"How is life here?" Like springs, all three necks recoiled. Faces flat as book marks, they appeared stifled.

"It's quality." The first frowned, "for this we are grateful."

Compared to their fine physique and porcelain faces, I felt clumsy, a cumbersome, overweight cob. I righted my gait and gave new strength to my feet. The swelling in my shin gone, I was getting there. I was trotting back through the trees when, LA appeared.

"So, shall we see how you fair on the beach?" she held out a handful of pony grain, "Come, my friend..." I followed her, towards a trailer and went in. Ten years old, I was probably a bit long in the tooth to race, but addicted to the sport, LA didn't give in. Instead, she put a snaffle in my mouth and a slim saddle on my back. Joined by one of her jockeys, he got on. Pulling and pushing me, he made me jog on the spot. Heels sinking into the softness beneath, it felt like quick sand. Gently, the jockey urged me forward. Using a side step swivel, and as if scooping ice cream from a container, I learnt to churn walk in wet sand. Spear, swivelling, digging and flicking, I char, chared, half a mile before turning back. Breaking into canter, breeze in my main, I felt fantastic. Giving in to gallop, I mastered my movement upon difficult grounds.

"His potential is profoundly pleasant!"

Nodding, the jockey agreed with LA.

"Cool him off." Pleased she crossed her arms and watched as we went. My legs absorbed the salt water, and with a more positive heart, I tried to enjoy the endurance work. I was into week three, when I woke to the smell of cream tea, coffee and cheese. Nicely dressed as always, LA had company. Tightening her head scarf and raising a coffee, the visiting couple stared at me. Stood twenty feet away, nibbling on an almond tree, I felt uncomfortable.

"So, you really think he can race?" The wife clacked her cup and saucer together, but never took her eyes, from me.

"Faustino against the fine breeds," her husband cocked his head to one side, "Interestingly, brave, I must say!"

"Do you really think he can do something darling?" The wife searched her husband.

"When you've as much money as Abs, it's neither here or there." The man made them all laugh.

"I think it will be fun!" It wasn't, what I expected from LA.

Alicante was all brick and tower block tall, but on its far side was a flat track. We arrived at ten. The first race was at twelve. Although I was pure Andalusian, I was still classed as a half breed amateur. I knew the jockey, his moves, what he wanted, and when. Arabians either side of me, the flag went up. Fast off the mark, they disappeared like dissolvable tablets. Reins thrashing my neck, my rider spurned me on. Stocky legs eating the ground, I caught the first, on a bend, overtaking, I hammered the ground for more. Hooves beating their own drum, I shadowed a chestnut mare before making a swift move to my left. Weaving like a cobra, I sped past a further two. At the finish, I arrived fourth.

"Moi Bien!" Pleased with the result, the rider leapt from his saddle and waved recognition to LA. A flanking belly and heaving nostrils, I gulped air, as though it were grain. Undoubtedly, I needed my saddle undone. Sides heaving, I wondered how long this would last. "As long as you can run..." My subconscious whispered back. At the villa, I was put in a stable. I watched LA, and the lad chat. Everyday thereafter, he tendon, trained me in wet sands.

"If you can trot through this for an hour a day, your legs will fly along the flats."

Indeed, it was hard, but boy, did it build hamstrings. Tendons tightened, Lungs bolted to my ribs, I felt like a tin horse. Pushed to my limits, my perception of people changed, and I came to realise that, humans needed one of three things. Money, power, or face. I think LA wanted all three. And so, the big event arrived, and in the lorry, I had company.

"They started this IOTB, stuff, last year." The pure breed, began.

"The, what...?"

"Integration of track breeds."

"Oh..." My jaw dropped, and my hopes of a happy ending fast disappeared. Instead, I was tied in tight expectations. The horse red me right.

"You don't stand a chasing chance, Faustino, so why put you through it?"

I pondered on his words, he had a point. Humans, they had to experiment with everything. Talk of prize money emulated from the front cab. I was hot, sticky, even tired of standing in the same spot. My mind and body swayed, until, finally the wheels stopped. Tied and tacked up, my rider went to be weighed.

Consciously, I glared at the circular track and the closest contenders. Swans on spindles, lubrication in every joint, the words of my companion resonated. Untied, I felt the contact of my feather weight rider. Wearing purple and yellow, we were number seventeen. I was led towards the stalls. Branding cages, I bulked out. Bunched and bouncing against the others, divots of dirt flew. Protesting, I watched as they bundled in. A lunge line behind me, and I was steered forward. Peddling invisible wheels, hot competition lava leaked from every stall. The flag and front gates went up and we tore, like tin foil down the track. A cloud of mechanical legs collaborating, the fine breeds clumped into one mass of movement. Ferocious, I felt teeth from behind. Angry, I was ahead, the lorry companion was furious. I began moving towards the outside. A spur in the ribs every few seconds, it brought back memories of arrogance. Like a thousand beams of lightning, we tore around the track. Overtaking and dodging one, I counted eleven others. It was in the midst, of the madness, that I felt for my life. Dangerous to slow down, fatal to drop out, I had to stay on the running machine. Imaginary monsters behind me, crushers either side, my bionic legs breathed renewed life. The first lap behind me, I felt my lung cells begin to shrink on the second. Huff struggling, blood entered my mouth. Strained and pained, fluid flesh, fell from my nose. It merged with the sweat on my face. Eyes full of brow foam, I ran blind. Like sheets of sharp metal, I felt some of them overtake. Colliding, the shoe clipped my fetlock, an angle grinder, it removed my scar. Wound re-opened, I buckled and fell. In the way of would be winners, I felt legs lunge, dust and dive over me. Bodies bolting like bullets their hooves trigger tore into the bend and bolted to the finish. I managed to get up. My rider brushed himself down and took hold of the reigns. Moving off the track, we hobbled, towards LA, and the lorry. Swarms of sweat gathered, his hand was frothy. He flicked it across the floor and led me up the ramp. Ragged all over, the pinching in my heel was excruciating. In anticipation of the pain, I hitched the leg up and then down. I just didn't know what to do with it. No antidote for my agony, I leaked blood, from at least two places. Veins inflamed like a swollen road map, my nose was a messy motorway. I knew companion had won, by the way LA praised him. And so, the king of shine, entered his lorry lane. Full of himself, he beamed.

"You took a real fall, Faustino. For that, I admire you!"

"And you didn't need to bite."

"I'm sorry, I get carried away out there." He lowered his voice, "Guess, I've got used to the good life and don't want to lose it."

I knew all about that. But, every time I found decency, destiny stole it back. I bowed my head. Back in the orchard, birds failed to flutter, and the cat, cringed. Battered, I was left beneath a tree. I had a migraine, and someone was using a cheese grater on my gaping heel. Loneliness replaced the pain and my insides cracked with the quiet seeping of soul tears. The sound of a rustling rabbit accompanied LA.

"Yes, he did his best, but unfortunately, is knackered." There was an intermission, then. "The only thing left is breeding, which is why I thought of you." The voice of LA was vulgar. I watched her pace, shirt collars flapping like sheets, she nodded continuously, into the phone. Audible, her voice went up an octave. "I was trying to achieve something!"

I couldn't believe her cold-hearted audacity. There was a clack, she slammed the phone shut. Her eyes met mine, a falcon in mid-flight, a battle ship about to sink, she appeared embarrassed. Lip quiet, she disappeared like a dawn mouse. I lay down. Spirit, and his ordeal, sprang to mind. Persecution and punishment. An onslaught of hate, about to overcome me, a fluffy faced kitten spared me the stains.

"Cute aye...?" It was cat.

Two more fluff balls behind her, they nestled inside my neck. Enticed by a feather, the first, chased it. Intrigued, by its innocence, my heart lifted somewhat.

"Enjoy..." the cat cleaned her whiskers, "they'll be grown and gone, within the blink of an eye."

The kitten chased a further two feathers. Fetching one in its mouth, it ran towards me. Skidding a few inches from my face, it tickled my nose. I sneezed, I smiled, I felt family feelings. They stayed for over an hour, before cat bid me good night. Only when they had all disappeared beneath the olive shrub, did the intrusion of fear arrive. Fear of the unknown, the wicked slaughterhouse and starvation, but biting me hardest of all, was loneliness. The lack of compassion, consideration and damned right neglect, needled me. Nothing but money, mattered. Marina was an exception. Still, magical, her mind wasn't yet shackled to adulthood. Detached from humans, I lost all hope of finding another genuine one. Awkwardly, I tried to sleep. There was silence until five, when distracted by a saw, I sat up. The grooms were shortening the hen house. Leg stands, a foot shorter, its top was then covered in tarpaulin. To keep the sun out, I guess. Gourmet grass only feet in front, I limped towards it. Schedule, unknown, I did my upmost to stay, people proof, and positive. Three further nights passed. Then, destination unknown, the lorry ramp was undone. It was a big one, cost a few bucks more than any before. I stared at the racing stock. A moment exchanged, and I entered. What really did me was that folks didn't even have the decency to say thank you, or goodbye. Doors closed, and I put aside my lingering doubts. What will be, will be. Let's, do it.

Just maybe

Acoustic music, easing the wheel motion, it made a more interesting journey than usual. Busy, Benidorm was full of bumps, but finally we arrived. Arched gates behind me, a display of carriages and cars, ahead, the posh pad stood between a pet shop and private bar. Separated by livestock, the fields were full. Not so lucky, others stood stagnant, in the stables. Hay and straw in abundance, my astonishment, became alarm.

Mateo, had yellow teeth, sun wrinkled skin and disrespectful hands. Hard hitting, he pushed me towards a stable. Door shut, I spun to see out. Wearing a hat that didn't match his boots, the rich dealer lacked both pride and presentation. Ill mannered, he picked his nose and belched. I didn't like him one bit. But, use pain powders he did. Not because he was kind, but, because it kept face. The next day, a groom came and got me out. A beverage in one hand, Mateo used the other to belt me about. Picking up my front foot, they forced me to stand on both backs. Injuries extensive, Mateo excluded me, from immediate work. In the name of recovery, I was stall tied. Only straw on offer, for sure, the guy didn't like me. When they came to muck out, movement was minimal. But, a good whack around the ears, forced me to quickstep outside. Once in the air, I admired those able to roam, better still, be together. Daydream discarded, I felt a thump on the forehead. Jumping fiddle sticks, what was with this groom. Hungry, I reached for some alfalfa, on the floor.

"Behave." I was hit again.

Avoiding another whack, I bolted on three legs back to my stall. But, I got another clack anyway. After a week of this, it was safe to say, I was completely-head shy. So much so, that when they came to get me for the breeding programme, it all went to pot. There was nothing wrong with the eye-catching mare, she was magnificent. A bellyful of Bute, my legs moved in mechanical motion towards her. It was the twitch that did it. Nose exposed, they noosed it. Twice, it twisted before I went up. Taking the torture stick with me, it slapped me clean in the chops. I saw stars, heard the handle hit the floor and spun fear into authority. The mare neighed submissively, but I wasn't having a rope, rip my nose to bits. Like buckaroo, I threatened to box the men. Waving arms of white flags, they let me float in my own time, back to earth.

"Stupid horse," Mateo lit a fag and fumed smoke at me, "don't you know where your breads buttered?"

Exuberant, they let me calm down, before entering my space. Mateo didn't like dilemma, or defeat. Four feet firmly on the ground, I could almost hear, the grinding of his thoughts.

"Public parade!" Mateo punched the air.

Reputation, contacts and the face thing, was important to him. Paid, or unpaid, so was getting some work out of me. Fiesta season about to start, Mateo had more than just one, appearance to make. I'd never seen a suit of armour. A tart in tinfoil, I found the outfit heavy going, especially, the metal balaclava, bolted over my face. A lance in hand, it took time to get used to my rider. Once ready, we joined a colourful cavalry. Unable to see anything beside me, I learnt to trust my feet. In between stuffing sweets, the people cheered. Street after street we went. A public farcical, I didn't like the crowds, or the bolt tight cramps. Two hours into it, we turned off. The cobbles were hard to cope with. Shoes sliding on concrete bubbles, I bruised my soles several times. The smell of sweet corn, conveyed with soft music, soothed my senses. Craft stalls all around, the medieval square, was bee hive busy. Beer for the riders and big troughs for us, everyone received refreshments. Proud of this seasonal sensation, the public stroked the horses. Some even posed while others snapped their cameras. Then, out of nowhere, there she was. Like a ghost from the past, my beautiful, Marina, was right in front of me. She touched the armour on my face and sighed. I nuzzled her like old times, but her smile became sad and she pressed her lips together. She remembered.

She just didn't know that it was me under the armour. Oh, why can't we talk, put our feelings into words. I was frustrated. Wanted to know all about her dad, her exams and current life. Then, cruising like two big cart wheels, a wheelchair approached. Running beside it, the baby had grown into a boy. Candy floss in both hands, Tia too arrived. Happy for the family, I felt something I hadn't for a while, alive. And just like that we left. Uncomfortable in the fact we still had miles to go, I was grateful for the pain powder. Standard on every parade, Mateo always put it my food. Shoes wearing well on the roads, we trundled on. But like everything, Fiesta season ended. Wanting his monies worth, Mateo put me in harness. Impressed, with the coach, I hit the road. All the way along the promenade I pulled. Back and forth, I got to know every pub, club and restaurant. I knew when the sea went out, when the lager louts arrived, and when the doves took advantage of the tourists. Hundreds of them, they flocked in the square to be fed. As I trotted past, they would rise like a giant fan into the air before again landing. On a Saturday, the market would set up. Afterwards, arms full, people cued to be taken home. A slim city, cluttered in cars, the coaches were always popular. Safe and scenic, Mateo's new business didn't go wrong. In fact, it got so busy that it hurt. Regimental, the routine was strict, hot and sweaty. But, anything, was better than being on the end of the twitch. I only had to think of it and my legs turned to jelly, then steel. I pulled consecutively for two years before being sent to a show jumping yard in Calpe. By now my legs were conditioned and could cope with the landings. The lad gave me a good hammering for six months, before sending me back. I later learned, he'd been the nephew of Mateo. He received a call from a friend the next day. Her circuit cruiser was lame, and the summer shows were looming. She needed something willing, who knew the ropes, would get on without retaliation. I didn't think there was anything left, until Mateo loaned me to the circus. Money mad, the man was. A giant ice cream cone, the tent twizzled into the sky. Inside it, was pure mayhem. Peanuts, monkeys, magicians and tight rope walkers all in action, my head spun. I was handed to a girl in a body stocking, who checked me over.

"He'll do just fine, have him ready for seven."

Plaited and polished, I felt a fancy bridle on my face. Packed full of people the place was loud. Spot light on an empty circuit, the girl took over. Peacock feathers poking up from her hair, a riot of red ribbons holding her striped corset together, the candy girl was given a leg up. Vibrant, her softness energised me. Cantering into the ring, she had me circle it in style. On the correct leg I knew when to come down. Then unexpectedly, but gently, she put her knees into my back, and knelt. Exquisite, she extended her reigns, barefoot firm, on my fur, she stood up. Frightened and flabbergasted, I moved tenderly. Two laps complete, she swung her legs left, and sat. Leaning, arms reaching into nowhere, she hung like a petal. Carrying my tulip, I took her round again. Normal position resumed, and I was relieved to stop. I had palpitations, the crowd applauded, and the elephants entered. Exploitation in process, I was glad to go out back and pretend, I was elsewhere. By the end of that summer there was little I hadn't seen, and nothing more I wanted to.

Mateo knew everyone, even friends of their friends and families. On my return, he was having a party. Music mad, it continued into the evening. I heard the bolt go, a minute later a drunken groom grabbed me. Outside, I was paraded before a young lady.

"I don't want a horse, especially a grey."

Indeed, I was, a snow white, stallion, with speckles.

"Go on Bianca," Mateo burped, "ride him!"

"No, I don't want the responsibility, tie or burden!"

At least she was being honest. She reached out and touched my neck.

"How old...?" She softened.

"Nine."

What a liar. Amusement on her face, she wasn't as stupid as he thought. I was fifteen, and she knew it. More drinks and a dinner on the agenda, they put me away. An hour later, Bianca was back. Was my luck about to change? They tacked me up. Kind, she rejected the whip, took me by the reins and walked beside me. Bearing a piece of apple, she led me into the school. I came to life, felt vibrant and happy. A lamb on a carousel, I cruised on air. Eagerly watching, I noticed her children, Lotte and Annie. Like, Bianca they were a bundle of fun, even reminded me of, Marina. Ignoring her feelings, she hopped off, and handed me over.

"I'll think about it." She gave me to Mateo, of all people.

Pulling on my mouth, he shoved me fully tacked away. The girls cooed at a Jack Russel and her puppy. Only weeks old, and the only one, it shouldn't have been out. Not a heart in him, Mateo scooped it up, handed it to the kids, and sent the mother on her way. The complexion of Bianca changed. Unhappy with his behaviour, she looked me over, had the puppy put back, and bid everyone, goodnight.

My lucky star

Without any warning, I was bashed out of the stable and onto a lorry. Two more on, and the sardine tin was full. I've no idea what was on the agenda, only that the angle, forced my feet to seriously splay. Plunged backwards, sideways and face down, I felt disfigured. A slow vertical chug, my legs didn't appreciate the leaning. It got so steep in one place, that I had a touch of vertigo. Bones stiff stuck, I had to almost do the splits to stay in place. Hooves drilled down, the mares mirrored the same fears. Determination grounded, our legs gained new stand up skills. For to fall during such a trip, would for sure, be, fatal. A sharp left, onto even ground, and we were righted. Thrashing a thousand loose chippings aside, dancing to the bends and skating on a wet floor, we finally stopped. Mateo wasn't familiar with gentle. Lunge lines attached, he literally yanked us backwards. How we turned didn't matter. What we twisted, was unimportant. If we fell in the process, it was tough. The mare must have caught her back on the bar, because it bled. But oblige the order, she, then the other mare, did. Neck folded, feet trampling over one another, I managed the turn.

Abstract, all around me, the mountains were figurative. A bit shaken and stifled, I found myself face to face with Mateo. A bald overweight man with more attitude than moral, he was a complete control freak. Delighted with my frightened features, Mateo sneered. Then, just for the sake of it, raised a hand to my head. Fast as a fly, I flinched three steps away. Fidgety, the mares stared over the new paddock he'd put them in and at the oblong house opposite. Feeling fiendish, I filled my lungs with immaculate air, and backed away from him. Awaiting instructions, Mateo let the rope go slack and slipped a cigarette into his mouth. The side of the paddock was separated by a gated walkway. Behind it, newly built, was a wall dorm. Reaching to the end of its layer, it was long enough for over a dozen inmates. A tug, and I was led up a path around the side of the house. The place was made up of three layers, the stable block had been built on the second. Fortunately, for me, Mateo placed me in one of three front stables. Horses either side, they were silent. Parallel, with the house roof, the view beyond was paramount. Roots too deep to remove, an established pine tree was wedged between the bank, and the back of the house. Gemstone green, the air was needle sharp packed. Clack, observations out of the question, I ducked from another, Mateo clout. Hurrying down the slope, he rubbed his hands together. I glanced to my left. I could just see the dorm roof. I had hoped men would stop building them, but business is business, and horses stood side by side, easier, and cheaper to maintain. Jeepers creepers, I'd really gone back in time. Free of Mateo, I felt fluffy. From behind my wall, I could hear hooves and the neighing goat. It reminded me of mother. Overwhelmed, I tried to open the others up to answers, but they didn't respond. Flustered, I felt an awkward outcast. I was new, they would come around. Ingesting, pure oxygen, I let its silky textures, send me to sleep. Breakfast caused quite a stir. Grace, in my feet, I got up and tucked in. Captivated, I saw a toad on the roof. An extension of my layer, it was easy for frogs, cats and insects to access it. And, as I soon found out, caterpillars too.

I looked to my neighbours. On my left was a white mare, to my right, a Lipizzaner stallion. Posh and pure bred, he was as black, as I used to be. Lineage, like Monty, he made me smile. But, still, none, of them spoke a word. An hour later and Mateo's, lorry returned. Malignant, the man was back. Three more unloaded, the black mare came out last. Front leg, hanging as though severed, her eyes severely told off, Mateo. A quick examination, and he pointed his groom towards the lorry. Lazy, Mateo poured white spirit into her frog. Retaliating, the mare went up and shunted backwards. Letting the rope go, Mateo lip, directed, her into the paddock. Gate slammed, he was done. I got the impression the new owners were not the only ones pleased to see him go. Five in the paddock, it was full, had to be the last of his visits. But like a bad omen, he returned the next morning. This time, instead of horses, he unloaded a coach and a cart. Finished, he reached into the cab. Paperwork in hand, he, and Ron went into the house. Yes, the new owners were, Ron and Sally. Arriving outside my stable, Sally, made her acquaintance. She then, led me down the layer and let me loose between the paddock and new fence separating it from the dorm.

"Go stretch your legs." Sally encouraged.

Endeavouring not to fall over my own feet, I felt lively as a cricket, but shy as a beetle. Underweight, the black mare was by no means unintelligent. She was the surrounding air, the iced gem on the mountains, a snow drop in spring, and just like the shooting star on her face, she was spellbinding. An exquisite, filly, she was taller than all the others. Was charismatic and elegant, had an awesome, aroma about her, and despite the cold, a cheeky grin. I named her star. It was barking, that snapped me back into reality. I glanced down the track towards the fork. There, my eyes followed the bend. On it, slept a cabin. Double cream whipped, its layers surrounded it. From its slim chimney, chugged smoke. I moved to the end of my passage to see better. There, a small dog antagonised its owner. Yapping mad, loud as a bell, it was. I nicknamed it, Barker. Axe in hand, the man chopped a trunk into logs. He shouted for Barker to stop, scooped up some wood and went inside with both.

"Faustino...!"

Oh, he told you my name then. Deal done. Mateo gone. It was Ron. Led away, butterflies in my stomach, I sighed against my stable wall. Enticing, Star made me smile. Sent electric shivers down my spine. Connection, stronger than the cold, she was special. Unlike the summers that breathed fresh hay and herbs, the altitude offered only snow and chimney smoke. I thought of star in the open paddock, I shuddered, felt guilty that I had somewhere sheltered, to eat from. That I didn't have to hasten my intake, for fear of it being blown away or stolen, by the other horses there. How long would I last, if someone stole my food? My fast, lasted till three in the morning. The next day, was even colder. Because of the elements, extra alfalfa, was applied to all of us. Once lunch was done, Ron fought the easterly winds and went into the warmth of his house. Paddock horses huddled together, my heart went out to Star. Some hours later, I heard voices. Sure, I knew them, I strained against the winds. They disappeared into the house, but an hour later, returned. Accompanied by Ron, coats zipped tightly up, two girls got out the goat. On her back legs, she boxed the air and bunny hopped to the tune of mischief. Leading her up to the third layer, they let her scoff grasses. What came next was a sight I won't forget. Coffee in hand, cream coat to match, she chatted incessantly to Sally.

"Oh, he came up too?" It was my beautiful rider from Benidorm.

"Yes, cheeky, Mateo, sent him up with you in mind."

"Did, he now!" Bianca chewed on one side of her mouth.

"Oh, can we mum, pleassssee..." Overhearing us, Lotte, left her sister with the goat and came back down. "Can I, at least brush him?"

Sally obliged and out I came.

"Just look at his main," Lotte couldn't believe how long it was. "He'd do well in the show ring."

Unimpressed, Bianca was silent. But behind her armour, I got the impression that like me, she was worn and worried.

"You know, Ron could do with some help while I'm at work." Sally could see how capable Bianca was. "Can't pay much, but you can ride all you want..."

"I Can't, commit permanently," Bianca sounded bashful, "but I'll help for a few months."

Annie put the goat away. The weather worsened, and the paddock mares were put in the dormitory. I heard the engine start and was sad to see them go. Arriving again the following morning, Bianca led the stallion next to me, out. In the paddock his body, bounced and bronked' with delight. Arms crossed, a toothpick twiddling between his teeth, Ron said nothing. A change over, and it was my turn. Unclipped, I was glad to see Star on the other side of the fence. Her nose nestled in chain link, it looked like dough in a pastry cutter. Pretty dough too. Fluttering, in the bottom of my belly, I moved closer. She had great legs and solid feet, that would never need a nail near them.

"So," I managed to muster, "Where were you before?"

"Auction..."

"Awful!" I cringed, "and before that?"

"With show jumpers."

I pulled a face.

"My parents were professional!"

"Oh...?"

"The owners didn't think I'd make the same grade, so got rid of me."

She didn't look a failure to me. But, then I didn't have human formality. It was time to go. Not wanting to get Bianca in trouble, I obliged. The week went quickly and on Saturday the girls arrived.

"Can I ride Faustino?" Lotte, the eldest was keen.

"A few things need sorting first." Bianca did up her hood.

110

Lotte pulled a 'what,' face.

"Shoes, for one…" yes, they needed a trim. "then there's worming."

Ron pouted in contemplation. "Can you get them?" He put the proposal to Bianca.

"I'll go tomorrow."

The kettle whistled, Sally, made coffee.

Now to my knowledge, I'd never been wormed. But, someone must have, because unlike 'Star,' nothing showed up. Long as bamboo shoots, but even whiter, they were. Yuk, yuk. Yes, I must have had something over the years.

"No wonder Star's so thin." I spoke to the dog outside my door. "I bet she's had terrible belly ache!"

"Hmm, pregnant with parasites," the dog scratched a tick from its ear, "they're everywhere."

I arched my neck and sniffed at my belly. The only person kind enough to care, could have been Carlos. Feet trimmed, and I was ready to roll!

The Breeze

Like, the girls, Saturday arrived, and they got me out of the stable. But, before they could ask, and because I'd been in a while, Bianca got on to try me first. Bareback, she encouraged me down the drive and onto the mountain road. On the bend, the middle-aged man, with his dog came out. A big grin smothered his face, hatless, his silver hair was flecked with sawdust.

"I'm Jed." Camel boots, pale jeans, patchwork shirt and scarf, he was a colourful character.

"Bianca..." She sounded, shy.

"I often see you drive by." Ruffling my neck and fur, he maintained eye contact with Bianca, "are you riding for Ron?"

"Ahh, huh..." Awkwardly, Bianca kicked me on. We'd gone ten feet, when she turned right into a little loop.

The gush of water came from nowhere, and I do believe, had Bianca not been looking behind at Jed, she wouldn't have fallen. I swerved. Unseated onto uneven ground, she hit the deck. Terrified, I was in trouble, my immediate reaction was to run. Bolting blue bottle fast, I halted outside the cabin. Fast off the mark, Jed jumped on his bike. Taking Bianca with both hands, he helped her up, dusted her down and did a wheelie. Safe on the back of his bike, I scarpered so fast that I must have left a trail of sparks behind. Firework fast, I raced up the drive and past the girls. Worry all over them I charged to where I'd last been tied and lowered my head. Ron snatched up my reins and raised my head to tell me off.

"It wasn't his fault." Intentions intercepted, Bianca leapt from the bike. "It was an accident." She got her breath, "Don't you ever get scared?"

"Course he does." Jed kicked his bike stand out and reached for Ron's hand.

That was the day, I melted like butter towards Bianca.

"If I take Billy, can I ride to the cabin and back?" Lotte was keen to get on. Billy wagged her tail in anticipation, brown stripes wriggling, she encouraged the fun.

Ron went into the house and returned with a saddle, that he, and Jed did up around me.

"Cross country will be safer?" Sally pointed to a track, etched in the hill above my stable. "To get to it, go around the ruin," she pointed to the left of the drive. There, rooted upon dry mud stood a derelict mansion. "Keep going, all the way around, eventually, you'll see your nans house. You know where we are from the village."

Ron handed me over. Relieved, I carried Lotte down a layer. Hooves beating to the sound of Billy's barking, I curved right and around the building. Gradually, we climbed upwards. Different grades of grass either side, it decorated an otherwise, bleak surrounding. Swollen from rain and snow, the ground was plump and pleasant to pace upon. But, unlike the scent of summer, the cold was cutting edge. Abandoned, rustic homes caught my eye. Oh, to be self-sufficient, with 'Star,' of course. Lotte sang. Good too, she was. The louder she got, the faster the dogs tail propelled. In-fact, at one point, I thought Billy, was going to take off. This made Lotte laugh hysterically. Infectious, the two of them restored some of my faith and sanity. It was good, to meet her nan. Afterwards, I took the narrow slope into the school square, where, there, the only school in the village stood. Plodding through painted side streets, I then headed up towards the cabin. Jed came out. An apple in hand, he gave half to Lotte, the other to me.

"I don't have anything for you." Jed bent down and scratched Billy on the neck.

Ten more minutes, and I was back, untacked and put in my stable. Bianca and the girls left. Their car disappeared, before reappearing on the bend where it stopped. A conversation with Jed, car parked on the gravel and inside the cabin they went. Summer seemed to draw a long straw, and like a pair of loose soles, winter dragged its feet into February. Unlike the evergreen pines, life on the lands had stumped their growth. I wasn't quite sure of the cotton wool nesting in the pine needles. But like a balloon, it expanded, and for sure, something inside it, was growing. Heavy, the white hive stretched. Ron spotted it and shooed the ground sniffing dogs away. An aerosol to hand, he sprayed it, clicked his lighter and burnt it. The smell of candy floss didn't fill my nose, instead, fried insects did.

"Caterpillars!" It was the first time the mare next door had spoken. "It's kill or be killed." Wistfully, she stuffed her face with straw.

"Toxic fibres," the stallions voice was authoritive, "they get in your throat and swell up. Fatal for humans too they are."

"They're, a rotten ending to every winter." The mare finished chewing. "be careful till March."

On the other side of the house, another pine overshadowed the dorm pen. My thoughts turned to Star. Please don't sniff, or eat any, I thought. Bianca settled like snow into a routine. Riding routes established, I was pleased when winter ended. At last, with field mouse magic, spring, and its wild herbs arrived. Boggy ground drying, feet as fresh as the font water, Lotte, and I, flew along the hardening tracks. Not wanting to miss out, Annie borrowed the mare. Carried by whispering winds, hair blowing like fondant icing, the girls were a portrait of time. No longer a muddle minded mess, I embraced my good luck and broke into a comfortable canter. The mare caught up, she overtook. Stuck to her like a suet pudding, Annie urged her over a small gate. I followed, and so did a gaggle of laughter. Fluttering birds and blooming plants, it was a pleasant place. Yes, I was the most privileged horse in the yard. I don't know why, but the butterflies reminded me of blinkers. Perhaps it was the shape of their wings, perhaps the oval patterns, I didn't know. Hills behind us, we headed down, and into the village where we drank from its famous font. As always, we passed the cascades of land that led towards the cabin. I could see Jed. He was carrying a sheet of timber, not far behind, Bianca followed. There was a whistle and a wave. Like me, the girls didn't know what was happening either. Seasonal changes in the air, Ron expressed the importance of cooling down our tendons. Opening my mouth, I beckoned for the hose. Sucking on it like a lolly pop, I gurgled and glugged at it. Top lip curling like a half-opened tin, I had them in hysterics. Totally soaked too, the girls put us away and left for the cabin. Not long after, the farrier arrived and went around the back of my block. He returned with a stallion called, Rumba. Tied to my door, we were face to face. Old and worn, his legs, were riddled with arthritis. Nervous, he shifted his weight every few seconds. Complacent to the nail pain, his eyes were stony. And if my eyes didn't deceive me, I swear, he was surrounded by orbs.

"Bull ring." He snorted, "I'm the longest server to survive."

"Survive what...? I was bleating now.

"Death." The hammer hit, and another nail went in. Brave, he glanced away, then back. "I've seen it all. More horses gorged than you've had meals." The orbs

116

appeared to flutter about his face. "Nightmares every night. Spears, spikes and screaming. No matter what our state, we still have to trawl."

Mother, of mine. Did, I really want to know the details?

"Hit me with it." the hammer thrashed at another nail, "everything else has." Knots of pain swallowed, I felt nothing, but respect for him. "What was her name?" He was sharper than the rasp ribbing his hooves.

"Othelia..." My throat swelled. I couldn't swallow, "Andalusian, all white, with the brightest of..." I choked, I trailed off.

"Bold mare, she was. Hated humiliation, as much as me. The taunt and tease, the blood bearing holes that trailed veraciously behind its body. The bull will always be a victim, hurting horses, just a way of offloading his own anguish. Even when injured, she endured the stitches, stood another round, and pulled the carcass with dignity. But disapprove, she did. Often, she tugged on the reins, reared and heel dug, played up merry hell. Demonstration meant a lot to the mare." The last nail driven in, he shuddered on his own weight. Untied, Rumba was turned back towards his block.

"What happened to her...?" I couldn't help myself.

"If," he called back in a totally different tone, "the grey was your mother, she was sold to someone in

Segovia. Famous for its architect, life there, wouldn't be all bad."

Rather than the real one, he put a better picture in my mind. With gratitude, I wholeheartedly accepted it. I envisioned mother. War wounds heeled, she halted her Brougham, right outside a Romanesque church. Overshadowed by a famous aqueduct, it protected her eyes from the sun. Moving on, her and the passengers approached a gothic cathedral. My imagination fizzled out. Bingo, it was Bianca. But where was Lotte? School holidays weren't over yet. I was looking forward to my ride out. Finally, I spotted her, but instead of being up on my bit, she was below, grooming star. I felt something new. I felt jealous, left out and afraid she would abandon me. Only two years old, Star took to Lotte. Ears going up and down, she paid her an enormous amount of attention. Even picked up three of her feet for cleaning. Thanks to white spirit, impatience and Mateo, the mare flat refused, to pick up her front left. Ron put her on the lunge for Lotte to observe. Back legs beating the air, she played a drum, performance. Unimpressed, Ron tried to change the rein, but reel her in, he couldn't. Instead, fast as snow off a shovel, she entered his space. Ears disappearing into the dimples of her head, miss, wild retaliation, went for him. Lunge line raised, it was Ron's only defence. Screaming Spanish obscenities, it worked. Dancing back into her dizzy circuit, Star created circles of entertainment. Unlike the others, she fought for her rights, and wasn't afraid to show her guts. Not even, if it got her a good beating. Exhausted, Star stopped and prickled her ears. Expecting a reward, she nuzzled the air.

"Who the bells, does she think she is?"

Sniggering, Bianca disappeared down to the cabin.

"It's not funny!" Ron barked after her.

Lotte took over, tied Star to the paddock rails, and brushed her. More interested in the new mules, Annie conversed with them. I heard a door slam. House windows open, I heard every word, Ron vented.

"She won't conform like the others. Teeth barred, she's always ring tugging, foot tapping and throwing tantrums."

"I haven't noticed." Sally was calm.

"You don't deal with the miserable mare every day!"

"I've got to go, or the shops will shut." I heard the door close. Sally appeared in a pair of pretty shorts. Engine on, she stone surfed down the drive. Having fetched her coat from the cabin, Bianca was on her way back. The women waved at each other.

"You okay?" Bianca asked Ron on her return.

Deep rooted, Ron was planted outside his front door.

"I'm going to sell a few..." Ron twisted his jaw to one side. "Perhaps, I need a few smaller ponies for our plans."

"Can I have 'Star, mum!"

It stung my soul. Lead rope in her hand, Star hurried after Lotte towards the house. Then, quickly looking up at me, I could see, Lotte was torn.

"I like Faustino..." It was Annie. Miss observant had an opinion, and voice it from the dorm she did.

"I didn't mean to put you in a position." Ron heaved a bundle of air.

Feelings

As if on purpose, it rained, and they all hurried home. Not just large drops, but torrential sheets, one could barely see through. For days it poured, penetrating the land, making life almost impossible. It was so heavy that the stables only got swept out, once a day. Umbrella blown upside down, food bucket quickly filling, the grain was drenched before Ron could dish it out. Hungry, soup slop we did eat. Drainage over spilling, it merged with the rivets of loose mud and mountain muck. A water fall, that couldn't be turned off, we got flooded. Ankle deep, for days, it was a wet, and worrying time. In plastic coats, I watched, Jed, and Ron, dig a trench. Faces dripping, they didn't stop until it was wide enough to divert danger. April arrived and finally, the rain stopped. But, the land, like my stable was slippery and far too unsafe, for Lotte to ride on. Talk of landslides and overspills had frightened Bianca. Instead, she brought me a bag of carrots. These, she, shared out.

"You are lovely Faustino." She gave me a hug. I chewed the carrot continuously, mouth dribbling, I made her laugh. Jed appeared. He put his hands on her shoulders.

"Just buy him."

Bianca smiled, but said nothing. Saturday arrived, and at last, so did Lotte and the saddle. I'd been in the stable for weeks and my joints felt hinged together. Moving, like a horse made of Lego, it took ages to shift the stiffness in my limbs. Billy dog beside us, we enjoyed the transition of colours. The grass was much greener, dashed in heather and laced with lavender. Combined with pony perfume, it was a scent that would have sold worldwide. Exclusive to us, we were exceptionally rich. The cabin stable, was as much a surprise to me, as it was the girls. Childhood dream come true, all Lotte had to do was choose a horse. Unlike my snow-white status, Star stood on four black legs that would eventually, lighten. Intrigued by the transition, I wondered if all horses changed colour, or just some. Confused, Lotte turned her face away from Star, then, back up to me. An uneasy call, choices loitered in her brain. The air was full of treasure, but Lotte couldn't choose.

"Can we go." Head hung she was confused.

It was mid-afternoon, and I didn't want them to leave. From my stable, I saw them stop, and stroll across the cabin layers. Jed threw a stick. Dogs barking, they sounded puppy happy. I gazed at the carriages. I'd pulled the big coach along the coast. Unfamiliar with the smaller one, I decided, that if I had to go back to driving, I'd choose the larger. Just not the blinkers. Please, not them. Or any angry hands, I added. Past penetrating, I felt clouts around my head and ears. Instead of a brain tumour, I'd been left with a head of shaken clotted cream. Desperate to dislodge such thoughts, I drank from the water dish for longer than needed. Belly gurgling, my eyes followed a spider over my stable door. The cat crept across the roof tiles. A squirrel in view, it stalked it. A tile creaked. Startled, the squirrel scurried past my block and up into the hills behind me. Hills, that for a time, I, and Lotte had loved. Slowly, I was letting her go. Saturday came, and so did the girls. Earlier than usual, the morning was yet to evolve. Small talk and strong coffee, Bianca drank hers before the dorm fence. A bucket of grain in his hand, Ron brushed past and opened the gate. Hungry, the horses began treading the ground. Head hankering up and down, Star, ruffled her rope and called out.

"She doesn't like waiting, does she?" Jed sneaked up on Bianca, like a wild jaguar.

"Effervescent, isn't she."

"Faustino," Lotte sang, "Faustino..." My heart sang. I was on the stairway to heaven. But what about Star?

"How about you buy one," Jed put his arms around her, "and, I, buy one?" The girls ran clapping towards Ron and Star.

"Now just a minute." Bianca swung around to face him, "you only built one stable." But, her tone soon softened into the souffles of his eyes.

"You worry too much," His tanned boots, hare thumped the floor. Besides, I've been thinking about your idea." Jed was pushing.

"What's Star's name in Spanish?" Annie abandoned the single stable subject and ran after Ron, who was now heading towards Sally and the coffee she was holding out for him.

"Estrella!" Sally was happy for the girls, Bianca and the horses too.

Happy to explore new places, Estrella, followed Bianca. Graceful as a lily, I watched her leave. But call out she did. An orchestra, her voice ventured into every rock, crack and crevice. Though out of sight, she was never far from my mind, and never would be. The next morning, Bianca came back to borrow a broom, and see how I was doing. She explained, that I would be joining them, just as soon as things were sorted. What, things, I thought. Three days later, the vet brought a metal carrier case and colleague with her. Undoing it, she loaded a syringe. The twitch made me go cold. They were all armed and I was alone. I tumble shot to the back of my stable. I was sold, surely this isn't right. Rigid like snakes on a stalk, I stood frozen solid. Pine leaves shook, and not even the deadly caterpillars posed a threat compared to this. White flag raised hands, Ron, neared me.

"It's okay!" He took me outside and tied the rope short.

Mind, soiled with bad memories, my guts became a plate of mash. My stomach twinkle twinged, and my nerves now, shook like winter leaves. The colleague coaxed me with words. While I tried to control my heaving lungs, Ron raised the noose. Rope beneath my nostrils, he encouraged me to sniff it. Still loose, he slowly raised the chord over my mouth. Tricking me into thinking it wasn't going to be tight, he gave me a treat. Mouth slightly restricted, eating wasn't easy. Unlike Mateo, who had no patience, Ron at least used some trick tactics. Fast winding his handle, it spun my nose into a golf ball. Immobilized. Pure evil pain entered. A bolt tightened pony tail. Pork tied up for the oven. I was left wide open. My teeth sunk my gums. Stood before me, rooted to the spot, Ron held onto the twitch.

"Did, you have to use that!"

Hallelujah. I couldn't move, but Bianca's voice was music.

Injections and incisions, I didn't know what was going on. The correct procedure in process, it was a painless practice. I didn't feel the scalpel, but liquid I did, and for once in my life, was grateful, I couldn't see behind me. For two hours instruments clanged, and scalpels were clinically cleaned. I felt nothing, nothing, until the anaesthetic wore off. So, why the damned twitch? Job done, the rope was loosened. No longer numb, the blood slowly flowed back. Sewn up like a kipper, I swayed from the drugs. The vet took her money and left. In I went, and down I did go. Ron loaded a barrow and sprinkled some straw around me. But the concrete had already housed my aching limbs. Nostalgic, none of the usual damp or dirt bothered me. And just as the owl came and went, so did the night. Still eating her boiled egg breakfast, Bianca entered. Tight lipped, she acknowledged the after pain, knelt and shared her toast with me. I got up and nuzzled her for more. Rattling a yellow bottle, Ron arrived and nodded for me to be brought out. Once tied up, he sprayed betadine on my cuts. Disinfectant, it stung like bees. Dancing, I shuffle stepped to one side. A diversion needed, Bianca pointed at the trees. A pink bouquet of almond blossom had settled. Pretty and pungent, I inhaled its cologne. Lungs full of fragrance, I held it for as long as possible. Because, like my pain, the blossom would only last a short time.

"So, how's it going down there...?" Ron wiped yellow stained hands down his jeans.

"We haven't built the second stable yet."

"Have all summer," Ron put the bottle away, and patted Faustino. "All summer my friend..."

That night I had two privileges, a shooting star and an abundance of straw. I was just falling into a hazy state, when I heard hooves. Leaping to mine, I saw Estrella outside the main gate. Pushing them with her nose, the unlocked padlock fell beside the barking dogs. Flung open, she barged through them, and up to where I was. Untroubled, she brought high spirits and happiness with her. What a joy. Ron came up in his PJs. In bare feet, he put her in the front paddock. From there, she called out all night. The next day Jed came to get her. But Estrella was nosey and got loose. Running off, she skipped left along one of the ridges. I don't know, how she managed it, but she slipped and fell into an overhanging bush. Unable to go up, a five-foot drop below, her legs disappeared, until only her body was visible. A giant bird in a nest, she did look silly. Jed and Bianca arrived beneath her. Protruding trunk, tea pot sprouting, Jed dug his feet into the bank and grappled for finger holds. One hand on the overhanging branch, he reached out and up with the other. A foot from her headcollar, he reached up and clipped a lunge line to it. Letting go, he landed gymnastically, on both feet. Bianca beside him, the two of them pulled on it. A further tug, and out she tumbled. Legs splayed, Estrella, dropped five feet, landed on all four hooves and shook. A hard, little mare, she didn't seem to have a care in the world. My antibiotics lasted a week. Finally, able to leave, I felt nervous. Having spent most of my life in different places, the potential of a proper home, filled my belly with buttercups.

Heart to heart

I kept snatching the reins from Lotte. Not nastily, but excitedly. Oh, hail, ye auctions, wheelers and dealers, whip handy wickedness, and brain blinding, blinkers. I think, I've found some sanity. We reached the bend, and as we tiptoed down it, the petals of paradise opened. Mounted on mountains, the cabin was set on god given ingredients. Limes and lavenders, oranges, lemons, almonds and olives. Covered in bougainvillea the cabin was one big bowl of blossom. Excited, Billy and Barker, broke the silence in a greet and meet mannerism. Eccentric, man's, toyshop, there was an eclectic collection. Generators, tractors, trailers and tools, all littered one piece of the plot. Lower down, paddock posts in, Jed and Bianca, busily sloshed them in engine oil. In the same paddock, stood beneath the pine tree, a tinsel shiny face, freshened the land. Whinny, whining, Estrella, encouraged me down the road and towards the entrance. A left turn, and two white boulders marked our new territory. Beside them, stood a small empty barn. Blue eyes awaiting, how my heart did sing. Estrella took to her heels. Playful, she ran up and down the enclosure, spinning the stable end, she tore back towards the entrance. A few more strides, dogs yapping at my heels, I was there.

"Looking good!" Jed raised a paint brush to the air, then Bianca.

She smiled, but still looked unsure.

"Don't worry," Jed blew her a kiss. "They're home!"

In a kind of neck and neck standoff, the stables backed onto the neighbours, land. The shape of an Easter egg, the paddock was held in place by cable ties. A second stable in rising process, it just needed a roof. Tack off, Lotte opened the gate and let me go. Two tornados, we air pinned Jed and Bianca against the fence and tore towards the stables. A U-turn, four heels bunny hopping the air, we sprung up and down until breathless. Free of caterpillars, and feeling like two tired tortoises, we stopped to rest beneath the pine. My neck snaked like an ancient nagger around Estrella's. Indeed, history had been made. Painters finished, oil, dry, the posts enriched the paddock. A beer in mind, they pranced up to the cabin. At five, it was feeding time. Still under the tree, they came and got us. Rope on, Jed led me towards my stable. Two feet from it, and I began to panic, needed to get in there, stand to attention, and all that jazz. Nervous, I ran rushed away and into the stable. Speechless, Jed stared at the rope burn on his hand. Stood facing the wall, one eye guarding the door, I quivered. Expected a beating, or belt.

"Men made him that way." Bianca finished tying the mare up outside. "It's okay, Faustino," She entered and reached out, "your safe from the world now."

I swung my head, but the stocky sight of Jed, set me off again. I felt her touch, soothed, I started to trust.

"So," perplexed, Jed rubbed the rope burn, "a little patience is needed?"

"Yes." Bianca nodded compassionately. "Perhaps, you could work with him."

Bianca opened a back door in my stable. I poked my head inside. Tightly tucked together, stood several full feed bins. Nice touch. Oats, barley and bran filled buckets, the atmosphere healed. Bianca took me back outside and fed us both in the sun. Bellies full, they unclipped us. Under our feet, the dogs sniffed the ground for leftover granules. Thirsty, I drank from a hand built and filled, trough. Beside it, stood an iron gate. Beyond it, a slope to another layer. Conveniently, it was used as a muck heap. Stable doors pinned permanently back, we had the choice to choose. The cool stable, or shade beneath the pine. Separation or sunshine. Exercise or easiness. Fox nosy, Estrella loved to be out. Older, I would watch her from under the pine. Eating, adventure and entertainment in mind, she scrutinized every inch of everything. A picture of her picking grass from under the fence cable, I finally fell asleep. Bang! My eyes and feet actioned the sound. Stretching my neck, I saw two baths. A bed of bricks either end of the fence, Jed and Bianca, eased the baths onto them. Not as cultured as it looked, the cabin had no water. But Hey, have no fear, to the font the trailer did go. Drums full, water was plentiful. And not just any old water. Straight from the belly of the mountain, it was clean, fresh, and full of minerals. Outdoor barn built, our first food delivery arrived on Monday. Fifty bales of alfalfa and straw, Bianca and Jed, barrowed it into the stable store room. Yes, we were extremely lucky, had won the horse lottery.

Coffee in hand, Jed and Bianca, sat on the top layer. Legs dangling like loose wires, over it, they appeared content. Contemplation all over her face, Estrella had their attention. Head going under one of two cables, she edged for the shrubs on the other side. Then, pushing her body between the cables, she proceeded to step over the first, and under the second.

"The grass is always greener!" Jed got up and growled, for her to go backwards.

Bianca took out her telephone and called the builders. The next day several rolls of chain link fence hit the deck. And so, a silver lining sealed us in. Job done, exhausted and sweaty, Jed gave Bianca a high five. Collapsing, they shared a beverage.

"What about this idea of yours?" Jed lit a cigarette.

"Thought you'd never ask."

I listened in interest. Situated on the bend and only seconds from the village, our location was excellent. Fruit and veg, basic tack items, bagged almonds, free range eggs and figs. It was a good plan. The only thing they lacked was water. Jed loved the idea, supplies and solutions in mind, he said he'd apply for proper permission. Sunday invitation received from Sally, the girls rode me bareback and joined the adults up there. Apart from the lovely spread Sally put on, lots had changed at Ron's, including a very fine pony, he'd purchased. Tiny, stood 12HH. All ears and mane, she was prettier than the hills. A ride and drive purchase, Ron, suggested Annie have a try. Together, they tied 'Tiny' to the house. Attention all around her, she seemed to thrive on it. Tassels swinging over her face, the Spanish bridle, whipped the flies away. Tacked, and taken into the school, Annie got on. A lunge line clipped to her bridle, Ron asked her to make a circle. A little full of herself, Tiny, moved quite fast. Then, without warning turned into the unbroken bronco, she was. Thrown sky high, Annie came down with an almighty thud. Shocked and jarred, her back hurt. A whole lot of hugs, and two cream cakes later, soothed the situation. A little sore and shaken, Annie was going to be okay. Ron was sorry and gutted. Purchased with good intentions, he had no idea, how green she was.

Monday morning, Bianca tacked me up. Saddle bags, empty, she filled them. Water, pen, pad, lunch and sun screen, she threw it over me. Billy beside us, we headed for the big house, beside Sally's. There, we ventured upwards, until on the hill treks. Once there, everything behind, seemed to shrink into miniature sized models. Even the sound of Estrella's calling eventually calmed into the morning pollen. Jed was there, she wasn't alone. Fully fleshed flowers, summer smelt of poppies and purple thistles. Honey comb, lemon and limes, nature had a personal punch, that I was pleased to be a part of. We passed several trees, reaching out to one, Bianca picked an orange. But where was Billy? Somewhere behind, she'd diverted. I turned to see. Sniffing the carcass, of a wild boar, the hunters had been out. A strong pong and a mound of maggots, it wasn't pleasant. Billy in tow, we turned back onto the track. On the top ridge was a house. Empty and derelict, we headed towards it. Finally, on top of the world, we chose a quiet terrain. Untacked, I adored the trust, Bianca had in me. I snorted, assessing, what was, and wasn't, safe to eat. I wandered. Saddle on the ground, its high sides offered shade from the sun. Nesting inside it, Billy slept. Bianca guzzled water, poured us some, and nibbled the end of her pen. Creativity, her soul food, she leant against a trunk and put pen to paper. Only the sound of my heartbeat, we enjoyed the silence for over two hours. Free as a bird, I nibbled on sunburnt grass, bits of bark and wild weeds. It was a baby snake that spoilt the morning. Zebra markings, it cruised through the grass, winding its way towards Bianca. Holly hailstones, I'd never seen her move so fast. The finalities of her notes put away, she threw the saddle on. Girth still loose, I galloped away. Billy bowled after us. An amicable pace resumed, we collectively slowed. Going down the rough surfaced road, we finally reached the bend and could see all beyond it.

'Little house on the Prairie," I felt her arms around my neck, "isn't it, Faustino!"

I'd never heard of it. But like her, had never been so happy. I loved the font water, being allowed to sleep under the tree, the alfalfa and grain, but most of all, Estrella. Unlike the usual brutes I encountered, even the company of the dogs was a pleasure. Turning towards the last stretch, I tiptoed down the hill. Inquisitive, Estrella was into everything. Even the lunge line Bianca put her on. Mischievous, she was obedient one minute, obscene, the next. All ears and legs, excellent entertainment, it was hilarious to watch. Body weight better, she was turning into a beautiful horse. Bigger than me, she stood at 15.2. Once worn out, Bianca put an old English saddle on her. Not in the least bit bothered, Estrella enjoyed the attention. Increasing the work each day, it wasn't long before she was following me. A long lunge attached to her, and she came everywhere with us. Up the hills, through the village, along the tracks and around the mountains. Memories, of magnitude, I cherished every minute with her. Totally motivated and feeling brave, Bianca one day asked Jed, to hold Estrella. Entering her personal space, Bianca dared to lean over her. Totally acceptant, Estrella never moved a muscle. A big breath, and Bianca, climbed onto her unbroken back. Spellbound, Estrella was stone still. Amazed at how accepting she was, Bianca repeated the process every day. Born to be brushed, Estrella loved the attention. A sophisticated creature, she was very special. Able to sit on her, without any kind of fuss, Bianca just needed someone to mouth the horse and finalise the last bits. Bianca was doing our lunch, when the first stray appeared. A big white mongrel, it was thin and frightened. Accelerating, Billy and Barker chased it away. Hungry, it returned until they allowed it to stay. Bianca opened a tin of food to feed it. Never, have I seen anything eat at such speed. Stable roof finished, Jed sat on it. A cigarette in his mouth, he overlooked the situation. Lowering himself, he rubbed his chin and walked the length of the paddock.

"He can stay if you want."

Before the big entry stones, stacked like a deck of cards, sat several pallets. Taking two, Jed bashed them together and made a kennel. He then hammered four posts into the ground. Snug against the big right boulder he built a compound. Using up the leftover chain link, he laced three and a half sides. A gate, and there it was.

"A guard dog for the horses." Jed lit a cigarette.

Last screw tightened, and the gate swung open. Annie loved the new dog and named it Ted. Took it on woodland walks and brought butcher bones to bridge his boredom. Every week Bianca would sit on the bank and flick through the newspapers. Only once, did she turn back to the previous page.

"Fortuna," she yelled to Jed on the top far layer.

Jed looked up from the generator. A spanner in his mouth, he lit up for more.

"Stock clearance of tack for the shop."

"Then let's go!" Spontaneous, he spat out the spanner and smiled.

And go, they did. I remember it well, because Ron did our lunch that day. He also tried to check our feet. Old school, I didn't mind. Estrella, well, she was another matter altogether. Both hot headed, they were doomed from the start. Try as Ron may, she refused to lift the front left. And the look in her eye said, beat me to death, but I'm not giving in. Ron cussed her, let her go, and lit a cigarette.

"Chica's," he mumbled while watching her wander off. "Faustino," Ron joined me under my tree, "you're my friend, aren't you?" Stroking me, Ron chimney smoked. Impertinence indeed established, Estrella deliberately endured the sun. Evening came. People free, we settled beneath our tree.

Additional

August was my favourite month, and with it, came many new things. The trip to Fortuna was successful. Boot full, seats piled high, tack wasn't all they brought back. Though large, the puppy was silent. Arms full, Annie, carried her for us to see. She was beautiful, but, had a breathing problem. The vet issued antibiotics and within no time, the bear cub was up and about. A Doberman cross, she was quite a chunk that Bianca named, Sheba. A second kennel built, and she nestled next door to Ted. Night arrived. Settled beneath our pine, nocturnal creatures came to eat. Like a silver biro, the fox dashed the land. A hoot and branch hop, and the owls arrived. And so, to a tooting choir, we did drift. A week later, a trailer pulled up. A standing ovation inside, hooves hammered the floor. Excited, the girls stood like two electric lamps just been switched on. Ramp down, and out he came. Shining like a conker, the pony was the brightest copper in the world. What his 12.3 status lacked in height, he made up for in looks. A star dripped across one eye, breeze blowing his colourful forelock, highlights of silver extended into his main. Legs dashed black, the portrait was complete. Barking mad, the dogs were as excited as us.

"Meet Mr new Darcy." Bianca stood him before our fence.

Opening the gate to the layer on our left, she let him in. Surrounding the far half, the embankment made a decent wall deterrent. A stringent little soul, Darcy attempted to climb it. Impressive, he got half way up it before losing his footings. Rigid as a mountain goat, the bank gave way and he tumbled back to earth. Hooves beating the soil, he trod it down, bent his knees and rolled in it. Falling about laughing, I nicknamed him, 'Little legs.' Happy and hungry, the adults and kids, wandered up to the cabin. Darcy mooched a further five minutes before returning and peeking through our fence.

"You aren't Spanish, are you?" Estrella quizzed him.

"New forest..." 'Little legs' sounded lost.

"Where's that?" I was completely clueless.

"England..." His confidence collapsed.

I sniffed him. He didn't smell any different to us.

Getting as close as he could, Darcy curled up beside his gate. Voices on the veranda, they continued until late. A pleasant energy all around, everyone slept into the morning. Breakfast served, dogs straddled, Bianca, and two smiling girls, topped up our water butts.

"Carobs, r, in season." Jed put the big dogs away, "what say, we go get some?"

Bucket in hand, Jed swung it. Yapping mad, Barker leapt up and down. A little gang about to go scrumping, they cruised up the hill and around the bend. Chuckling, Bianca, went back up to the cabin. Car backed onto the drive, she raised the boot. Unloading it, she carried various items into the under-build. Unlike the heat of upstairs, it was made of stone. Perfect for keeping things cool. There was, rugs, bridles, brushes, headcollars and reigns. Even several sets of boots, Hats galore, it was, a golden shop start. All they needed now, was a colourful collection of fruit and veg. High on life, she knelt to stroke Billy.

"Come on," she skipped down the hill. "let's go on a walk."

A chunky cherub, Sheba scuttled to her feet. No longer gaunt, Ted was the first to cross the road. Ribs well coated, he cruised up the bank and spun to see where the others were. On his heels, they nipped him playfully and waited beside the neighbours finca, for Bianca. Hat straightened, she caught them up, going over a slope they all disappeared down the loop walk.

"So," Estrella nosed after Darcy, "what's the story?"

Sketchy, his eyes fluttered.

"The woods were a wealth of health," He frowned, "at least until man came." He batted his lashes, "I recall the round up as if only yesterday. Separated from our parents, they were real picky." A sadness washed over him. "Split in two, some of us were for the auction, the other half, the meat trade in France." The, life left his eyes. "I didn't know, I was in the meat section, until half way there when the lorry stopped."

"What happened?" Estrella pressed a lot harder than I would have.

"One of the first on, I was crammed to the back. But as it thinned out, those last on, leapt, like lambs towards the ramp. Pushing and worm weaving, I was nearly there, could smell the cold night air, possible food and freedom. Clunk! Partition closed, it sent us scrambling back. Tin tight, it was horrible. But, for the opinion of one.

"You, not leaving it open…?"

"What for?" The driver had no heart.

"They might be meat mate, but they're alive, till you get there!"

"They'll also run amuck in extra space."

"If you're leaving them like that, at least lighten the rear end."

Preventing possible, prosecution, two more had to come off. Documentations selected, so, was I."

"I didn't like the ring. Its hammers and meddling men." Darcy was hyperventilating, "Fully registered, I fetched three hundred." Darcy wet his whistle. "At his yard the dealer pulled out a pair of clippers. The noise terrified me. Blunt, he managed to claw clip most of my back. But, blades tearing down my legs, I leapt all over the place. First pony, prospects, put to bed, I was labelled unsafe, and left half bald. I remember feeling sleepy, the slip of a leash around my back shins. They couldn't sell me as a stallion, so castration it was. As I came around I heard voices.

"Let's put a bale of straw down for him?"

"He won't lie down!" The rowdier of the two voices was being ridiculous.

"Why would anything sedated stand up?" Mate.

I must have gone back onto the floor because that's where I woke up. I stood in for a further three days. I was just beginning to heal when I again felt sleepy. Easy to handle. Placid and patient, at least for the first part of the journey. Aroused by awareness, I came around. It was cold. Road roaring, the lorry was going far too fast. How many times I lost my footings, I don't remember. There was a stop check. We broke too hard. Still hazy, I stumbled. It must have been loud, because the cab men came to see what had happened. Pinched between one of two partitions, it was removed. Like a sack of spuds, I hit the deck. Legs tied, a lump in my throat, I was left there."

"Mental scars stay, don't they!" I felt sad.

"For hundreds of miles, I lay like that."

"All the way over to Spain?" Gobsmacked, his story hollowed out my heart.

"Darcy bowed his head.

"Humans!" Estrella didn't need an excuse to despise them.

"Eventually, they stopped, stepped over me and loosened the ropes. Alive and alert, I grappled at dry patches, and stood. Marked for different destinations, there were others breeds on the lorry too.

"And..." I was now intrigued.

"Bought and paid for, I was first off. The pedantic buyer was potty. An ornament in mind, she tied me to a tree beside her pool, and patio. Cut lawn crucified, the idea wore off. A month later, I was sold on."

"More money than sense," Estrella sighed.

"It happens." I, fidget frowned.

"Absolutely." Darcy picked at an apple on the ground. "The last lot were ok." He munched, "but on taking up her dental course, had no time."

An accident, the fruit hit me in the face.

"They look scrummy!" Just as Bianca came over the hill, so did a shower of carob chocolate. Runner bean, lookalikes, the sweets rained over our fence. Buckets full, Jed and the girls fed Spanish treats to us.

"I found some help with Estrella." Smiling Bianca put her phone and dogs away. Shoulder brushing Jed, she joined in.

"Shoeing tomorrow!" Ron pulled up and poked his boat race through his window.

"What time?" Bianca put the carobs down and went to greet him.

"About lunchtime."

"Whose, that?" Reaching into the back of the jeep, Jed, joined them.

"Just another dumped pup. Pound job I think."

"She's cute." Jed pulled the pup from the car and put her down.

Excited, she circled the tractor. Rolled into a ball and put her paws over her ears.

"She looks like a muffin." Just as the girls got close to the pup, she popped up and ran a figure of eight. "Just wants to play all day." They laughed after her.

"Leave her," Jed said, "if she fits in, we'll keep her."

Nodding approval at both the dog and new pony, Ron pushed back his cap and pulled away. Jed knelt, opened his hand and held it out. The puppy flew straight past him and chased her tail.

"Cute, isn't she?" Bianca flumped onto the ground and joined him.

"What was you saying about Estrella?"

"Oh, a lady called June, can fit her in next month, finish off the stuff, I can't."

Chewing on sweet carobs, we dribble drooled content.

The farrier arrived and began with Darcy. But, it was always the same, tense legs, frozen hips and a fearful face. Bianca comfort, Darcy came to a compromise, fronts fitted his backs were fast flash rasped. Evidently Estrella was next. More interested in eating than visiting the shoe shop, Estrella face engaged the man. He didn't like the look of her. Entering the gate, he approached where she stood open eyed over him. If, she obliged, it was pot luck how long she'd hold up her hoof. Some days, she'd stand angel still. On others, her hoof came crashing down like a crane. They were the days she remembered the sting. Cool as cucumber Estrella crossed her legs in a cocky stance.

"She's a self-maintenance mare," he caught me, "no need to go near her."

Taking me out and tying me to the tree beside the tractor, he began changing my shoes. Going up to the house, Bianca made him coffee.

"What the fiddle sticks..." A cup in each hand, her return quickly became a rant.

"Kipasa?" He yelled.

"They're odd!" Bianca slammed his coffee on one of the white boulders. "even worse, ones rusty!"

"Shoes are shoes." He didn't understand her. Didn't compute or comprehend her insistence for balance. How would he like one heel shorter than the other?

"If they don't match," she frowned, "neither will my money."

The farrier was furious. Lifting my foot, he removed the shoe and replaced it. Grateful of good hooves and wanting her peace back, Bianca got out her purse. Ponies put away, she waved ten fingers at Jed, and drove home to make them lunch. Outside the school, the kids were cooing over a baby goat. Its owner had one, too many, and needed to lessen his load. Taking its leash, it happily ran up and down the road with them. Miniature, in size, it was cute. Bianca opened her door, and according to Billy, in, they all went. Clambering over furniture, a chain of children on its tail, the goat played hide and seek. Running riot, they went through every room.

"Can we keep it?" They pleaded...

"Course you can." Jed arrived. "I'll build it a pen by the house." Jed buttered the bread and lunch was served. Like the dogs, the goat made himself at home and neighed for scraps.

Bianca worked hard with Darcy, removing him from the greener stages of his life and lifting him into lighter, better, shades of education. There were a few hitches, but that aside, he accepted Annie on the lunge. By October, he was lifting his back legs, listening, and walking peacefully alone with her. A time slot in her dressage dates, Joni, finally came to collect Estrella. Unimpressed, Estrella refused to enter the trailer, ripping the rope from their hands, she abolished the idea. Practical, Joni persevered. One foot on, two steps back, Estrella wasn't sure. Half way in, and she went to pieces. Pulled back and ended on her hocks in the road. Not wanting a fight, Joni, tied her up and had a tea. A bucket of goodies and Estrella responded. Left right, left right, she loved the apple best. Back up, engine on, I had no idea, how long she'd be gone. Or, if she was coming back at all. I felt empty, hollow as a drum, and if honest, couldn't, function without her. Disheartened, I stood beside Darcy's fence, and waterfall wept. I didn't just pine, I counted the hours, then the days. I remember the fifth well, because Jed was singing. "She'll be coming around the mountain, when she comes."

Souls, like plants and people, need air, and she was mine. Neck arched, Estrella came out of the trailer. Prancing on the spot, she was every bit as beautiful as spring, soft as the day and smooth as butter. Immersed in her energy, my heart sang to the tune of her neighs. Never, in my existence had I felt so full field. While she relit my life, Joni, informed us of a new law. Chip and passports compulsory, Bianca, began the process. A week later, the vet arrived. Instead of her horrid castration case, this time, she brought a long metal syringe with her. A strange sensation, it was sharp, but harmless, bloody, but painless. A scratch, and it was over. The vet flashed a machine over my neck, I bleeped. I didn't like it. One mug shot for the passport and I was released. Estrella didn't play up, good as gold, she was a diamond. Strange as it was, little legs, didn't need a chip. Not of Spanish nationality, it wasn't compulsory.

Back and backed, the girls made the most of Estrella, and brought a friend out on the rides. Exploring the mountains, we climbed for hours. When thirsty, we drank from the fonts, when hungry we found fruit and on the days they had homework, we did a shorter route. Through the neighbours and up nan's hill where there we panned right. Off road, we headed down into a valley and across its half-moon, flat lands. Circuit met, our track grew thinner and began to spiral upwards. Leafless and lifeless, dozens of trees, paved our path gently guiding us along our journey. Spindly, they reminded me of readymade

149

brooms for light weight witches. Several turns later, and the trees receded, refused to go any further. On the other side of the avenue, the uneven ground opened into a smooth mouth-watering gallop. Side by side, we took charge, and cruised to its top. Taking back the reigns, the kids halted us just before meeting the mountain road. The nights drew in and like many things the half, moon, ride was put away. Copper coat converted, Darcy took on the appearance of a grey sheep. Projects put on hold, another Christmas came and went. Submissive, Bianca embraced another spring. And us, another moon ride. Only this time, the witch like trees, were covered in blossom, a few weeks later, gobstopper sized cherries. Farmer free, the girls threw down their reins, leant over our necks and filled their mouths with crimson treats. Estrella especially, couldn't get enough of them. Flesh, pip and leaf, they went down a treat. Sweet as honey and plumb soft, the girls filled their pockets for later. Rising red berries, we trotted out of the orchard. On the hill we flipped into cowboy canters. An extension, in mind, the girls rode us back along our old track and around the 'Big,' house. A connecting road bend, and we were back.

Sweaty, Bianca used some of our emergency water to cool our tendons down. But, the bricks the butt was balanced on moved and fell over. Water being an issue, her and Jed, had words. She left. Fun over, we waited for him to feed us. Days went by, but there was no Bianca. Only Jed, who used his phone a lot. Finally, she returned. Jed beside her, they together searched our surroundings. Clomping over baked soil, Darcy clambered close, so he could watch them. Rummaging through shrubs and rocks, they tooth combed the hedgerows. For two days they did this. On the third, they danced delight. I don't know if they had dug into it or just got lucky, but a mountain source they discovered. Fighting the gushing surge, Jed, fitted, a connector to it. Hose pipe in place, he ran it towards the stables. Large white container purchased, it was camouflaged from the sun and filled. An adjustment fitted, bingo, we were in business. Jed twiddled the knob and produced a spray. Like cold pearls, the droplets hit my back and rolled down my belly. After having no supply for so long, it seemed a crime to see it soak into the floor. Hot, Estrella was happy to be hosed. It was at least ten minutes before she got down and rolled. Dusted in dirt, she looked like a sherbet dip.

"No more font trips." Jed gave Bianca a high five before squirting her too. He turned to find Darcy, but he was gone. Jed smiled, he admired the pony.

"Maybe, we can grow something now." Bianca embraced him. "Even get some hens..."

Through wet eyes, I imagined it. Yellow and green peppers, apples and potatoes. Peaches and pears. Jed gave her a high five, one of his winning smiles and a hug. Bianca checked the time, late, she kissed him and left.

Belly spice

A soft spot for Darcy, Jed sat beside the water butts, opposite him. A bucket of carobs at hand, he fed us, happy, he forgot to stop. One of my favourite sweets, I gorged. Bucket, empty, Jed took the dogs around the loop. While he was gone, my belly began to hurt. Stomach contents separating like curds and way, I fell to my knees, there, I buckled good and proper. Lassoed, my organs grew tighter and tighter, until like the branded calves, I could barely breathe. It hurt. I felt sick. I couldn't throw up. Dizzy, things started to sway. Frantic, Estrella circled me.

"What is it?" Hazel nut pupils pitched, Darcy glared at me.

"I don't know!" Estrella neighed. High pitched, Jed heard it. Could see the situation from the hill top.

On his phone, he rushed back. Confused by the dialect and coupled in pain, I just wanted to die. Flustered and heated, Jed shut his phone and put my head collar on. He pulled, but due to soggy stools, belly ache and butt clenching cramps, I couldn't budge.

He wrapped a lunge line around my neck, leaned backwards and began sawing. Flecks of fur fell away, then growing closer to the skin, it tore like paper. A potato peeler in progress, it skinned and split my neck, until finally I got up. Like a racing circuit, my neck was covered in open roads. Once on my feet, Jed found a whip and forced me to walk around. Crunch, my stomach biscuit broke. Crumbs, scattering, they settled in all the wrong places. Estrella, on my tail, she followed us up and down.

Hours felt like days, until finally things settled, and it was safe to sleep. Estrella stood protectively tall, and with hooting owls, stood over me. It was seven in the morning when my stomach finally settled. Gingerly, Bianca approached, accepting her company, Estrella let her sit with us. Astounded, at the state of my neck, she reached out. Hand hovering over raw flesh, she cried.

"I had too." Jed came down from the house. "it was the only way of getting him up."

"Why didn't you call me?"

"Closest, I rang Ron. Out, he told me to get him up before he died." Jed paused, "as you can see I needed two hands."

"I wish, I'd been here to help." Tired, her tone faded.

Sad at the mess, but pleased he'd saved me, Bianca nodded. Sunlight on his shoulders, Jed went up to the house to make a drink. Bianca consoled me, stroked my face and neatly folded legs. My head fell into her hands and I licked the salt from her palms. Protruding teeth, they grazed her skin. Cups clanging, she jumped up to meet Jed.

"His teeth need doing." She took the tea from him.

There's nothing wrong with his teeth!" Jed had a way of weaving bad situations into light banter. "He eats like Pacman." Indeed, we all smiled.

Out of her region, Kay didn't cover our area. But as she stated, it would be nice, to see Darcy settled in his new home. I'd never had my teeth done. Tied up, I shuddered at the mouth clamp Kay produced. Estrella frowned, and I pulled, not carriages this time, but the tree we were tied too. Wide, it was deep rooted and stuck fast.

"I thought you meant people," I scowled at Darcy, "not ponies."

"No, equine dentist. Sorry!" Darcy scarpered across his paddock towards a shower of shrubs.

"Don't be rude!" Going after him, Jed, caught and brought him back.

"He looks happy." Kay patted him.

Shocked by the gag, I couldn't believe how wide it opened his mouth up. Worst still, she put what looked like a foot rasp in his mouth. Motoring up and down, I cringed. An examination, and they said he had wolf teeth. Well, he didn't look like a wolf to me, but hey ho. An instrument inserted into his mouth, it pushed and pulled. Ouch, out it came. A small unwanted tooth, that was taking up gum space. Space, the final frontier, oh, beam me up Scotty before it's my turn. Unlike Darcy, who'd arrived with passport and paperwork, Estrella's age was estimated to be three. And like her feet, her teeth were healthy. Like a hollow cave, the clamp came closer. Tingle tune active, my brain and pulse raced. As it engaged, the confines of my mouth grew dryer. It clipped my front teeth and tightened. Uneasy, my ears filled with drums and my pupils, strained to see what was next. Apparently, I wasn't a wolf, just a bit wispy. Rasp, raised, Kay filed my enamel, tin foil on teeth, I hated every second of the shave. Gadget out, teeth clamped together, Kay examined the shape of my fronts. Accurate advice, I guess, I probably was getting on for sixteen or seventeen. But, surrounded by youth, it, kept me young. All done, I couldn't wait to get back in my paddock where, Estrella was waiting.

"It's stunning isn't it?" Kay absorbed the mountain moss, its riches and secret forests. Unlike us, not everyone knew their way in, or out of them.

"I could have sold him several times over." Kay continued, "But all of them were drivers and would have just worked him and the carriage into the ground." She smiled at the copper conker hoovering for shrubs, grass and anything able to withstand the baked soil.

"I was so glad when you guys came along." Kay scooped up her bucket. "I hope, this is, his forever home.

Forever is a long time, but I liked the word, as much as Estrella.

"And, what of the farm shop you had in mind?" Kay turned to Jed.

"Awaiting permission." Jed carried her dentist case to the car." But, you know how long they take here, don't you?"

"Yes, I do," Kay laughed, "but worth the wait, I'd say!"

"Come and see the goat." Billy beside her, Bianca ran up the hill and across the top layer. Panting, her and Billy paused outside the pen. Surprised at the sight, she smiled.

"Where did they come from…?" Speckled white, four black chickens circled the goat.

Having caught her up, Jed crossed his arms, he smiled, but said nothing. Thirsty, Darcy booted his bath and didn't stop, until, he had Jed's attention.

"It's truly beautiful!" Kay's eyes followed Jed down the layer.

Hauling out the hose, he was at the command of little legs. Bianca invited Kay, into the kitchen and poured juice. From its window, they watched Darcy. Sniffing his pocket, he knew, Jed had an apple in it. And appease him for it, Darcy, did. Juice done, kay took happy memories away with her. And as always, the days quickly became months. November brought cool, but muggy, energy. It also invited over a week of heavy rains. Not any old rain, but big billowing sheets that saturated everything, including our hay and straw. Mouldy, Bianca had to bin it. Unable to get up the mountain, the next delivery date would be a week or so. So, instead of straw n alfalfa, it was oats, bran, and more oats. Cold to the bone, I think I must have shown shivering signs. In the stock boxes downstairs, Bianca dug out the rugs. I'd never had one before. Never had anyone care, enough to cover me up. A new and welcome, experience, I felt duvet snug. Enveloped in comfort, I felt secure beneath quilted buckles. The other fitted Estrella. Grateful, the mare nuzzled Bianca, who turned to Darcy.

"I'm, so sorry," Bianca uttered to him, "but, the boxes only contained big sizes, I'll feed you more to compensate."

Bianca opened the adjoining door and swept some emergency straw out for him to stand on. But the rains flooded both stables and washed it all away. Ankle deep, a trench was needed to divert it. A shovel in hand, Jed, dug towards the muck heap. Receding out of our stables the water clattered under the muck gate. On the lower layer, it dispersed into different directions. The dogs too, were flooded. Perched on dry spots, they barked to be rescued. To be put somewhere dry. Battling the rain, Bianca arrived. Compound open, they flew up the hill and into the under build. There, I imagine, they shook like ducks and shone like sequins. Like two wet bats, Jed and Bianca waited on us. Even held our feed buckets up, so that our grain, didn't get washed away. Shutting us in, they left Darcy's door open and disappeared. Momentum gathering on every mountain layer, the water created landslides. It growled, it spoke, it washed away past pains. Rabbit still, we glared out, over our stable door. Lightning capered storms, the passing swirls, brought rocks, wood and debris with them. Darcy didn't like the high wall that separated our stables, it made him feel shut out and alone. Too little to see over his stable door, it had been left pinned back for him. Fretting, he stepped into the soup mud and leant upon the cable ties that created two paddocks. Near on neck and neck with us, his forlorn face and body, was saturated within seconds. From the cabin window, Bianca could see him. Braving the elements, she came back down. Splashing, through the sea of mud, she was soaked. One hand clutching a bag, she grabbed Darcy with the other. Out of the overspill, she closed the door. Nosy, Estrella, peeked through the partitioning wall planks. The place would have been better built with lower, more social sides. But, then a third pony had not been on the agenda. Nor, his obvious, insecure needs, to again be a part of a pack. The heard, and even the house, had he been able to get in it. Bianca removed a blanket from the bag and tied it onto him with bailing twine. A coat of many colours, the dog blanket did the trick. At one with us, Bianca, dug her hand under a sheet of ply. Pulling hard, she snapped the plank of wood in half. A window, and we were able to poke our heads through it. Comforting Darcy, she chatted and fed us. Explained her feelings, and how she related to me. How pleased she was to have us as friends, and how she felt about Jed. Undoubtedly, it was how I felt about Estrella. A ray of light in the rain, she was engaging. Pockets empty, treats all eaten, story time was over. Chucking a second blanket over Darcy, she fastened it with bailing twine and left. Finally, the next day it stopped. But the earth was wet, so much so, that the smell of damp stayed till spring. And oh, what glory it brought. Birds and bees, nests and nuts. Squirrels and bobcats, thistles and figs. Bianca removed our rugs, and unlike us who'd lost winter weight, our new forest, still had a nice round belly.

Time had no meaning, and another year began rolling by. With it, came bad news. Shop proposal finally reviewed, the authorities refused permission. Though disappointed, Bianca dusted herself down and went for a walk with Jed. Every night I said a prayer. Winked at the moon and thanked my lucky stars. Peace prevailing, life was being kind. Not once, had a single caterpillar ever fell from our pine. Its shade constantly cool, Estrella at my side and Darcy opposite. Life had a lot of meaning. A stray from the village arrived with the girls. Ragged, the kitten had obviously, had it rough. Named Gizmo, the kitten was anything but slow, and as she grew, the rat population lessened. Quick and clever, not much escaped her. Not even the baby spring snakes. An expedition in mind, the girls rode until the road ended, then met, with the highest hemispheres. Magnetic mountains, whistles wet at the font, it took us a full five minutes to take them in. Unlike the baron wilderness of winter, the enormous plain was aesthetically pleasing. Almond blossoms everywhere, alluring pollen fairies filled the air. Coupled with cherry trees, the two tickled our senses. We moved along the first sand track in awe. Pine needle fresh, the air was sharp, then, in one big berth opened up. Overlooked by the mountains their protective walls were all eyes. Setback, from its many sand tracks and trees, heaven laid before us. A spring in my step, and I took off. Pink blankets either side, the blossoms made even the thistles appealing. Excited, Estrella took over. Darcy on her toes, we left a hoof happy melody behind. A change of direction, and so the scenery did too. An infrequent sight, we halted. Beautifully blended, the fleeting fox, froze. Humans and horses together, his ears flickered with little response. Confused, but clever, the fox, Counted the snow drops between us. Tail held high, he pawed and padded the floor. One, two, three, he straddled towards a shelter of trees. Silver sight gone, we thundered on. Doing her best to stay on Darcy, Annie held his main too. Free as a bird, the little guy, could give it some. Scooping and spitting sand, our hooves left happy holes, behind. There were tulips too! Touché, Life, was cool.

Wheels

A proposition in mind, one of the villagers arrived and chatted with Jed. The owner of a nice flat plot, 'Antonio,' has some very powerful horses. In summer he owned the rights to drive them around the lake. Apart from the boat, it was one of the top tourist attractions. Having been asked if there was a smaller pony, to fairy tale take the children, Darcy, was now top topic.

"A carriage?" Jed rubbed the stubble on his chin. "Just think," he joked, "I'd be able to drive him to the bar."

"It could have shopping benefits too." Bianca added to the banter.

Knowing nothing about driving, Bianca didn't see the harm. A plan in mind, they agreed to begin the very next day.

Bianca watched them walk Darcy down towards Antonio's. Hot and bothered on his return, Darcy appeared distraught. Complained, he had a headache, and went to sleep under the shrubs beside his embankment. Curled up like one of the dogs, he wasn't right. Bianca arrived that evening and went to see him. Skin lesions on his nose, she fed him treats and gazed deep into his eyes. There was hurt and humiliation, a riot of harassment, a chisel on the soul. The next day, she went to watch the training technics.

Strapped down tighter than a biscuit tin, Darcy was fighting the metal teeth. Biased, Jed, didn't see the problems, Bianca did. But, unlike her, he knew very little about horses, even less regarding long reins. Bossy boots, Anton marched Darcy around the school. To raise his head rip hurt, to keep it tortoise tucked stopped him from swallowing. Bianca intervened. Brandishing both men, impatient and incompetent. She was about to call time out, when something else did. Torn, Bianca couldn't ignore the howls tearing the air apart. Running towards the yapping, she was drawn to a water tank. Submerged, it was easy, to see how the husky had fallen in. His spine was twisted, and age, like his thirst, wasn't on his side. Completely frazzled, and cripple crying, his legs didn't have long left. Reaching for the large lump, Bianca, pulled him out by his scruff. Howling happiness, the dog, followed her back. Debilitating and drenched in sweat, panic took hold of Darcy. Defensive and defeated, his back legs lashed out. The men loosened the line and backed up. No, he wasn't mad as suggested by Anton. Just a little legged soul, who'd buckled under pin point, pressure. A paradox of paradise! An experience of all things not nice. Bin tops and blue bottles undo his brain pain. Bridle removed, his nose was a smeary, mess. But, oh, to breathe, feel diamond cut air, and daffodil freedom. Senses, still in order, dignity, was smelt. Bianca took his lead rope. Husky shading himself beneath her straw hat, the two animals, followed her up the hill and home.

"Ouch!" Estrella wasn't impressed by the imprints. Sadness, hidden, she squashed her eyes into two tiny slits and turned to face me and the faded zebra, crossing my nose. "I guess, that's how you got yours?"

Opening his gate, Bianca let Darcy go. Suddenly, quiet as a church mouse, not a chime was spoken. Not one word wittered. A tough little blighter, Darcy dived into a bucket of food and tried to forget. Unlike my taxing youth, he endured two days only.

"Think yourself lucky," food finished, Darcy stared at Estrella, "hopefully, it's a ritual you won't go through!"

Bashful, it was the first time, I'd seen Estrella bat her eyelashes. Sat outside the compound, howling for attention, the big husky whined while thumping his tail at the same time on the floor. Barking at Bianca, Sheba wanted an explanation, Muffin her dinner, and Ted a walk.

"He was drowning, Bianca looked flustered, "I couldn't leave him. You will have to share until something bigger is built."

Fur wriggling with parasites, the Husky, was anything but presentable. Hose out, Bianca covered him in soap, lathered him up and let the others out. Rinsed off, the land reined suds and bubbles. These, the dogs bounced in and out of. Unable to keep up with the others, the husky was put away to rest and dry. Bianca took Estrella too. Bridle on, she went bareback. Coupled with high banks and trees the little loop opposite, was a fast, and fantastic ride. Three Dogs and Billy on her tail, Estrella set off. Bianca put Estrella before an embankment. It was steep hill high. To do, or not to. Like a million flustered ghosts, the leaves spurred them on. Barking dogs on dancing heels, Estrella conquered it within seconds. Wow, what a horse. The potential was profound. But the thrill of it, far more important to Bianca. I estimated by the barking, that the dogs must have followed her up it several times. Hot and happy, they returned with a thirst. Lunchtime, the men appeared on the porch and poured a beer. Unimpressed, Bianca had to go. Back at five, she didn't expect Jed, to play jump out on her.

"I like the new addition," He turned to where the husky was sleeping, "I guess, I'll have to extend the dog compound..." Jed rummaged amongst his off cuts, "We might need some cement and a bit of chain link." Bianca frowned. "And what about pony," Jed did like to tease her, "do you really think you can do a better job?"

Bianca didn't speak, she just smiled. The next morning, she set to work. Leaving a plain headcollar on Darcy, she clipped a lunge line either side and long reigned for the first time in her life. Maintaining distance, she whispered softly, until he responded. Relaxed, he obliged down the hill and into the village. There, they turned around and returned. This they did for a week. Then, confidence gained on both behalves, the village route was extended through the slim streets and up the first, of the horizontal hills. Steep, Bianca let Darcy pull her up it and into the level school square. Playing outside it, children flocked to praise their efforts and offer them drinks. Darcy did well, but diversity was needed. The next day she directed Darcy up the neighbours drive and through the short cut. But, instead of going straight on to the connecting road, she panned left under the trees and upwards. Bumps and boulders, beneath her feet, it made the ground, hard going for them both. Patiently, entering a penny flat circle, they were able to look down and see us below. Work revised, Darcy, could reverse too, and by the time July descended, was ready to pull something other than Bianca.

Another August arrived, and with it the desert heat increased. Stifled, it was impossible for anyone to indulge in anything. Deflated, the cat didn't bother hunting, flumped like a little rug in the shade, she was happy to be warm tin fed at ten. Ten was a better temperature, one, we all gladly, gulped. Hypnotised, by the gleaming, star lit sky, I was able to give in to sleep. Dusting herself at dawn, Gizmo loved the dry dirt. Grass gone, the land was bare and Estrella, bored. Jed opened the layer above Darcy, there, we foraged for shrubs and leaves. Blackberries in bloom, we ate them too. There was other stuff, but we didn't like the taste, and left it. Due to different soil types and tree shade, the neighbouring bank still displayed grass. Permission granted, we were able to graze it, but, there was one problem, it was fence free. Unaware of my past leg cuffs, Jed used a lunge line to tie me to a tree. He'd barely crossed the road to fetch Estrella when... I loved the fresh tips, but quickly got tangled and in a two and eight. I panicked. Legs caught in the lunge line, I was back on the flatlands. No mare to guide me, she was gone. Alone, and unable to move, I began sawing at the tangles. By the time Bianca got to me, I had ripped off my scars, and given the flies an open house to squat in. Gently, she calmed me, untied the tangles and took me down the bank to my bit. Sympathetic, Estrella, nibble soothed on my neck. A course of antibiotics, and the flies were evicted. Jed thought Estrella, might like to try the grass. But, Bianca said it wasn't worth the risk of possible accident. Determined, Jed took Darcy instead. Intelligent, Darcy used the lunge line with exceptional care. Fear exempt, he raised his head, Line lifted, he stepped a few feet at a time over it. Grazing a complete, compass, the circle became bare. In-fact, he was so damned clever, that Jed tied him to a different tree every day, until the whole bank was baron. A lawn mower service in action, it was one less thing the neighbour had to maintain. Confident, in their saddles, the girls took all, but one dog, on the rides. Over hills and tracks we went. Giggling and tearing at the ground, the dogs, gave good chase. It was a Monday that always springs to mind. Scuttling up the hill, we all stopped at nans for drinks. We were heading for the cherry orchards, when... Realising the compound gate wasn't properly locked, and refusing exclusion, the husky had escaped. High pitched, his calling cut the air. We halted and turned. Not far behind, a very jovial, but jaded, husky hankered after us. Sticking to a walking pace, he was pleased to be a part of our day. It was good to have water, but by the time we had husky paced home, we were pickle parched. Exhausted, but satisfied, the dogs slept long and hard in their pen. A new one in its early stages, it would provide more space. The husky hated being left out, but his back legs deteriorated, until even the little loop, was too much for him to walk. The vet diagnosed a bone disease. Responsible for his spine, the hindrance on his legs would only worsen, but the dog refused to give up his right to life. Pain killers and snail paces, he took up residence on the veranda where he was able to watch the passers-by. Satisfied, there he stayed.

It had taken over a year, but, finally, nan had built her corral. Complete with a shaded kennel, it was the new pitstop. We didn't mind being tied up while they had tea and toast. Usually, we got something too. The sun shone approval, leaves fluttered musically, and shivers of yellow and green dashed the landscape. Sometimes, nan, stripped the tree of Bramley's, offered us the peelings, and cooked crumble for the girls. Bigger compound built and occupied, Jed took a peculiar interest in Darcy. Daily, he took him to the penny flat circle, there, he lunged him. Tip toe tasty, Darcy gave him the run-around. Dashed off in all directions, he did. Line tight, energies taunt, it was a punch-drunk performance. Unimpressed, Jed reined him in. Nose to nose, Darcy's eyes were butter bright defiant. Before Jed could say a word, Darcy run rushed backwards.

"Patience," Bianca shouted up to him from the goat pen.

"Is a little thing I don't possess!" Echoed playfully back.

Persevering Jed made it his personal project and eventually pulled it off. Good too, he was.

"Maybe we should try driving him now?"

"Only, if you ride out with me first."

Random, and spontaneous, Jed got me out, tied me up and asked for tack. Too wide, Jed found the saddle uncomfortable. Bianca had barely removed it, when he got on bareback. Adoring his bravery, Bianca beamed all the way into the village. He looked admirable, riding suited him. Chatting away, we made it all the way to the cherry orchard, before turning back. Through the village and onto the home stretch hill we went. There was a splash of energy and Jed took off. Cantered all the way up it, he did. A born natural, he really loved it. Unfortunately, his pelvis, prevented him going again, but for sure a carriage was on the cards. So much so, that Bianca, found him one, the very next day. Pleasantly priced, it was purchased and delivered. Unlike the giant thrones, I'd pulled in the past, I found its light frame work impressive. Inspired by the gift, Jed beamed. The metal frame measured, the arms didn't quite fit Darcy. An extension in mind, it was wheeled towards the work shed, where there it sat beside the welder. Still too hot to work, they had a rifle shoot instead. Target boards battered, they then let the dogs out and enjoyed the embankment. Once it was cool enough, they walked the dogs and loop. Devoid of vegetation, the dry banks appeared steeper than usual.

"You never saw her in action, did you?"

"Then go get her!" Sophisticated, Jed always made her smile.

Bianca returned with a twinkle in her eye and a star in both hands. Bandana bright, sat sardine tin tight, Jed was cushion comfy upon the top of the bank. An exhibitionist, Estrella didn't let her audience down. Tip toeing on the spot, psyching herself up, the dogs tore around the side path to join her. It took exactly two seconds for her to leap climb the twenty-foot bank to where Jed was observantly sat. Dogs still following her, synchronized barking and Jed's clapping, it, echoed through the trees to us. As if she'd just conquered the scariest ride at the fair, Bianca went around for another belly buzz.

"She'd be great at cross country!"

"Yes, but she's staying here, and so are you."

School and work balanced, Bianca ventured further afield on Estrella. I must have made a lot of noise in her absence. To stop my anxiety, Jed put me in the stable and shut the top door. Not as silly as me, Darcy kept quiet, his liberty too. Sensible, he shared his embankment with the goat until we got back. And, then just like that, we got busy. Stories of the strays travelled, and people came to visit us. With them, came generous donations that were stored in the under build. Blankets and biscuits in abundance, winter wasn't looking as bleak as the one before. On Darcy's layer, the dog compound was spacious, big enough for them to sprint around in. But, not everyone dropped off problem solving pieces. It was about five, when the car pulled up. A man got out and hovered nervously, between our boulders. I stirred and stood up. Shifty, staring up at the cabin every two seconds a man approached. Awake, the dogs barked. Basket in hand, the muddled human, placed it inside our paddock and fled. I was sniffing the air, when nosey barged me out of the way. Estrella was about to nuzzle it open, when the cats choir began. Inquisitive, Gizmo shot across the land and circled the carrier. Darcy was nod fishing for an answer, when Bianca hankered up her car. Billy beside her, they approached and opened one of the basket flaps. Sensitive, like a nest of new born sparrows, five scrawny felines, sorrow stung the air.

"Poor things, what a predicament!"

Billy barked at the contents. Black, blue, grey and two, tortoiseshell, they were a colourful combination.

"They'll be safer in the emergency straw store..." Jed, threw her a tin of chum. "I'll walk the dogs while you whisk them down there."

Holding the flap down, Bianca, scooped up the basket. Scooting after her, we all followed. Going along the inside of his fence, Darcy met us down there too. Billy wagged her tail for a second glimpse but, was pushed away by Gizmo. Carefully, Bianca concealed the black one between two hands. Head peering out, it looked like a tiny terrapin. Happy in heart, Gizmo purred.

"Look Faustino..." Bianca held it up. A lump of coal with eyes, it was cute. Feeling tender tight, and terrified of it, I stepped away. Estrella laughed her one white sock off, squeezing past me, she arched her neck over the feral nest. As if she'd found a bowl of cultured pearls, they prickled her pupils in pleasantries. Gizmo circled the mare, scarf style, her tail curled around her tendon.

"They're weak," Bianca looked up to Estrella, "and smaller than your hooves."

Bianca opened the tin of chum and laughed at the speed in which they ate. Surveillance, her new name, Estrella, stayed close to the straw shed, and watched where she walked. Though the girls mothered all five,

Annie became especially attached to the blue one. As it grew, so did their friendship. Alive, the dry lands breathed animal magic. Energies harmonious, we even slept at the same time.

Always something to do maintain or clean, we kept Bianca and Jed busy. A peaceful place, Bianca would often take a break on the opposite bank. Free of serpents and insects, the circles Darcy left, made safe platforms to sit upon. And on the days, he was tethered, she had shadow shade too. She was eating a sandwich, when the kittens appeared. Fluff on legs, they fidgeted just inside the open stable door. Cute and dreamy, they made a peaceful picture. Unaware of the situation, Jed and the dogs returned from the loop. Bianca stood up and pointed towards the stables, but it was too late. Snap hot fast, Sheba, spotted them and lead the way, through the boulder entrance, under the gate, and down the paddock. A pack in tow, the cats scooted back into their boxes. Right behind them, Jed arrived and called them off. From their pen, they watched him measure and cut wood. Cat flap inserted, they had a chance. Sedated in seriousness, Gizmo chewed on the situation, dogs secure on the upper bank, she called to the young cats. Quite amazingly, she showed them how to climb a telegraph pole and reach the stable roofs. From there, they could see the whole world, including, dog location. On occasions Sheba sneaked down to the stables and barked up at us. Safe on the roof, the cats laughed down at her. But the laughter didn't last. It was dawn when I first saw the three dogs, thin as fierce, they prowled on the opposite hill. Starving strays, I knew trouble was on the horizon. Our dogs crazy barked and tension tore down the layers like furious rain. Startled, the dogs disappeared, unfortunately, so did Jed that night. Alert and undernourished, they arrived. As if they knew, no one was about, they floated onto the land past the dog pen and towards the goat enclosure. There, their emaciated souls burrowed under the erected fence. The commotion sent us all into a frenzy. Fire in my hooves, I bolted back and forth along our perimeter. Estrella in tow, our neighing must have been horrendous. Stock startled, Darcy didn't move. Barking dogs and squawking hens, they were in! It was the squealing and shrieking of the goat, that scarred us all. Attacked from three angles, shy and timid, he didn't stand a howl in hell. Blood on their lips, the strays made off. Closer than us, Darcy dared to go and see the mess. He returned, with mist melted eyes. Fast mauled to death, the dismembered goat was in several pieces. Feathers floating, the hens had died of fright. I felt nauseous, and sad. Heads bowed, we all did.

"People!"

"Oh…?" Estrella pressed for me to finish.

"If they didn't starve and dump their animals it wouldn't happen!"

I was glad to see Jed arrive alone. Screaming a language to foul to publish, he cleared the sad sight

174

away. It would never sit well with Bianca, let alone the girls. The heartache enough, she didn't need an envelope of evidence to go with it. The rare night out, ruined, Bianca was shattered. There was talk of a fox, but we knew different. Had seen the culprits come and go, twice. Eyes red as cherries, Bianca dragged her feet towards the new compound. Opening it, the dogs consoled her. There was an eerie energy that evening. Stopping longer than usual, the girls silently stroked cats beneath the stars. Another lesson, I realised that time, has no schedule, and life no guarantees. Grateful of mine, I intended to live it the best I could. In a bid to bring back some clarity, Bianca bought a caravan for the girls. Parked on Darcy's layer, it overlooked the stables. Close to us, it got a lot of pit stop use. Doors open, dogs inside, the caravan indeed, brought us all closer together. Darcy loved sleepovers, because he got fed extra treats, crisps and bread crusts. I even saw him eat tomato once. Beneath the stars, the night sky was incredible. Paramount, even the dogs seemed engrossed to an extraordinary point. Husky hot, Bianca bought some clippers. A perfect gentleman, he didn't move a muscle. On the contrary, he thrived on the attention. Impeccable manners, someone, had once, loved him to bits. What a shame, they saw fit to dump him. We all knew his spine wasn't working, but he clung to life, like a wolf with a bone. Going a few feet after the other dogs every day until he no longer could. Unable to even get down the veranda steps he was in more misery than pleasure. I knew by the look in his eyes, that he wouldn't be coming back. The vet agreed that he was in significant pain. Old, a decision was made to do the right thing. Red eyed, Jed, and Bianca brought him back to the one place, husky knew as home. He was buried, beneath the big tree, beside the goat. Bianca painted a plaque she put there, on it she wrote, "A perfect gentleman." And a perfect gentleman, indeed, he was. One, who always said please, sat, without being asked and begged for nothing, but love. Sewn into every grain of soil, not even the breeze could remove his soul.

Energetic, Estrella constantly stared upon the lowest layer. It took a month for them to farm it of stones, sticks and boulders. Finally fenced off, the frustrated, Estrella, called out to explore. Gate pinned back, we skidded down the muck heap. Spacious, it allowed more room for us to eat and exercise on. While grazing the lower banks, the little black cat approached. A live beard either side of its mouth, the curly critter squirmed up and down. I shuddered, firm stepped away and let the feral pass. Unfazed by the snake, two feet firm on a steep bank, Estrella's only mission was to munch the grass growing beneath the overhanging bushes. When that was all ate and gone, her nose endeavoured to explore some more. Sensing an exit beside the muck heap, she went to investigate. Barging through a thicket of stinging nettles she snuck into a slim space and disappeared between two thorn bushes. I headed after her, but Darcy called out and tugged on his tree line, he too, wanted to come.

"Back in a bit, sshshs."

Darcy refrained from further noise, wide eyed, he watched me disappear down the side of the stables. I escaped the stinging nettles, but not the thorns. Sides scratched to pieces, the tears in my skin were long and open. We'd used the neighbour's drive as a shortcut to nans, but never had I been upon their lands. Wow. It was worth it. Sea weed green, grass, parcelled every platform. Eyes big as saucers and planted like a garden pot, Estrella gorged before a pretty house. Totally engrossed, she swished her tail, shook the flies and swapped the foot she was resting. I could hear people, if caught we wouldn't be allowed out again. Coaxing her, wasn't easy. Attention gained, she gave in and backed up. We were sneaking towards the avenue, when we were seen. Intrigued, and swift as a sword, a piebald Shetland shuffle shunted our way. Chain, attached to a barn, it tightened before us. The size of Sheba, he nuzzled Estrella's knee. One eye smaller than the other, I noticed it wasn't right. Possibly contagious, I urged Estrella not to make facial contact. I knew the sound of cubes in a bucket. Fast on our heels, we battled the bushes and hurtled towards the muck heap. Rushing down it had been easy, going up, not so. Cream cheese soft, our legs sank knee high. Several years old, it was nutritional soil. Perfect, for spreading and planting. So, much so, that it was bagged up and sold from the side of the road. Lunch eaten, and I went back down the muck heap, only this time, we stayed within the boundaries set. I was munching beside the road gate, when chain rattling behind him, the poorly Shetland came trotting up to it. Shaking hair and flies from his face, I got a better look at him. One eye now completely closed, he looked uncomfortable. Happy to be caught, Bianca put him in my stable. Indeed, it was conjunctivitis. Desperately uncomfortable, he'd pulled the loop out of the barn side and done one. Bianca contacted his owners, they called by after work. Admittedly, they, didn't have time for him, and asked Bianca to fix him up. A visit to the chemist, cotton wool and cooled water, he got his help. We nick named him, 'No Name.' Happy to be in company, he got better in no time at all. Only little, Jed put him in the dog compound. Accepting him, they enjoyed his company, and when they got walked, so did he. School-holidays brought the usual regular riding. But not all school friends, could ride. Going too fast, Tina fell from me. She wasn't hurt, but I was hungry. An edible patch to my east, and I was there. Easy to catch, we continued along the top tracks. Afterwards, the girls would crash in the caravan. In the morning, Tina came out to use the portable toilet. Loving the early atmosphere, she came to see us. Totally, out of character, Estrella chased her from the paddock. Shaken, but not stirred, Tina caught her breath and called up to the cabin for help. Bianca didn't believe it. There was no reason for Estrella to eat small people. Perhaps it was just a playful gesture, mistaken for something else. Bianca walked with Tina back to the caravan. Famous for her cooking the girls all went cross country to nans. Canoodling, outside the stables, Bianca opened the store room and dished up grain. While Estrella ate, Bianca, brushed her main, chatted and did the usual daily check. Leaving us all with a slice of alfalfa Bianca wandered down the paddock. She was half way, when Estrella rushed her. Spinning, with raised arms, Bianca waved her back. Hormones. The mare was being a bit of a diva.

On a morning walk with Jed, the land was dog and Shetland, free. Exuberant, the cats one by one came out of the cat flap. Then, like the Aristo-cats, ambled across the road and dashed into the woods. Still finding their feet, they were funny. I saw them return. I also, saw the car cruise around the bend. Going too fast, the little blue one Annie liked, went under it. Bianca sprinted towards the scene, but it was too late. Dead, on impact, the cat didn't have a chance. The returning dogs and Shetland raced towards the body. Entrails everywhere, it was a disturbing sight. Tear-choked, Bianca clutched the little cat to her chest. First the goat and now this... Crying upon the white boulders, the cats grieved. Gizmo wailed. High pitched, it sent shock waves through the ridges. The graveyard was growing, and for the following few days, things ground to a halt.

Cute

It was while picking wild asparagus, that Bianca saw the advertisement. Intrigued and on foot, she entered the finca gates. Sat on his porch, the man had two puppies. Bianca scooped up the smallest. Tiny, it sat in the palm of her hand. And, oh, how cute she was. Arrangements made, health food under her arm, we watched her return from the village to get her car. Still upset, Annie was in her room. Going in, Bianca put the puppy on Annie's pillow. Like a light bulb, she lit up. Aromatizing the air, puppy perfume spread to every room. Annie called the dog Bella, put it in her pocket and took it everywhere. And so, for a few months, clarity returned. That is, until the big fire unleashed itself.

The breeze brought a strong strange smell. An invisible chimney, on the far road, a reel of rogue cotton drifted high into the air. Then, feasting on the bush shrubs, it rainbow reached out. Jutting left and then right, its limbs moved like elastic. Burnt orange strips, sky blues and tinted tulips, it held the hands of a hundred ballerinas. Dazzling they did a lot of dancing. Falling and rising, flames prickled the skies, worse still, they were prancing towards nans. Like starving strays, it ravaged her entrance. Smoke in its gallons, nans road was no longer visible and for a bit, neither was the fire. Together with Bianca, Jed came running down the hill. Opening her car door, Bianca started the engine. But by now the hill opposite was engulfed in smoke. Instead she took out her phone. It rang. Nan was fine. Said, that the wind had turned the fire just in time. Watch out it's on the flat land now! Unable to see the flames through the smoke, Bianca was for a second stumped. Then, raising its red head like a dinosaur that had just spotted its prey, it tore down the separation land and filled its furnace. Spearmint and sparkles, it spat tantrums across the south terrain and headed straight for us. Fast consuming the vegetation, it was feet from our bend, and depending on which way it cruised, only minutes from the cabin. Made of wood, it had no chance. Wings widening, the flames filtered closer, then, faced with the concrete road gullies, was forced to halt. A candle wick stuck in sinking wax, a thousand blue and red dancers performed. Inert, the confused fire, put its feelers out for fuel. Then as if the devil was orchestrating, it turned and raced right towards the neighbour behind us. Not far from the stables, the situation was serious for all of us. Pacing and prancing, the dogs tried to climb the chain link fence. Going to the compound, Jed let them all out. A race against the dogs, 'No name,' ran towards me, equine security needed, he huddled against my fence. Unsure of everything, Bianca even let Billy out of the car.

Fire was all new to me, the others too, fear burning through our blood, my heart heat hammered. Inhaling smog, my head felt thick. Stood on the bank across the road, the dogs panic barked. Out of control, the fire escalated in to a fully scaled tsunami. Hoping it would miss the neighbours, Jed ducked under Darcy's gate and waded up the land to try and see where it had fled. Wide eyed, I huddled against the gate, Estrella beside me, she didn't move. Oppressed, Darcy had a long distant stare, I'd not seen before. The cats crossed the road and quickly took up resident in the furthest, and tallest loop trees. Back and forth, the dogs didn't know which way to turn. Tails between their legs, anguish was all over them. Jed reached the boundaries. Smouldering, the land streamed smoke sediment that made it impossible for him to assess anything. Arms raised, his hands swivelled from side to side in uncertainty and turned back. Bianca held a hand out to Estrella.

If I let you go, head for the village. Bricks burn slower than forests, and there's water there too!" Eyes, full of endearment, Estrella understood. Bianca was focused on Jed when her phone buzzed. One arm around Darcy, she answered with the other.

"It's incredibly smoky up here!" Sally panicked, "where is it…?" She was frantic, tearful and totally bewildered.

"It's hovering," back, Jed breathed heavily into the mouthpiece, "not sure if its heading here, or there."

Screaming neighbours slapped our ears. Unable to fight the situation an engine roared and a barking dog followed them up to ours. Just then as if the fire had heard Jed, it stalled, it spat, it backed up. The phone went dead. A red rabbit running from a gun, the fire headed back the way it had come, passing the gullies it began nibbling her land. A tail of smoke following, it blew thick until the air was nothing but killer fog. Jed kicked our emergency barrels over, dampening the ground it kept the temperature at bay. I could see a roof burning red, the neighbours had just anchored up their jeep when it caved in.

"My boy panic fled." Petrified the mother pointed towards our muck heap, "he's stuck! We can't get to him by foot, or car!" Stroke material, she was mad, muddled.

"Where is he?" The situation upset Bianca.

"Barn roof," the father barked, "but, he's got vertigo, and frozen." Totally tear jerked, terrible vibrations grew stronger than the fire.

"Isn't there a passage through the nettles, to their place." Bianca turned to me, "you went there a few weeks ago, didn't you?"

Bianca grabbed a bridle hanging on the tractor, scarf soaked, she tied it to my nose band and got me out. Estrella tried to follow, but Bianca quickly shut her in. Leaping on bareback she pointed towards the new gate on the renovated layer. Beside it, the boy's father undid it. Kicking me through the boulders, we panned left. Dogs in tow, she galloped towards the muck bank, slipped past the stables, and into an avenue of smoke. There, the nettles bit me all over. Dogs on my heels, they urged me on. I knew I wasn't dreaming because the thorns, cut me to ribbons. Smog, candy floss thick, visibility was vague. I halted. I shook my head until the scarf covered my nostrils. Head low, I breathed filtered air. Straight ahead, the roof remains glowed a million rubies. Still separating the house from the barn, stalk sized flames fluttered. I sensed something to my right. Yes, it was coming from one of the two barns. Bianca called out and the boy answered. Face flat upon my neck, I nearly hesitated, but Bianca anquored me right. To smoggy to see, his voice, was all I had, a few minutes on top of that. Checkmate, there he was. stuck some several feet up, his legs dangled over the roof lip...

"Hurry." Bianca splutter waved.

"I can't..." It was lame.

Buttercups and buttons!!! The boy wasn't helping. Had less time than a deflating balloon. Bianca jumped off, righted a step ladder, while at the same time using it to get back on. Afraid, he came face down. Bianca reached for his hand, booted me sideways and demanded he jump. Both on board, chests heaving like fish out of water, I ran blindly back. Air a priority, I didn't feel the thorns pulling us backwards, or the stingers that deliberately zapped me and their legs. I slowed at the muck heap and breathed. Barking dogs and bawling parents, I proceeded to the exit. Ecstatic, Estrella and the family were overwhelmed. But where was the fire? Having eaten the right-hand side of Sally's fields, it now tunnel visioned for her house and stables. There was scary shrieking, door banging and shouting. The stable block was beginning to burn. Thick as clean white sheets, the smoke smothered everything. The boy's father and Jed fought their way towards Sally's drive. Thinking she'd never see them again, Bianca painfully paced. Then, as destiny would have it, the helicopters came. Containers attached, millions of gallons swung from their bottoms. Falling like hail, the water hit the lands. Retaliating, the fire hissed and fumed fury. Two hours later, it was tamed and contained. Told to stop what it was doing and die. Job done, the helicopters left, unfortunately they didn't take the heartache with them. Jed and the father returned. Stun gun shocked, the family drove downtown. Easing his butt onto the bank, Jed was sad. Ron had lost one of the horses, the goat too.

I didn't know how to feel, and I, didn't want the name of the deceased horse. Speechless, I ingested, hot mist melts. Jed waved the dogs away from all licking his face at once. But where was Billy. Bianca leapt to her feet. Oh, no. She'd let her out of the car. Frantic, Bianca broke down. Running blindly into the mist sizzle, she called for her. While she searched the loop, Jed did our layers. Bianca must have been gone for over an hour before returning tired and distraught. Devastated, she went up to the cabin and searched it. In pieces she shook. Jed frowned, told her to go while he continued to look. At home, Bianca told the girls Billy was asleep in the caravan. Restless, she couldn't sleep, got up and fetched water, but it didn't put her stomach fire out for long. Billy was no fugitive and Bianca felt her to be alive. A selfless and receptive dog, she was somewhere out there. Up at dawn, her and Jed let the dogs out, leaving no stone unturned they searched until lunchtime. Bianca refused to give up. The loop ledges were steep in places. In need of sturdy solid feet, she jumped on Darcy. Daringly, she rode along every edge he could lay hoof to. Side winding and ledge trawling, Darcy went that bit higher, than she could. No joy, she went into the village up the hill and along the back tracks. Tiptoeing over tarnished lands she even went into the neighbours burnt kitchen. Three days passed in which time everyone in the village was informed and all the farmers asked not to shoot, if she was seen. By day four, little Billy was becoming a ghost. It was hot, nothing could survive this long without water. Energy diminishing, day five became a funeral. Dogs at her heels, Bianca did one last search. Dejected, she fell onto the cabin steps, welled up and washed the wood with tears. She'd lost her best friend. The phone irritated her. She didn't want to answer, but it might be school or work.

"I've found her!"

"Where are you?"

Adhesive, her energy spread like glue. Glory in her feet, her sprint was of Olympic standard. Over the road and into the shrubs, she ran. Deprived of proper paths, it was made up of rocks and skinny spirals that eventually circled the face of a canyon. Gloating, Jed caught her in his arms, gasping for air, she followed his finger. In between them and the sheer drop off, was a brown and very white face. Bianca was astounded. Somehow, Billy had fallen during the fire, scramble, scratched at the wall, and against all the odds, hoisted herself into a small hole. Tucked tightly into the cave sized cage, she was truly stuck. Heaven knows how she had managed to turn around. Impossible to get back up, her only option was down. A sheer drop, death was inevitable. Too frightened to lean out, to hoarse to bark, I think, she was in shock. How, she'd survived with no water, was indeed a miracle.

"Faustino can pull." Bianca ran back to get me.

"Hang on a minute." Verbally on her heels, Jed wanted to know the plan.

Bianca grabbed Darcy's harness and two lunge lines. Securely fitted, she led me up the hill.

"You're not serious!" Hands on his hips, Jed was on the bend.

"I know how to get around there. Come on."

Bianca went up onto the road bend and panned left. Going down a gridlock of obstacles, and onto gritty ground, we arrived on the other side of the drop off. Bianca threaded the harness rings and clipped the lines either side of my headcollar. Only the dog in mind, she proceeded to tie a bowline knot around her waist then, ankles.

"Too risky!" Jed wasn't happy.

"He's the most benevolent horse in the world." Bianca paused, "I trust you and him, with my life."

"Well, that's exactly what you are doing."

"It's either him, or you," Bianca winked at me, "but he's stronger than you, so let him pull."

Bianca leant over the ledge. Billy was the length of her body away.

"I need five feet."

There was a jolt. I felt the lines tighten. Body pancake flat upon the rock, arms outstretched, she reached into the hole and fumbled for Billy's scruff. There was squealing. It took me thirty seconds to drag them up. Bianca, let the dog go and lay on her back. Dewclaw torn in the fall, Billy held up her front foot. Getting up, Bianca tucked her under her arm.

"Let's go get a drink," Full of praise, Jed led me back, put me away and got out a couple of beers.

Settled, on our bank, Billy between them, they hugged her while sipping bubbles of satisfaction. Originally from the rescue pound, eyes, bigger than her body, she'd used them to get out. Nine lives. She'd been lost and found at a car boot, eaten rat poison and had her stomach pumped. Sneaked out of the car on the school collection. She'd run some way behind the car before being seen in the mirror that day. Had gone after a cat down the beach and disappeared for two hours before returning to the car. Found her way home through harsh terrain from the highest font ride. And now this... Yes, Billy was doing ok for life lines and friends. Subject changed, Jed and I, were intrigued to hear Bianca talk about barefoot. Unlike Estrella, I had endured nasty nails most of my life, and Darcy was just beginning to. Recommended by Ron, and intrigued with a natural method, Bianca, gave him a call. John arrived a week later, stood before me, he discussed numerous benefits and restrictions. Navicular, being the top contender inside a cramped foot. And yes, in the wild, horses did wear down their own feet. And walk, I had no idea we went so far when wild. Not, until he told us. Fifty kilometres a day. Suddenly, the phrase, "horse power," had new meaning. Coffee cups empty, the conversation was put into practice. Shoes removed, John did a grand demonstration. One hoof perfectly rasped, he handed the other over to Bianca. I could tell she was nervous, but file it, she did.

"As long as the foot is flat round and even," John squinted sunshine, "it will always be balanced."

He left her, with a smile and a complimentary rasp. Bianca held up my worn shoe. Estrella sniffed at it. Hooves hard as nails, she was proud of her rock-solid feet. At first our hoofs felt soft and a little sore on the hot roads. But as time went on, they hardened, eventually clay, clattering upon the concrete, without pain or pressure.

The helicopter soared towards us. An undercurrent of hot waves created, it descended like a remote control, toy.

"Wayne's, here..." Jed waved to the pilot.

Our neighbour didn't come often but liked to make an entry when he did. Parked up, engine off, he came across.

"The horses look handsome." He had a likeable accent and strange sense of humour. "Were having a party. Will they mind?"

"Not if you share your carobs and apples," Bianca made light of it.

"Not, so many of the carobs," Jed shook his hand and thanked him for the use of his embankment.

"Is this him?" Wayne moved a few feet to the other gate. Behind it, bright as always was Darcy.

"Yes," Jed roared, "he's your, hoover!"

We watched Wayne, go across the road and up his drive. Out of his rustic house, he pulled two full sized speakers and a BBQ. Us animals all fed and watered, Jed disappeared for the night. Sure enough, people came, a mini rave in the making we didn't get much sleep. The morning however, was somewhat different. Hung over, but happy, they came across and fed us all we could manage. Going only, for the apples I gave the carobs a miss. 'No name' neighed for his share. Going through a little gate in the hedgerow, Wayne fed, him too. Careful not to overdo it, Wayne emptied what was left at Darcy's feet, locked up and left. I don't know how it happened, but while sniff snuffling up apples, he got his head collar clipped to his hoof. To begin with, we didn't believe he was stuck. Merely thought Darcy was trying to make us laugh, as he sometimes did. But, as panic, turned to pain, Darcy was dead still.

"How on earth..." Gizmo, examined the catch closely.

Somehow, while scoffing, his headcollar clip had got caught, opened, and embedded itself into the sole of his foot. Head secure, there wasn't anything Gizmo or the other cats could do. Poor Darcy, I didn't like it. The adults rarely left us alone, but it seemed each time they did, disaster struck. For over an hour he stayed in that position. Poor thing must have had head, neck and back ache. Anxious, not one of us relaxed, until finally, they arrived. Stuck fast, they had to push his head further down to pull out the clip. Inner hoof wall pierced, it left quite a hole. Plugging it up, with her finger, Bianca steadied the seeping blood. Going into the store room, Jed grabbed a bandage, that he wrapped around it. A better option than the dusty soil, they helped him limp onto the green embankment. There, Darcy forgot his woes, and ate.

Neighing next to Sheba, 'No name,' wanted feeding. Flicking his ears in sequence to her tail, the pair of them, froth foamed for attention. Bianca collected up the bowls and began washing them with water from the big buts. Opening their gate, Jed let them out. Squatting like ducks before him, their tails fanned the floor for food. "No, Name," however, had other ideas. With button bright eyes, he scurried over the road and hid behind Darcy. Bianca tried to bring him down, but he dug his heels in and asked to stay. An hour, she smiled, that's it. Impunity, granted, No Name, gorged. Animals and another day done, Bianca opened a bottle of wine with Jed. Unlike the stars that barked Bianca to sleep, Estrella had totally other ideas. In their haste, someone, had left it open. Unbolted, the muck gate flapped to and throw. Pushing against it, Estrella watched the metal frame swing slipped, over the muck heap. Engulfed in devious delight, socks sinking into muck silk, we skidded to its bottom. Like two kids playing truant, we took off in defiance across the lower layer. Only held together by bailing twine, Estrella used her teeth to undo the far gate. We tottered onto the empty road. Grateful of barefoot, respects to pay, we went unheard, up the hill and around the bend. Interested in our fleeting shadows, 'No name,' and Darcy, watched in dismay. Cabin behind us, we headed for the u bend. Newly planted alfalfa, it smelt candy, dandy, sweet. Enveloped in the quiet, we tickle tasted, its green tips, and ate, all we could. Startled, all four of Estrella's feet left the ground. Looking like a cardboard cut-out horse, she finally touched base. Moonlit cute, the mother boar, had brought her babies beside us to eat. A silver fox and some rabbits too, it seemed that night was day for many. Hiding from the hunters, who could blame them? An owl also came and a hare, greeted her too. Excited, Estrella's eyes were saucer wide, and though her soul had always been free, I think she lost it to the wildlife that night. It was a scene from the Lion King, where for a short valuable time, everything was at one with nature. I think the fox stirred Ron's dogs. Silence broken, we fled. Sensing something not right, Bianca ventured onto the veranda. Stood in her pyjamas, she listened to the stillness. It was chilly, but she knew something was out there. In flip flops she padded across the shingle and onto our road bend. The stars her only headlights, she sniffed cool air. Squinting, up the hill, her eyesight strained. Flying around the bend like birds we saw her, slowed, and ghost floated towards her silhouette. Arms held high, Bianca waved and whispered.

Gradually, we ground to a halt before her. Coaxing us with words, she walked between us, until back on the second layer. Gate closed, I heard her sigh the word, safe.

New and Blue

Due to bad memories, the neighbours put their place up for rent. Roof patched, and land no longer parched, it offered a lot of privacy. Set back from the road, it meant we could roam. So, Rather, than renting her flat any further, Bianca traded landlords. Sold to a German lady, they came to collect 'No name.' It was a sad day, but Bianca couldn't afford anymore, and accepted he was going to a good home. And so, our belongings were moved around the corner. Doubling up, the girls, rode Darcy up the derelict drive and put him in, 'No names, old paddock and stable. I could hear him calling. Demanding, Darcy didn't let up until we too, arrived. Though I'd had a sneaky preview with Estrella, nothing could have prepared me. Apart from a little shed on the top layer it was totally wild. Ten thousand square metres of meringue, a staircase rolled towards me, split around the house, then, swirled down to the barn. Shag-pile soft, my feet relished upon green sponge. A natural boarder between us and the cabin, it was wide and thick green lush. Made up of secret avenues and arches, my imagination disappeared into Autumn coloured coves.

Invitation put aside, it also offered peach and pear trees, for immediate eating.

A little damaged and fire smelly, the renovation, was stunning. One big window instead of a wall, it brought us all inside out, close. A pretty terracotta patio, it reminded me of a pink, cupcake. There was a hose, it worked, hallelujah. The girls loved every inch of the place and with them, the dogs followed. Not just one, but all of them. And just like us, they had no desire to stray. Sprawled out around the house, the only one restricted, was Sheba. Unfortunately, she chased cats, also considered a dangerous dog, the leash was for her protection too. Perforated, the small shed on the top layer provided the perfect cattery. Just till they settled. Content staring from its one window, the cats cooed and slept. Olive trees on the house layer, Bianca open tied, her first washing line. Never had we felt so content or been anywhere so angelic. The only thing connecting us to the outside world, was the break in the trees behind the shed. Had it not been for that little bit of road disturbance, we'd of had a sealed and private world. Using heavy duty cable, Bianca tied it between the furthest trees. Perky, and feeling utter joy, we had no urge to go under it. And, what's this. Estrella was growing dull. Not in character, but in coat. Somewhere in mid transition, black mottled patches mingled on her grey surface.

The bus dropped the girls and a friend at the bottom of the village. School done, bags dumped down, they vaulted on and rode into the hills of history. Hosed, on our return, we loved the cool showers. Peppered mist absorbed, appreciation glistened upon my old skin. Pounding the ground, I rolled. Legs reaching into the sky, I wriggled like a lost worm. Squirming left and right, I smiled at the sun. Unlike, Estrella, who was frightened of water, Darcy didn't mind it, not so long as it didn't hit his back legs. Perceptive, Darcy didn't want to go back into his paddock. A pack pony, he tugged sharply on his knot. Continually nibbling on his rope, he finally undid it. Scarpering like a naughty kid, he caught us on the second layer. Estrella chuckled. A kick in the air, and we took off. Darcy in tow, we headed for the highest bank and hid behind the cat shed. Bianca clambered after us, but as she got close, we took to our toes. Exhausted, but glad we all got on, she let us be. Warm nights, only lizards and bees in the air, we grazed our dream. It was about nine when we ventured down to the house. Not because we were hungry, but to be nosey. Bianca was folding her washing and as expected the dogs were sleeping. A precious moment, we lie down beside the patio and breathed integrity. Complete, I again, slept as a foal. The sound of croaking frogs, morning birds and a faint meowing, woke me. Coffee in hand, girls still asleep, Bianca came out and sat between us. Together, with the dogs, we watched the sun rise, and the breeze collect, and carry fairy pollen away. Thirsty, I got up and made my morning introduction to the trough. Savouring every cool wave that trickled through my teeth, I drank easy. Estrella arched her back, a half-moon on stilts, she was funny. Still on the ground, Darcy ate at the grass around him. Kneeling, Annie brushed his back.

Bianca set off to let the cats out. Had a week passed already? Coupled in happiness, my inbuilt clock was no longer needed. Nosey, Estrella followed her up the layers to the shed. Not far behind, I followed them. There, like china cats behind an old net curtain, they were china still. Waiting. Not only for their food, but freedom too. One by one they came out. Huddled together on the same step ladder used to rescue the boy, they brushed shoulders. Confused by the new scenery, they cleaned their whiskers and whispered to one another. The sound of oncoming dogs, and they shot up the tree. Billy, Bella, Muffin, Ted and Sheba arrived, a few minutes later so did Jed and Barker.

"I wondered who'd let her loose?" Bianca fussed Sheba and hushed her noise.

I gazed at the cats and felt for their fears. But where was Gizmo? On the shed roof, she was in ocean deep thought. Then leaping from the roof into the tree, she enrolled the young cats into feline cadets. Five or six feet apart, the trees ran directly down the layer, before circling right, towards the house. Taking the lead, Gizmo lily pad leapt, the first. One by one, the cats skip, hop, sprung, after her. Spellbound the dogs watched in wonder as they catapulted the lot. Nine branches later, and they were overlooking the patio. Feeding the cats and dogs so closely, wasn't going to be easy. But, Jed came up with a solution. Wood samples sawn to shape, Bianca held them in place. Platforms, in position, Jed screwed them to the trees. Entirely safe, eating was no longer a chore. Towels, to lie on, and they had sun beds too. Intelligent, they would wait for the dogs to integrate with sleep before indulging on the ground. Young and adventurous, plant life exuberant, they all loved to explore. Adventurous they sometimes went, even further than nan's. Growing fast, but still only an overgrown sausage, Bella wandered onto the patio. A smile on her petite, face, she beckoned, Estrella over. Cool as cucumber, Estrella, towered over the oblong pup. Nose to nose, all creatures great and small, it was a cute sight. Confidence, growing, the pup played with the bigger dogs and explored the land. Rain fell, bringing the faint smell of summer forestry, it grew heavier. Lightning and thunder struck. While, the dogs took shelter in the house, we took off and searched for shelter. Stables, prepared, Bianca called to us in her rain coat… But, by then we'd entered the secret avenue for the first time. Ancient, the roots had outgrown the earth, risen and taken up residence above. Branches, sweeping the earth we stepped over them towards a less leaky cave canopy. There, cocooned in green moss, enormous, willows sheltered us. Through the lashes of rain, we saw the lantern. A tiny torch, it bobbed towards us. I felt bad, but, could hardly see to help her. It was heavier now, sweeping over the log roots and making them ice slippery.

Torrents, streaming over her cheeks, Bianca straddle swished forward, without tripping on graphic root obstructions. Leg over the last log, face battered by hail, hair hanging like a hundred wet tails, she'd shrunk.

"There you are!"

Too heavy to turn and go back, Bianca stayed. Finally simmering, summer sprinkles fell from the moss and leaves, offering Bianca a better understanding of why the English, call them weeping willows. Following her, back towards the house, I saw my first rainbow. Bella loved food, so when she stopped eating, I knew it was bad news. Jed arrived and tried to encourage her with treats, but tempt her, he couldn't.

"Perhaps, she's just having a bad day." Bianca sighed.

But the next morning was a none starter too and her weight began to deteriorate. On top of that she oozed a nasty smell. Away on holiday, Bianca couldn't reach her vet and left a message for, Tim, to get back. But he didn't, and by the third morning, Bella was a bag of bones, held only in place by fur. Removed from Annie, Bianca rushed Bella to the animal hospital. Unlike her usual vet, they were cold. Bianca didn't like the drip they put in her tiny arm or the fact that there wasn't any bedding in the observation bay. Bella shivered, eyes bigger than her body, Bianca, still saw life there. The smell was unbearable and according to the vet could possibly be parvovirus. Survival rate wasn't great. They were closing, it was time to leave.

"You damned well live you hear me!" Bianca sobbed.

In the morning Bianca attended alone. Upsetting, the dog was dying an undiagnosed death. Frail, weak and unable to even raise an eye brow, Bella closed her eyes. Bianca rang Tim. This time, he answered.

"Bring me the dog!"

Annie felt unwell and was rushed to hospital. Lethargic and white, skin hot enough to fry an egg on, it took three doctors to diagnose glandular fever. Medication followed by milk chocolate, she sweetly swept into morning. Responsive to the antibiotics, she was a much better colour and altogether stronger. Sitting up, Annie asked after Bella. Unable to answer, Bianca said nothing. Whatever the outcome, she knew, Tim's decision would be the right one. Another night passed before Annie was discharged. Open minded, and on the mend, she asked they stop at the vets, before venturing home.

"Stay there!" Tim immediately disappeared. Annie felt nervous.

There was a scuffle, a whimper and whine. Then, thin as a wish bone, and smiling, just like one, out came Bella. Scooping the pup into her arms, Annie was overwhelmed. We were lazing on the grass, when they pulled up. Reciting everything on her return, Bella explained the force feeding, the tubes and stomach stalling. But, throughout all of it, the fear of not returning had been her biggest enemy. On the patio lemonade was poured, the rustle of a crisp packet and the dogs left us to see what they could scrounge. After, camped on the settee, Bella by her side, Annie was able to see us through the big window. From there the sun sang approval, leaves fluttered, and small birds twittered the same musical, 'get well.' From between the aloe Vera plants a very brave rabbit sniffed the nose of Estrella. Nature at its best, animal magic helped Annie drift off. Three days of cinema rest, and her and Bella were back on form. Sat on the lip of the empty pond, the girls were joined by Jed. Good at making stuff, he knew a place to fish. Homemade nets in hand, we watched them drive off. The girls returned with five fish, an additional two in his bucket, Jed made it seven. Alive, like the land, the pond became an additional treasure to our attractive home. Happy, none of us realised how fast the time had passed, not until the grass thinned and the flies grew fewer. Bianca was washing her car of dust when the phone rang. Foamy fingers, they fumbled in her back pocket for it. Almost in her face, I searched her for treats. She was nodding and smiling at me. Then, half way through the conversation, it was wiped from her face.

"I didn't know the house was up for sale. Let alone sold!"

Hardening like rigor mortis, I saw the anxiety set in Bianca. A handful of dreams built on someone else's banks, she was sinking. Blotting out the news, she was pleased when her friend and daughter visited. Harper and Hailey loved the enclosed privacy. While the girls explored picture book scenery, Harper and Bianca, did the daily chores. Harper loved the cats, their platforms and purring, she also loved me. Taking my fancy Spanish tack, she saddled me. Leaping on little legs, Bianca walked beside us. Weaving around the trees, we showed her every inch of our haven. Even some of our hiding places. Cool from the sun and dry from the rain, we had a few secrets spots. I'd covered every layer, but, where, was Estrella? Harper urged me onto the last bank for a better look'. There, grass belly swollen, legs splayed before her, Estrella resembled a black handbag dropped by a giant. I say black, but it was more chocolate to be precise, dark chocolate with a tad of milk mixed in. Long days on the patio and BBQs in the evening, eliminated, some of Bianca's worry. But, when Harper went home, I think she felt half empty. Like me, Bianca's life seemed to swing between heaven and hell. I don't think either of us wanted to go back to hell.

Different

A move in mind, Jed needed more help than he could offer. Resigned to the fact that many of them had come as rescues, Bianca searched for special homes. Helpful, and due to the mouse population, the villagers were glad to house the cats, including her beautiful Gizmo who took up residence with an elderly lady. Endearing, Sheba and Muffin went to friends in one of the furthest villages. Though upset, Bianca was also punch pleased they were free to roam its grounds all day. Taken in by a local family, Ted became an indoor dog. Straight on their settee, this he loved. Billy and Bella, she was able to keep. Often, Jed would leave the linking layers open. When all of that was eaten, we escaped into an orchard on the right. Bianca, arrived, and came looking for us. Startled by her unexpected presence, I thought we were in trouble. Like the three musketeers we took off, charged past her and back towards our bit. Unhappy with the amount of fruit we'd eaten, the orchard owner pulled up, got out and slammed his door shut. Uncompromising, he yelled words that I understood better than Bianca. Worse still, he threatened to hurt us if we stole so much as another pip. The pressure of everything too much, Bianca took out her phone. I couldn't hear what was said, but a few days later a trailer pulled up. Shop stock removed from the under build, it was put on the trailer. Worse still, so was me and Darcy. Furious, Estrella raced up and down and attempted to jump the chain link fence. Opening her arms, Bianca calmed her, explained that Jone was starting up a riding school, and if suitable, could work something out for all of us. At least, until Bianca could balance everything. Housing for excursions, Estrella twiddled her mouth, snorted, and put away her mood. Curled up before the big gates, there, she waited. And wait, she did.

At Jones', I was put in a stable, beside me in the next one, Darcy. I'd never had a bed of shavings before, a sprinkle of sawdust, yes, but not shavings. Whiskers first, I put out the feelers. I sniffed the white bedding and opened my mouth, it didn't taste nice. Darcy rolled in his. Dusted in snowflakes, he mirrored a coconut tea cake. The food was tasty, but there was no freedom, and we were soon bored. I missed the girls, my blackberry picking, and scented herbs. My pebble dashed peaks, foraging ferals and hooting owls. I needed to stretch my legs, roll in the dirt, but most importantly, see, my dear Estrella. Gosh, she must be lonely. Jone had two yards and quickly realised she wouldn't be able to smoothly run both. Costly, we were sent back to the mountains, while she found someone to manage it. Ecstatic, Estrella went mad. Chasing her, our feet went like the clappers. Up and down we football thundered, lunatics, Billy, Barker and Bella followed. Doing circles, Billy chased her tail. Yes, they were happy to have us back. Broke, Bianca sold some of her possessions to feed us. Household goods first, then the gold from around her neck. The winter came again, but our rugs were worn and old, fallen apart in fact. Food more important, we grew long coats to compensate. By now you must be asking yourself why we hadn't been sold. Oh, it was mentioned many times, but Bianca switched off, collapsing any kind of conversation. Sometimes she would come down to the big old stables and sit with us. Hands in her head, a smile eventually surfaced. Getting up she stroked me, assured and adored all of us. Strangely enough, it was about this time that our passports came back. Put away, Bianca kept them safe. Hope, her second name, she tried to stay positive. Rolling around the bend and past the cabin, Anton pulled up beside the boulders.

"Why prolong the pain, just let them go..." He got out. "If you want, I'll buy the little one."

Bianca didn't answer, she just didn't hear him. He meant well, was only thinking of her. But, she couldn't stand the thought of someone mistreating us. Preferring to put a bullet to my head, budge she wouldn't. It was a strange thing that happened next, because, Jone called her back. The kids riding school was set up, and Elsa, the new employee was expecting us. Everything was catered for, food, livery, wormers and even shoes, if needed. There was only one problem, the lorry was temporarily elsewhere. It didn't matter, where there was a will, there was a way. And this time, we were all going. Happier alone than me, Bianca, rode Darcy first. Reaching the main road, coaches canoed them. Ears protruding, either side of the front screens, the new versions, looked like enormous beetles on wheels. Waving from inside it, tourists assumed Darcy was an attraction. Darcy shuddered, jelly shook on the spot, but coated in kind words, he trusted, and let them pass. For a pony who'd done little, or no road work, he was a star. Elsa immediately warmed to Darcy. Who wouldn't, he was smart, kind, safe and handsome. Elsa ran Bianca back up the hill, showing her a short cut at the same time. Just off the busy bypass, the slip road, cut a lot off. The next day it was my turn. In between the coaches, cars raced up the hill, taking the bends with a vengeance, I felt vulnerable. Bianca sang, chatted and talked, all the way to the short cut. A crooked, but flat piece of concrete, it felt pleasant beneath my feet. A few yards on, and barking made me jump out of my old skin. Chain link rattling, and I was pleased to get past the dogs. But what came next, stopped me dead in my tracks. Trees! Not just any though... An army of them. Marched into mid field, a twisted mosaic, stood spellbound in time. Waists wide as doors, the extraordinary tree trunks, birthed endless shapes. Formations, that beckoned and enveloped everything around them. Including me. Years of manifestation distinct, their heirlooms mastered, the landscape with impressive images. Moving on, the road became single track. I felt my feet trip with lightness but, had to shy away from a sheer drop. Like the breeze, I could hear Darcy calling. Going up a vertical hill, I turned left at the top. Below it, snug against the forest, stood a square stable block. Just before its wide entrance, a sand school. Sectioned off, the paddocks were outlined by hedges. Legs splayed, ears alert, Darcy x-rayed me. Bright eyed recognition, like a dog awaiting his master, he mooched back and forth. Lunchtime, the place was locked, but a key had been left out. Soaked in sweat, I felt crusty and couldn't wait to try the shower. A thousand cooling ripples, I purred. Released, I rolled my wet body in the school sand before nearing the hedge. Sun drying up the water, I chatted incessantly over it, to Darcy. Back on our hill, Bianca dumped down her tack ready for the next day. Estrella was the tricky one. Young and naïve, she knew nothing of road dangers, just mountains and tracks. Bianca saddled her, but something had got in the compound and chewed some of the girth off. Three inches short, she took hold of some bailing twine and tied it all together. And so, taking a leap of faith she directed Estrella towards a very dangerous, and busy, by pass. Everything was ok at first. A few flying cars and lots of one, to one, chat, seemed to work well. The coach roared long before it appeared. A skateboard with attitude, it fog, floated, around the bend. Estrella froze, she shook, and was ready to run. Bianca screamed kind words and tried to gather her up, but the terrified mare fled. Scarpering across the road, she swivelled in front of the oncoming coach and skated towards a sheer drop. Bianca kicked her boots out of the stirrups, over the saddle, and into thin air. Landing on her feet, she yanked at the reigns. Howling and shrieking, she jabbed jolted at her mouth. Carried along, for a few seconds like a rag doll, Bianca, saw the distance between her, and the drop off close in. Exhausted, one last yank was all she could muster before letting the horse go over alone. The coach stopped, and just inches from the edge, so did Estrella. Staring like a hare in headlights, she finally listened and let the coach crawl past. A collection of traffic behind it, Estrella didn't budge until every mechanical monster was gone. As you can imagine, they reached the shortcut, in gripping time. Spooking at the dogs, shying from the trees, she scooted up the hill, and stood statue still upon its top. All leg and lean, shapely and sweat shiny, I studied her silhouette. Profile, outlined, she had the finest of features. Porcelain fetching, eyes set like black pearls, she was for sure, the prettiest of them all. Yes, she was stubborn and sturdy, stroppy and strong, but best of all, all mine. A wriggle in her stride and she wandered down in style. She was a show off too. Mind boggled by her disappearance, it took me a full minute to figure things out. Unlike us, her full livery status, entitled, her to a stable in the yard. Separated, there was a lot of neighing. Not a suitable situation, it was for now, the best, Bianca could do. Unlike Darcy, who was in the paddock with the least shade, I had a shelter. I heard Bianca address the issue, but like most things in Spain, the word, Manana, became repetitive.

Estrella called out, until her tonsils hurt. Ignoring her, Elsa said she would eventually settle. Estrella wasn't used to being kept in a tight stable and found the boredom tedious. In-fact the only time we saw one another, was when the kids brought us into the stable square to tack up. Inquisitive, Estrella studied every single one of them. How they wore their hair, the bands used to tie it, what snacks they brought, and how they treated us. It was a long way from the mountain top, and commitments, meant that Bianca only came twice a week. A priority, Estrella was either ridden or lunged, but evidently, it wasn't enough. An unforeseen problem, Bianca was stood solemn beside her stable. Estrella was sucking an apple when Zoom entered. So many people came and went, that like Bianca, Estrella, lost track of them all. But, Zoom was fizzy pop, bubble gum candy. special is special, and that's exactly what she was. Conversations with Elsa ended, Zoom, introduced herself to the horses. Bright and full of life, her blonde hair hung in pretty curls. A permanent smile on her face, she was a real tonic. Three carrots left, she turned to Estrella, then Bianca.

"Is she yours?"

"Yes."

210

They shook hands and together stroked, Estrella. Zoom was easy to talk to, told Bianca to enjoy the moment and believe in dreams. Even better, she hadn't ridden for ten years, but now out of the blue, wanted to take it up again. All the kindness and energy of an angel, the only thing she lacked was wings. To some degree, Bianca had lost her way, but felt, Zoom had been sent to help. Zoom agreed to ride Estrella three or four days a week. And so, we were allocated a guardian angel and Bianca, a beautiful friend. Worried about Darcy being sun burnt, Bianca, asked Elsa to put him in with me. The baron ground grew hot and I was thankful of the shelter we shared. A push button pony, all the children asked after Darcy. Sweet, pea popular, he was the man. Sometimes, they chose me, but mostly, him. And work him up to a hungry appetite they did. It wasn't his fault, but hungry, he became mean on the food front. Ears flat, teeth barred, he finished much of mine off too. In-fact, the only thing we got lots of, was drinking water. Zoom, however, bridged, what gaps she could. One of them being, the carefully cut carrots she brought. Sweet and succulent, it gave us all something to look forward to. On the occasions she could get to us, Bianca brought her dogs and met Zoom. Sociable, Bianca shared the rides with her, on me. Free of the stable, Estrella was ecstatic, leg eager, she lanced into the woods. Scooting after her, I couldn't have been happier, for any time together, was better than none. Soil tracks and heavy trees, Billy, wagged her tail, and unlike Bella, raced in and out of

211

the woods. Legs stretched, lungs loose as grapes, I didn't mind the shower. Tied between two columns made up of breeze blocks, my body foam was showered, shampooed, and rinsed into a honey glazed diamond. I rolled in the dirt until baked brown. As if someone had used a sledgehammer, I heard the crash, and like Estrella, was up in flying time. The shriek was enough to stop even a storm. Hose pipe launched left, two arms raised, Bianca lunged before Estrella. Breeze block swinging on a length of line from her headcollar, running for sure, would have sawn her legs, hacked her bones to bits. Talking all the time to avoid a panic run, Bianca held her concentration. Cutting the rope from the block, the girls gasped relief when it crunched to the floor. A bag of cement purchased, and luckily, all was repaired. Estrella never went in the shower again.

Shaken not stirred

Lotte came to see me with a ride in mind. Unfortunately, I was on an excursion with little legs. Evidently, she rode Estrella instead. Full of beans, Estrella jugged out of the yard like a bouncing puppy on its first walk. Alert and alive, she was a red wire. On the first track, Lotte gave her the go ahead, but scented grass, and too much energy, had made her skittish. It was the sneaky guard dogs that did it. Leaping like Jack in the boxes, their paws rattling the loosely fitted villa fence. Estrella surged left, sending Lotte, right over her head. Ouch, on our way back, I heard the crying, saw Estrella spark sprinting for home. Rushed to hospital, Lotte, had a broken collar bone. Afraid, Estrella would be punished, me and little legs felt frantic. But, the stable hand was understanding, caught, he, put her away. Bianca blamed herself. It was simple, Estrella hated the stable, she needed to be outside, not on a bed of matting in a box. She was a free spirit, would never heed to confinements. Wasn't that why she'd bought her in the first place? A conversation with Zoom and Elsa took place. Space was short, but a sensible shuffle, and we had it. Estrella was trying to extricate herself from the stable, when Zoom, opened it up. It was fantastic for me, because Estrella moved in. Only big enough for two, poor Darcy, was placed back in his bottom pen. Alone, with an armless tree, the separation saddened him. But, on a brighter note, we were still together and could see one another over the thickets and fences. Work in Spain grew scarce and Bianca began searching further afield. There was very little to be found, and what was available was too far to drive each day. Employment found in England, dogs safe until fetched, they returned. I don't think Bianca wanted to leave her fitted saddles behind, but equally, didn't want our backs ruined either. Bianca continued with the arrangements, and Zoom, visited three times a week. An angel, she evenly spread her wings, and time. When we weren't being used by children in the school, she showered and groomed us. Amongst the children, was Lisa, who took to me like a duck does water. I got new headcollars, clean brushes and boots. And although she carried a whip, she didn't use it. We gelled like glue and she rode me all the time, eventually pretending I was her pony. Lisa liked to jump. A bright girl, she made everything enjoyable. A good combination, I comfortably flew over them. Not so lucky, Darcy attracted lots of younger children. Unable to ride, they tugged on his mouth and made it sore. In between lessons he was put away covered in sweat and still without shade. I saw his sadness, I didn't like it or those who took advantage of his nice nature and willing ways. The situation increased, until even Estrella became irritated by the excess of work he endured. Two months passed, then like a light, there she was. I could see Bianca wasn't happy with the situation. Obviously in her absence it had worsened. The sun was hugely harmful and Bianca again, asked Elsa to put up a shelter. Told by the groom that it was too expensive, Bianca offered to contribute. The stable hand agreed it would be done. But by the time Bianca left, nothing had been. Regular updates from Zoom offered reassurance. But, due to popular demand, Elsa was expanding.

Larger ponies purchased, I was pleased there was someone else to ease the burden for little legs. Thought, life would get easier for him, but due to his popularity, it increased. Not only did he work the school, but the excursions too. And with new adults, came ignorance. Tight reigned, heavy handed with lots of legs and sticks, we struggled over grit, sand and stone. Then something even worse happened. I was asked to integrate with my worse, enemy, man. And with them, came weight. On, the school surface I could cope, but carrying their corpses over loose chippings, and uneven ground, bruised my feet and back. So, much so, that it stopped me sleeping. I had permanent pins and needles in my soles, only the pins stabbed my feet faster than a starving dog eats meat. Fortunately for little legs, his feet didn't bruise, but weight, he did lose. Constantly hungry, he was sad. At night I would lie down and rest two souls. The first being mine, the other my pear prickled feet. Sleep, soothed, they lasted an hour, before again feeling gauged and grated on the ground. Zoom, suggested, I be shod as agreed. But the farrier was busy and couldn't come for a few weeks. And even offering to pay out of her own pocket, didn't speed things up. Great at telling jokes, Estrella endeavoured to lift my spirits, and if she was on real form, Darcy's too. Estrella even offered to take my loads and let me rest, But, I knew she'd never be allowed. Besides, they'd have only ruined her mouth.

I never knew who was going to arrive or which one of us they would be riding until they approached. Just the sheer size of the bloke, told me it was going to be back bending, foot squashing, stuff. Fifteen stone half way around a mountain in the heat and under a halo of flies, isn't ok. it isn't fair on my spine and indeed, as weighty excursions increased, so my back began to bow. Why they didn't use the bigger horses more, I had no idea. Zoom fought my corner suggesting the same, but, the groom said it was popularity and to mind her own business. Our only security, I was afraid Zoom would leave. Blessed by her happiness, carrots and positivity, her visits kept us sane. Thankfully, Saturdays belonged to Lisa. Unlike the other children who came, rode and left, Lisa had lots of time for me. Purring to myself, I loved her attention, the brushing and plaiting of my main. In the smaller of the two schools, I welcomed the sponge cake sand upon my soles and did my best for her. Afterwards, she would shampoo me. A water fall, of rain sheets, it gurgled, past my tendons, and into the tender parts of my feet.

Soothing, I stare stood and watched something new emerge.

The neighbours arrived and out of their trailer came a skeleton and story. Abandoned, the pony had been locked in a garage and left. A bag of bones with breathing problems, it was a sorry sight. Xylophone ribs, the rescue was in a pitiful state. Starvation had caused him to inhale and eat dirt, which had evidently damaged his lungs. Space an issue, he went down the bottom, with Darcy. There, he lay as an innocent foal. Just a shell of suffering beneath the sun. Oh, why did humans have to do such things. A darling, Darcy, offered friendship and support, even shared his food with the poor skeleton. The rescue pony saddened everyone, but as time went by, he got a bit better. They were side by side, when Bianca arrived. Sharing the sharp branches of a tree, the rescue and Darcy squinted into space.

I was taken out of the paddock and tacked up. Grateful of a private lesson, I skipped upon sand, until hot and steamy. Some people don't always have time to hose the sweat off. Its ok wet, it's when it dries that it becomes irritating. A crust of hard bread without butter. Rolling is one method, but you can never quite remove it all. Shoes and shelter, on her mind, Bianca brought them up. The next day one did go up, only basic it wasn't a solid structure, but shield the rescue and Darcy, it did. The week flew, and like a bird, Bianca was again gone. Finally, the farrier arrived and begun work on my feet. A blue, insert in between, I now had a sponge pantry of protection. Raised up, my bruises, breathed relief. It was so comfortable, that the cripple feeling, quickly passed and I was back on form in no time. Leaping and jumping like a lamb, Lisa put up some jumps in the big school opposite my paddock. Courage plucked, feet performing, I managed a three foot, spread for her. I loved the bigger school because Estrella could see me. Feeling energetic, I showed off, eventually reaching four feet. Though Estrella was pleased for me, lack of work, left her at a loose end. Bored, she begun chewing the paddock posts and sherbet sucking for minerals. When enough of it was gone, the stable hand replaced it with electric fencing. Zap, Estrella didn't go near it again. Three months had passed, and I was pleased to see Annie and Bianca arrive with Zoom. Spotting Darcy, Annie went straight down to him. A ride in mind, and they brought the three of us from the paddocks and into the stable square. But the pleasantries were quickly undone by the groom. A lesson after lunch, Darcy was booked. It wouldn't be the same on another horse, after all, he was still Annie's pony. Bianca perked her up by puting her on me.

I'd forgotten how kind and peaceful her energy was, and though, we were no longer in the mountains, it was just like old times. Trotting after Estrella and Zoom, I was bewitched. Disappearing into an alley of trees, I embraced my shoes and broke into a playful canter. All legs and a swishing tail, Estrella increased her speed and kept up her leadership. Playful, I pounded the ground, batteries in my toes, I tore after her. Disappearing into a cloud of mud dust, I took over wide and fast. A bad loser, Estrella tap danced on the spot, threw her hind at me, and caught up. Neck and neck, Zoom, let out a loud whistle. We had fun, enjoyed the moment, and made memories. When Annie, went home, so did the dogs. Just us lot left, I lived in hope. Holiday season on the horizon, excursion popularity increased. In flip flops and shorts they came. Hatless and hopeless, they pushed and pulled us all over the place. Riding is one thing, incompetence quite another. All hands and chat, I found their behaviour tedious. So much so, that I was glad of the odd summer storm that sent them packing or stopped them from booking. But not all bad weather brought comfort. One week for sure, sticks. It didn't just rain, it was a damned tsunami. Curtains, of it came down. Stood under our shelter we were shut in by four falling walls. Ripples of it running like syrup, it was impossible to see out. I heard the crash about two, am. It was as if a thousand cups had been dropped and all broken at once. Pushing my head through the ocean, I peeked out. The cloth sheeting on Darcy's shelter had filled, sagged and finally caved in. Bare, the little tree, offered only sharp branches that should have been cut back. Naturally, the two of them sought security beneath it. The rain didn't let up, and by morning, Darcy had cut himself. Deep and bloody, his hip wasn't a nice sight, but unlike the rescue, he had flesh to protect it. The rains didn't let up and the bottom paddock flooded. Nowhere, dry to even eat from, Zoom, asked they be brought in, but like the paddocks, the stables were all full. Up to their ankles in puddle slosh, straw afloat, I watched with a heavy heart as Darcy fished for strands of it. It was upsetting for us to see him struggle so. The weather finally settled, and the holiday riders returned. Hands higher than their heads, they tried my patience. Even more so, the lunge. I hated it. It was bad enough going around until I was dizzy, I didn't need yanking and booting too. I don't think there is anything worse than a novice abusing our services, just because its sunny. Still, I had to be grateful I didn't look like Darcy. Weight dropping, he was beginning to mirror his rescue friend. And for the life of me, I couldn't figure out why a pony so hungry wasn't eating. I should know, because I was dead opposite him. Even worse, the kids were still using him. Bianca came over. His eyes spoke in volumes, underweight and no longer the pony she knew, he needed help. Lunch served, and she watched him leave it. But his skin needed filling and his eyes were hungry. Hovering between the scoffing rescue and his bucket, his eyes wandered. Then, as if the bucket was going to bite him, and his mouth was wired, he nibble, nudged, a tiny bit of bran. It wasn't that Darcy didn't have an appetite, he just couldn't chew, for fear of pain. A native pony, it was his teeth. He worked so hard, brought the riding school in hundreds. Money didn't come into it, if it meant

Bianca had to pay, she would. But where was the dentist. Her flight left Tuesday. Zoom, made some calls, but, it was weekend, everyone was unavailable or busy for at least a week. Bianca was seriously stressed over the weekend. People again suggested she sell them, but to who? Spain was in recession, horses and dogs were being dumped all over the place. And at 22, I especially, was old. Estrella was stubborn and for sure would have been beaten for it. And as his previous owner stated, Darcy would have been taxi, driven to death. The dogs were gone, we had to be next. Didn't we?

I was in the yard Monday, when Bianca entered. Looking worse for wear she stroked my neck and chewed her nails. In the school, some ponies were going around its edge. Busy teaching, Elsa was pre-occupied. Bianca was at her wits end, when he entered. A silver case in his right hand, he headed for one of the livery horses. I watched Bianca approach him. Indeed, he was a vet, but not any old vet, a dentistry one. Bianca asked, if he would see Darcy. Fully booked, I saw her complexion change, saw the desperation kick in. He softened, it all depended on how long his clients horse took. No time to lose, Bianca brought Darcy in and tied him next to me. Eyes nothing but dead pools, scabs and sores around his hardened mouth, the sparkle was completely gone. The livery horse had good gums, time on his hands, the vet had a look. Indeed, it was his teeth. Middles ground into canals, the overlapping sides had become razor blade sharp. An anaesthetic injected, two ropes either side of his headcollar, they held him up. Rasp dunked in disinfectant, the vet switched it on. Like an electric drill, it motored down his gums, a twizzle twitch in my shoulder, I watched him file the sharp bits off. It took over fifteen minutes for them to become smooth and flat centred. No more pain, I saw a glint of the old Darcy surface. Rest, and repair, was the final word of the vet. On the plain, Bianca sighed relief and grief. The stress of it all too much, Bianca began searching for transport. In luck, a lorry called the, 'Pearl' was passing our part of Spain in three weeks.

On the move

Bianca arrived a week before the lorry. Paperwork to be done, Bianca and Zoom began the process. But, there is always something. The office in charge stipulated we had to be collected from our passport addresses. Well, Darcy was still registered in England and us up at the cabin. They wanted it changed saying the passports had to be sent off. But, there was no time. Zoom spent hours on the phone negotiating and trying to make them see sense. That Darcy was 'new forest' and going home. For heaven's sake! Eventually it was downgraded that collection and delivery, had to be from a registered address instead. But the delivery address wasn't coming up on their systems, and had it not been for Zoom, we may have been lost in cyber space forever. Post-codes updated and undisputed, they got out their official stamp. Bingo, we were in business. The office loved paperwork and of course every sheet had a price attached. Papers in order, we had three days to finalise things. I remember the vet, because he was very late. Chip, codes confirmed. Inoculations in date, the bills of health were dished out and our passports stamped. Time was tight, I had butterflies in my belly, but didn't know why. The next day the driver called Bianca. An eleven, horse lorry, the 'Pearl,' was unable to get down the lanes. Instead, he requested we be at the wooden bar on the main drag by seven. Only two hours to go, there was still so much to do. Bianca asked everyone with transport if they could run us to the bar. Ten minutes in a trailer, it wasn't asking the world. But, everyone was busy and couldn't help. Like a punch pushing paper, panic grabbed Bianca. I remember it well because it was getting dark and time, running out. Approaching Zoom, I could sense a deep conversation between her and Bianca. Reluctant to ride me in the dusk dark, I watched Zoom shake her head, the contemplation and eventual participation. While Bianca fetched in Darcy, Zoom, tacked me up. It had been eighteen months. The saddle was worn and crusty, and like my bridle, completely uncomfortable. Zoom tacked up Darcy and handed him to Bianca. Two disillusioned eyes, Bianca winked into them. Thinking we were going on one of our rides, Estrella quietly watched us as usual. Unknowingly, I rode the lanes for the last time. Into the village and over the bridge, until we merged with a wider road. The street lights stopped. It was dark. Darcy didn't care. Not even when the full beams of some cars blinded him. Ignorant, one driver even tooted for him to get out of the way. Bianca spoke to Darcy, and like the angel he was, he didn't bat an eye lid. Ignoring the dangers, he put one foot before the other, focusing on every word she said. For sure, he was protecting me and Zoom. I followed. No problem. But where are we going at such a strange hour in the dark? More importantly, where, was Estrella. We reached the bar. Zoom jumped down and went inside for refreshments. Outside, a horse in each hand, Bianca broke into a flurry of tears. Neither of us moved. Perfect gentlemen, we felt her anguish. A flight the next morning, worry streamed across her face. And by now, if anything went wrong the riding school would be shut up. Ears strained to the winds, we could hear something. There was road thunder, an earthquake of even tremors, all trundling under us at once. A minute later, the chug glug of a giant engine. Bianca beat back her tears, trying to swallow, she breathed. Gears going down one, it turned off the main road and rumble, strained into second gear. An uphill angle, momentum was minimal. A moving slinky, with two headlights, its metal face trudged towards us. Storm over, the 'Pearl,' pulled up. Behind schedule, they left the engine running. Two guys got out to greet us. I've been around a lot of humans and felt a lot of energy in my time, but never the emotions of that night. Relief, worry, achievement and loss, but most of all, the great unknown. Methodical, the men made light work of the situation. Tack squeezed into their living quarters, hugs and hand-shakes, the ramp was undone. Doors down, and Darcy spied a net of hay. Hungry, and as if he had wings, he flew inside. Cubicle closed, I was the last one on. A camera above me, it displayed a full house of eleven. The door went up.

Clack. But where was Estrella. Surely, she wasn't being left behind? Sad, I didn't get time to say goodbye, I felt numb. Catches all done up and the engine chattered fiercely to the road. Mystified, not even the summer hay in front of me cut it. Crushed, but curious, hunger eventually overcame me. It was certainly a lot tastier, than straw. The lorry reminded me of LA and my short, lived racing days. Of, how far I'd come since that awful fall. I closed my eyes. I was upside down. Thunder in the air, a thousand fleeting bullets, hollow hooves, again, haunted me. For three hours my thoughts wandered. It was just before midnight when we stopped. Legs wavering under the upright pressure, I was glad to get off and proceed into a barn. Though narrow and outdated, the stalls were pristine and well catered for. My little native friend next to me, and I relaxed. For now, we were safe. New teeth, Darcy didn't stop eating, but then who could blame him. I fell to my knees, tucked them under my chest and sighed. I tried to sleep, but couldn't. Estrella would be lonely. Would I ever see her again! Oh, stop beating around the bush, Zoom must have bought her. The thought saddened me, but on a brighter note, she couldn't be in better hands. The men woke us at six. Fed and watered, we were then, whisked back onto the 'Pearl.' None of us knew our destination, only, that we were sharing the experience. Tedious, the time dragged on for hours. Decent, the driver did stop to offer us water and refill our nets. One of them even took some pictures of us. Still puzzled, my legs found the standing

226

laborious. I was splashing a pee, when we abruptly stopped. Voices galore and the driver argued in French, against boarder control. I glanced at Darcy. Isn't France where they eat horses? Not wanting to remind him, or spoil the hay, he was spaghetti sucking, I held in my reservations. Passports in order, and we were ushered along. A total wash out, the traffic dragged its wheels until way past nine o'clock. Muscles marinated, joints jaded, I waded from lorry warmth, into a fridge, frozen barn. And, according to the horse beside me, the temperature was going to drop even more during the night. Combined with spooky air and musty smells, I wasn't comfortable. I looked left to Darcy. Only interested in what he could ingest, it was more important, than having an opinion. Opening my tired mind, I navigated backwards. Estrella would be sleeping, under our shelter. Probably still wondering when we would return. I supped on my water, like my thoughts, it hit my stomach hard and cold. Hungry, but stressed, I merely hen pecked my grain. Giving in to exhaustion, my thoughts were finally extinguished. A slush of morning water, and I was one of the first loaded. Little legs two stalls down, and our third day materialised. Ocean motion, I tried to catnap, but blundering across France wasn't as smooth as past roads. Jolting too and throw, stopping every few streets, sliding over speed bumps, it had to be a city. I'd pulled enough carriages to know the signs, time gaps between lights, turns and roundabouts. A sharp right, and my senses were alerted. The smell wasn't just unpleasant, it alarmed every organ inside of me. Brusquely, the lorry was jolt, anchored up. Feeling pessimistic, I watched them bring down the back. Thick as pollen, fear circulated. The end horse shied against his partition. Strained eyes, shifty shuffles and visible twitching, the horse knew. Knew it was over. Urine seeping, stomach flanking, they forced him off. Bolt guns, and blinkers, he didn't return. I hung my head, felt a thousand bad vibes, and to some degree, part of his pain. Undoubtedly, our destiny is in human hands. It's not always where you go in life, but who you meet and their attitude towards us animals. As I found out, man has few morals when it comes to money. And us horses only useful, for as long as we can walk and work. But he could work, so why make him walk an abattoir plank? Thoughts warren deep, I daren't let them wander, for wandering causes visions and visions, can stick like glue. I recalled our goat and the wild pack of dogs who got him. Quickly dismissing such misery, my old husky friend sprung to mind. The walks we'd taken when he could keep up, and of course, Gizmo and her band of merry bob cats. Residing in the good times, they would remain forever. We travelled all night, finally crossing the English border at five, am. London was busy. Standstill stranded, rush hour produced the stuffiest smog. Wheels finally mooching into first gear, we crawled towards the country side. I know this, because the air grew thinner and fresher, until cold, I've never felt, cruised down my throat and over my fine coat. Unlike me, little legs had youth on his side. Unfazed by the harsh climate, his only present passion was net nibbling. We pulled over. Through my window, I could see a rose covered cottage and a field of daisy's. Unlike the horse in France, two of our occupants had been blessed. Slightly lighter, the load skipped to the next drop off. Entering two white gates, another of the horses was engulfed in exit happiness. I needed out, my legs hurt. But it was another two stops before mine was met. As they untied my rope and turned me, I fretted. Tugging tussling the rope, I twisted my neck, hallelujah. Darcy was right behind me. Was going to be with me, whatever our outcome. Outside, waiting for us, was Bianca. I couldn't believe it. It was simply too good to be true. Exchanging us for an envelope, us and our luggage was taken down a lane. Gate passed, we entered a courtyard. Tidy and totally green, I loved this new region. In the stable, a thousand blades of barley bedding had been woven into a straw sprung mattress. Never in my life, had I been given so much to eat. Astounded, I didn't realise at first, that it was to sleep on. Hay on tap, the food was infamous, and for the first time in years, our bellies full. Morning brought even better events. Endless, the field, was awesome. Speechless, I couldn't believe it. Bushes running down one side, green all over, it had to be a trick. Tendon tense, I tore to its top, pivoted on two back legs and raced little legs back to its bottom. Ecstatic, I ran straight through the electric fence, tape tangle around my legs, I took out the middle post. Fortunately, for me, the battery supplying electricity, wasn't on. Running blind, I rid myself of the tape and didn't stop, till the storm of happiness, simmered into exhaustion. Never had I seen such an ingenious set up. The final frontier, my rocket had landed in unknown, but beautiful territory. The other horses and owners were nice too. Breakfast buckets made up, Jade arrived and fed us all at six. A kind lady, I looked forward to seeing her very much. Euphoria over, I began to feel like a Spanish relic. Cold! Crocodiles! It was freezing. I thought I'd got away with all the years of hard graft, but slowly like a cancer, arthritis attacked. Reputable rugs purchased, Jack Frost, took a small run and jump. But, not from my legs. Exposed, they felt like four frozen lolly sticks. I remember going to bed one night wearing a pair of travel boots. Fleece lined, Bianca made use of them. But, December arrived, and no cure was found for the damp that came with it. Entering my bones, it had no intention of ever leaving. Cod liver oil obtained, my first ride around the fields and lake, jolted the old joints.

I could cope. I was fine, until... Cows! Well, I don't know about Darcy, but the pigmented pigs, scared the life out of me. Closing and reopening my eyes, the black and white hippos, didn't disappear. Blinded by fear, I scooted across the corn fields. Bianca calmed me, saying I was being silly and that they meant no harm. What she forgot, was that these were the first cows I'd ever seen. It took me months to accept them and their calves. Calves, who deliberately hid in the hedgerow, so they could dive out and scare me. Other rides entailed using the roads. Shoes up for renewal, the farrier fitted me with two new fronts. It was a peaceful day, until they came. Tight lipped, I was stood in my field. A commotion on the river drew our attention. There was horses and hounds. Like card board cut outs, my ears stood to attention. Eyes wide as saucers, little legs, was glued to the ground. Beyond the river, an army of horses surrounded the small woodland. Mesmerised by what we were witnessing, we didn't move. Hooves of thunder, they darted back and forth, from the trees. At the command of their masters, dozens of dog feet desecrated the ground. Accompanied by terriers, they disappeared into the wood. Branch breaking and barking, it was a terrible commotion. I'd never seen such behaviour, didn't understand what was happening. Then out it came, mentally tortured and terrified, the red fox took to his heels. A horn sounded and off they went. Heartbeat and feet hammering the ground, his soul disappeared. Hounds on his tail, persistent riders pushed their horses. My heart sank. I didn't like it. Offended, I found it hard to eat even the green grass. Instead, I watched the liveries arrive and get their horses in from various fields. I watched one of them school her horse for over an hour. Full up, Darcy joined me. We relaxed, we played and were always grateful, beyond the bounds of expectations for everything. My thoughts turned to Estrella. Was she still in the same paddock? Still with Zoom? Oh, hail ye universe, how I yearned to know. Would have paid to see a picture of her. I understood Darcy had been a priority, that perhaps, for unknown reasons, she was unable to make the trip. Possibly poorly, or without papers. Either way, she was on my mind all the time. I thought about her every day. Like a magnificent poster, she hung in my mind. Never, would she be taken down and rolled up, nor would she ever fade. Holding on to hope, I nuzzled Darcy. Together, we wandered towards the gate. I was cold. Surely it was time to go in?

January brought snow and I think Bianca was more excited than us. Removing our rugs, she took us outside. I'd seen the mountain tips painted white, but never socked my feet into cotton wool particles. It was soft, crispy and crazy. Darcy tried to eat it. Coconut flaky, I copied. Nostrils stuffed, I accidently cough, sprayed it in his face. Then throwing both our heads into the air, we aimed for the top field, pivoted, and pranced back towards Bianca. Two mad frogs, firing off our back cylinders, we galloped up and down like lunatics. Loving, every second of our fortunate lives we jammed. Fine flakes still falling, Bianca had her own cinema. Darcy on my tail we stopped, stood up like stags and boxed. Little legs got carried away and I had to be careful not to retaliate with my metal shoes. We rolled, we ran, we loved every snug second of it. An hour of play and we were cold and wet. Happy to be brought back in we enjoyed a net of meadow hay. Bianca had to work away for a month and found us a surrogate mum. Lilly, one of the other girls, took care of everything, spoilt us rotten and when her daughter, Rose had time, the two of them took us out around the countryside. This, we totally loved. Spring put renewed energy into my aching bones and as the temperatures rose, the arthritic pain lessened. I learnt to love the season for more reasons than one. Spring didn't exist in Spain. Winter merely climbed over itself straight into summer. But, it was different here, and life flourished. I didn't at first know what the cheeping in my rafters was, then, circling the air, birds aimed and fired food into little fine beaks up there. Fascinated by the affair, I watched them work. I don't know how much of his 'forest' Darcy recalled, but the transformation of new buds, baby birds and spring bulbs, left me speechless. By May, a giant had painted the lands in rolls of bright yellow rape. A yellow brick road all around me, I just needed some red shoes to tap together. Evidently, my one wish would be to go back to the mountain with Estrella. Back, Bianca arrived with Annie. Tall and slim, how she'd grown. A ride around the land brought back fond memories but was quickly shattered by the sound of sneezing. I slowed, but it didn't improve. Darcy couldn't breathe properly. Pulled up, both parties got off. Better being led in walk, that's what they did. The stable invited improvements. Reading, breathing reviews and doing her own research, Bianca concluded, pollen to be the problem. Little legs had hay fever. The condition was eased with antihistamine and unlike my arthritis, the pollen season passed. Life is a strange thing.

Food had sometimes been scarce in Spain, but on our mountain, we never got ill. But then, not all horses are fortunate enough to experience, the exceptional, side of nature that we had. When, young Sarah's pony, became too old to ride, she asked to spend time with me. Grateful of the help, Bianca agreed. I didn't mind, I enjoyed the rides out, but began to struggle with the school. Fallen from grace, the flexibility in my hips strained and I found myself enduring circles, rather than enjoying them. Straight and direct, I faired, better over the odd jump. It was while spending time with Sarah, that Charlie began arriving to help Bianca. Mesmerised with little legs, they bonded. He'd never ridden before and his parents were safety concerned. But, I knew that her nephew, couldn't be in better hands, or hooves. Jumping jelly beans, daffodils and streams, Charlie was doing a sitting trot in no time. The showing season wasn't far away and against all the odds, Bianca convinced Lotte, to get back in the saddle. Collar bone mended, it was time to make amends.

She'd not been near us since her fall from Estrella. What a wonderful word, that was. Good old-fashioned fun, in mind, our first summer was full of baths and braids. But bathing at dawn, did nothing but make me shiver. I loathed the cold water and couldn't careless, for my colour, I just wanted to be warm! Stood drying beneath Sarah's sweat rug, I watched her and Charlie, do the same to Darcy. Half my age, it didn't bother him one bit. Polished and plaited, I tip toed towards a trailer. Pictorial, Charlie overtook with Darcy. But, just as they neared the ramp, his feet grew rivets, locking themselves to the floor. Catching up, I claimed my statue stance behind him. Two ice cubes, we refused to melt. The clock was ticking, the first class was at nine. There was panic and disappointment. Charlie held out a fresh cut carrot, extending his neck, Darcy endeavoured to eat it, but enter he wouldn't. Afraid we wouldn't be coming back, I didn't want to chance the trip either. Bianca empathised that it really was only a short trip and to trust. Carrot chomping, and foot mumbles, we went on. Tied in a field of trailers, it was another new experience. The old damaged saddle oiled, rusty stirrups sprayed silver, Charlie put on his hat. Buttoning the show jacket Bianca had bought for his birthday, he breathed. Suited and booted, he looked beautiful. But, little legs had a seriously hardened mouth and hadn't been in the ring before. Novice hands reliant on a hard mouth, the adults were nervous. But, as the little pony proudly proved, he still had a soft heart. Opening his walk, Darcy led the way around the ring and stood to attention. The judge approached, checked his line up stance and asked them to parade. At, walking pace they drew a graceful line around the ring. Tugging my trailer rope as far as I could, I watched them. Cool enough to put out a fire, they owned the ring. Ten minutes later, I saw him receive a red rosette, then with kind loving legs, Darcy did a little lap of honour. Like a beaming bobbing apple, Charlie held on to his trot. The moment caught on camera, Darcy didn't just win first ridden, he won first show, best behaved and biggest heart. I felt cold leather on my back. Turning I was pleased to see Lotte. Excited, I carried her around the warm up area. Then, endurance, replaced by my new existence, I went in. Alive, I felt that everyone in the ring loved me. It didn't matter that we came second. We enjoyed ourselves. Happy to share, Lotte handed me to Sarah, who took me in the clear round. None of us had ever faced a whole course before. But with happiness in my heart, it was a pleasure to prove, I could cope.

By June something called sweet itch sizzled at my skin. Like a mosquito bite, the rubbing didn't ease the itch. Instead, I ended up scratching my tail to bits. Bianca bathed it in aloe Vera shampoo, and what a relief it was. During the rinse other problems emerged. Lumps, under my dock they didn't feel healthy. The vet said not to threat, simply keep an eye on them. Perhaps I worried, dreamt and hoped too much. Either way, for now, they were dormant. An annual show in August and Sarah, suggested we attend. An open show, there were no age limits. Excited, Charlie wanted to go too. They worked hard cleaning us. Ears, and eyes spotless, feet and muzzles oiled, my fur was blue rinsed, white. Was I really, an old aged pensioner? Squeaky clean, I may as well of worn a skirt, instead of a saddle. Lilly loaned us her lorry, and off we went. Buckles and brass, oiled leather and class, plaits and boots, fly spray and hay, we had everything, but Star...

Darcy followed me into the arena. In the line-up, he never faltered. Five of us in total, we awaited our inspections. Then unexpectedly, one by one we were asked to trot around the ring. Praying, Darcy didn't follow, I took off. A perfect gentleman for Charlie, Darcy, didn't move. Full circuit done, Sarah steered me back into line. Then, with washing rein lines, Charlie steered his chariot without collision around his course. Concentration total, he somehow stayed put. On receipt of the red rosette, both Charlie and little legs lit up. Better still, they made the busy championship. Clutching my third place, I watched them join the merry go round of trotting winners. Trying to stay balanced and not greet the ground, Charlie was a jack on a brown box. But love the ring he did. Ears prickled like rockets, legs floating on fondant waves, Darcy did him proud. They came second, and so with blue and red ribbons, they did one last lap. It was an honour to watch. And yes, love does conquer all.

Forever friends

September brought intense brilliance. Showering the piebald cows, burnt orange leaves, fluttered about their feet and fields. The last attraction of the season, Sarah hacked to a local show. I think I must have been fit for my age, because she entered me in the veterans. One of the horses was vastly overweight, a domineering donught, I steered clear of him and stood myself last, in the line-up. To both her, and my, surprise, we won. It was my first, first. I felt vibrant, pleased and proud. In fact, Sarah, was so content with the qualifying card, that she forgot to collect her sash. With delight in our hearts, we headed home. Amateur showing available, Sarah made the arrangements. I have no idea why, but my Andalusian toes grow fast, which leave me looking like an equine ballerina. New shoes fitted, and the big day arrived. Bath, blue rinse, chalk blocks and blow dry. I looked like something from the ghost buster movie. Matching headcollar and rug, the trailer opened. I turned to see where Darcy was. Disappointment, disguised, I felt his anguish. I wasn't sure of the trip, and if honest, didn't want to go without him. Coaxed inside with goodies, I quickly felt alone and anxious. Bianca, read me like a book. Not wanting me to be stressed, she climbed inside and sat on the floor before me. Uncomfortable and damp, it probably didn't sit comfortably with her, but for sure, made a difference to me. Engines away and we were off! I glanced down, like a garden gnome, she was my guardian angel. A bend in the road and we swayed to one side. Legs splayed like two open pegs, I must have looked like 'Helen of Troy's,' horse, towering over her. More roundabouts than expected, the bends tested us both. Touching base, we stopped. While Sarah went to sort out her entries, her mum bought coffee. Out of the trailer, Bianca fed me sugar cubes and covered me with an extra rug. Aiding Sarah with her jacket, hat, make up, stock pin and scarf, mum helped her on. Young lady on board, we entered the ring and did our thing. Third place, everyone was pleased. Usually only first and second are allowed in championship, but this class was special, and third made it too. But not before four o'clock. Expectations exceeded, we got ready for the fancy dress. A running plait and my traditional tassels tickled my face. Sarah's transformation not only took my breath away, but back to my roots. A black bun on her hat, a rose in her hair, Bianca and mum lifted her into my old, Spanish saddle. Spotty Dress draped over my hind I recalled my dancing days. The deception and disregard put aside, my best foot went forward. Privileged to take part, I stood out as the purple, mountain thistle once had. Another second place, and time was against us. A change of tack and clothes, and we had one more appointment to meet. I had no idea the doors I'd passed all day were attached to an indoor arena. The bell rung, it was the grand finale, for me, anyway. As the dinosaur doors opened, I felt like a pea in a pod. A desert of sand calling, my heart and feet sank into a swamp of nerves. Three big horses passed. Legs like Estrella, I suddenly felt short as they entered. From the entrance my eyes cruised after them. Complimenting the pink bows tied to every wall, they walsed with elegance. The stewards, wanted to close the doors, overwhelmed, me and Sarah had grown roots.

"Believe," Bianca whispered to Sarah, "all you have to do is ask..."

Elimination only seconds away, Sarah snatched up her reigns. Sand on my feet, I was home. Yet, felt anxious and shy over pink bows and kites, cameras, and carousels. The ceiling was too high. And compared to the long legged-pros, who was I? One by one, the grandeur of horses, overtook. Trotting to the clock, I was all leg and extended hock. Had I lost my marbles, forgotten how to move, bat and ball. Sarah was too young to know anything I'd done. I would have to help her, we needed to be one. Ignoring the audience, jury and judge, I began to indulge in my musical stuff. Serious and synchronized, my legs did strut. Indulging in life, I once again pranced, on the corner I collected the perfect canter. Spanish roots regained, music in my head sustained, I began to move, flow and prance. A controversial spark, and the people did gasp. On the seventh circuit, we were asked to slow. The line-up decided, I was called in first. An inspection of horse, rider, conformation and tack, a solo lap was lit. Though hesitant, I didn't cut a single corner. Back in my place, I watched the others shine and dazzle. A combined circuit walk, and decisions were made. Adrenalin pumping, we took second place. I didn't need to see Sarah smile, I could feel the curves in her face. Four feet squarely positioned, this was my moment. I am, Faustino.

I heard Darcy's calls before we arrived, drumming on the door, he played a welcome back tune. Yes, I missed you too. Our second Christmas arrived and so did the blighty weather. Bone biting, it whistled through my soul. On brighter notes, my blankets and straw bed cushioned the old joints. Carrots and cards in abundance, we got to celebrate too. The first week in January, was mundane. Buckets frozen, I nibbled a hole in the ice. Ingesting an artic chill, frosted particles passed over my tongue. In the pit of my stomach they absorbed what heat I'd retained, and melted. Back biting, more nights than not, I found it hard to switch off the cold. I'd just drifted, into a damp snooze when… It was the spluttering, coughing and sneezing that woke me. I dozed, but there was something miserable about it. Dramatic, it spiralled into a fit of continual barks. A play with too much drama, the clogged drain, drew me to my feet. Fortunately, Holly, one of the liveries, looked in on Darcy. Head hung like a deformed pelican, he appeared peculiar. And had Holly, not made the call she did that night, I fear, Dear Darcy, might have been dead in the morning. I panicked, felt my head and heart spin, but ten minutes later Bianca appeared. By Now it had worsened, and phlegm was seeping over the door and staining the floor. Laboured breathing loud, it echoed into my ears. Bianca entered the stable and with parched eyes, he darted towards her. Stood rigid on the spot, he demanded help. Astonished at how fast he had gone downhill since she'd left earlier, Bianca consoled him and quickly called an emergency vet. Upset, beyond understanding, and unable to see him suffer so, Bianca even contemplated putting him to sleep. While waiting for the vet, the cough increased, and his breathing tightened to a critical level. Calm words, cuddles and support, was all Bianca could offer. I too, began to fear for him. He was my best friend, had he come this far to fade of a cough?

The vet arrived and quickly administered, the first of three injections, she suggested. Antibiotics followed by some pain relief. The possibility of laminitis too great, Bianca, passed on the steroids. Slowly, his breathing relaxed and a more balanced speed regained. Talk of strangles, bedding, dust and draughts, they tried to determine the cause from possibilities. But, more importantly, address the discharge icing the ground. Now I've never seen a horse be sick, and neither had Bianca, but like brown treacle, out of his mouth it curled. Spiralling like hot string cheese, onto the concrete his lungs strained and spew. Tubes blocked, airways gagging, Darcy gave us all cause for concern. Heaving like a fish out of water, his sides disappeared every few seconds into the caves of his ribs. Disturbed, every horse in the block observed him in horror. Reading Bianca, I could see her getting ready to say goodbye. Faced with the possibility of losing him, I began to fret, feel nervous, and if honest, lonely. Come on little fellow. I'd seen him half starved, shiver when wet, endure the sun without shelter, take the weight of those too big and put up with toothache. Christ, he was a winner, a champion! He had to pull through. It took a further hour of heaving, for it subsided. Drugs at work, he began to breathe. Differentiating between fact and possibility, the conversation came to a clear-cut halt. Highly contagious, strangles was overruled and Darcy diagnosed with pneumonia. Bianca's friend Jake, arrived, condoned, any talk of putting him to sleep and put the kettle on. Two, coffees later and she contemplated going home. But as Bianca left the stable, Darcy beckoned, pleaded support, company, and assurance with his eyes. Camped, down on dirty rugs, she stopped in his stable. But Darcy blind stumbled about and clipped Bianca's calf. His light left on, Bianca entered the empty stable opposite and left the door open for him to see her there. The morning consisted of hot bran and happy words. A week of medicine and Darcy made a full recovery. Shavings and haylage on his new menu, little legs, was spoilt rotten.

I wondered what Estrella was doing? Was she bored, hot and hungry. I thanked my lucky stars and was glad of the grazing. For a few hours at least. As always, Jade fed us at six, but unlike the others, I would always go back to sleep. Darcy didn't mind being up, young and nosey right beside the door, he enjoyed his people and pony watching. For me, age brought other delights such as the demise of loud Spanish voices. Replaced by Robins and sparrows, the block sometimes sang. Sarah still rode a few evenings a week, but it was when out, on weekend outings, that I sweated the most. I didn't like wet fur, it turned cold in the stable and made me shiver. Clippers purchased, Bianca plugged them in. An extension lead over my door and a buzzing was heard. Like a growling mouse, the slim, silver machine moved towards me. I felt a faint graze upon my skin. Sheared like a lamb, snow, fur began falling to the floor. A close shave, and I was partly bare. A blanket clip, she left my back and bottom on to keep me warm. I'd never had a Velcro scarf, but now in completion of this new art, I received a neck cover. By the end of March, Darcy was moulting mad. In view of his dust allergies and all the loose fur, it was decided that he should be clipped. Just around the edges anyway. Unlike me, he didn't accept the clippers at all. I saw him cringe and quiver, even once raise a back leg out of fear. Feeding him carrots, Jake, kept him occupied while Bianca worked with caution. Neck and back gone, he looked blinding. Often, Bianca would sit and sip a coffee with me. Towering above her, I sniffed the cup and searched her pockets for treat traces. If I was lucky, she'd have a jammy dodger or mars bar to share. And occasionally, she'd talk about the old times, the cabin and mountains. How we had to make the best of the breakages, but the brave face Bianca expressed, didn't fool me. And though I'd tried to blot Estrella from my mind, I couldn't forget her either. Picturesque, she was the embodiment of my soul, the epitome of my emotions.

Lilly helped us a lot, but firmer foundations were needed. And at times, I'm sure Bianca could have done with a lighter load. A popular pony, there had been many suitors after Darcy. One lady even arrived with her lorry and an open cheque book, but put him on, Bianca couldn't. How happy, I was when he was returned to his stable. Share him all day, but sell him, Bianca wouldn't. As the weather warmed up, I kept hearing Estrella's name. Every letter lingering, it coffee filtered through my soul, settling like cream spinach in my stomach. And oh, how lively she was, more energy than an engine, she was expeditious. Unspoilt by humans, she was unassuming, bashful and buoyant. There was a clunk. Day dream over, I addressed Sarah and the red ball now rolling across the floor. Engaging, I nuzzled it. Nuts appeared. Never had I seen such a delightful gadget. Once I had the knack, it didn't take me long to prize, and gorge its contents.

Magic happens

June, arrived, and with it, the juggernaut lorry. Then, without word or warning, there she was. All legs and eyes, she was much whiter than when I'd left her. Apple scented admiration, she smelt like summer. Stunned by her presence, I was again lost in her eyes. She hadn't travelled much in her years and had a nasty cut on her nose from the lorry. But, as beautiful as she is, clumsy was always her second name. The lorry contents all over her coat, it was a strong pong. Put in the stable opposite, I examined her again and again. Was it really her? I, reached out, and it was just like old times. Only she was older and wiser. Saddened, by our departure, she'd gone inside herself. Become a faintly glowing ever shielded candle, that only expressed sparks of gratitude, when Zoom was around. She told me of the move, and how much sunnier the new yard had been, but there was something missing. Friends and comradeship. The need for reconcile strong, this Zoom had recognised. Like our lorry, hers, also had to be met. Not beside our bar, but in a busy town. Led, on foot by the yard owner, she was unsure of her strange exit, dug in her heels, and held up the traffic. Terrified of the tail gate, she'd refused to enter such a contraption. Zoom had followed, getting out of her car, she took the rope and

246

led her on. Ramp up, Zoom was gone. Little legs stamped his feet. In need of attention, Bianca turned the three of us out. Fizz bombs and pony perfume, I was captivated. Flawless features, pounding hearts, and hammering feet, ooh, how we ran! Up and down we went, racing as one, instead of three. Blowing like dragons, but bouncing like lambs, our feet forever floated. Exhausted, our dancing souls came to an ecstatic end. Back in the stable, I wondered what planet she'd fallen from. I stared in awe, at my lucky 'Star.' Bianca took some pretty pictures, one of which was professionally painted. Unbreakable vowels in every stroke, the portrait speaks in volumes.

Mission achieved, Bianca needed some help. No one would ever replace Zoom, but kind reliability would help. Not for everyone, Estrella, chose her company well, and quite often her stubborn streak was mistaken for nastiness. But those who took the time to know, love and respect her, were well rewarded. Bianca, advertised, Kay, answered and arranged to meet the gang. You see it wasn't just about one of us. It was all three. We were a team, we were best buddies. What we really wanted was a friend who understood us all. Undisputedly, Kay did. Whenever we got someone new, we seemed to lose something old. Sadly, Sarah was moving. I wouldn't see much of her again. But the monumental moment we'd shared at the show would always be with me and her too. Kay hacked out alone and in company, and sometimes, Bianca and Rosie took us along too. And on occasions, the other liveries joined us, making long, and lively rides. They were the rides I cherished. Several hills to choose from, the gallops got us all going. Dancing on the spot, we dusted the divots, flaunted our front legs, and with excitable flatulence, hammer swept the land. Estrella drew momentum, then like a catapult, wings. Clumsy but classy, she clobbered the ground with excitable confidence.

Estrella hated, showers and clippers and was also clueless when it came to gates. But with time got better. Zoom arrived from Spain, but unfortunately, the weather, wasn't as kind as her. Snow fell in thunderous amounts. Choppy, the wind became a choir of cold whistles. But Zoom, had the weekend only, to enjoy the English countryside. So, brave it, they did. Kay loved little legs, as much as Estrella and brought him with us. Marching against the elements, not even our exercise sheets kept the rain out. Sophistication fighting the storm, Estrella lowered her head. Escaping the conditions, she pranged the ground in playful canters. Behind her, me and Darcy got splattered in muck and moisture. Sunday morning, we braved one of our hills. Neck and neck, we tap danced the same spots before splashing up it. Apart from being uncomfortably wet, it was just like old times. Monday arrived faster than any other had. Zoom spent her early hours with Estrella. Strokes and cuddles, chats and carrots they would always be buddies. Sorry to see her go home, we all felt saddened. It was while riding Estrella with a friend and her horse, that Kay caught her wrist in a gate. In pain, she went home. A while later and it was announced broken. Unable to come, we missed her, and I began to feel a burden to Bianca. Unlike the dogs, she couldn't take us home. No dogs allowed, I hadn't seen Billy for ages, but when everyone had gone home one evening, she came to see me. Grey and old, I didn't at first recognise her. But unlike her aging snout, her soul hadn't changed one bit since the mountains. And like me, I discovered that both her and Bianca, suffered from arthritis. Hips and joints, it was a joke that limited us all. Super-sized suppers, Bianca fed and chatted to us.

"Angels will come, you wait and see."

Not long afterwards, Bianca was approached by a lady. Her little girl was lovely and wanted to ride. Gina was a darling with Darcy. Kind and gentle, she was a willing student who consistently came every weekend. But what about me? I enjoyed the rides, but who would take me. Estrella wasn't one to sit in the background either. Too tired to ride all three of us as she had back in the old days, Bianca sank into deep thought. Too busy working, time wasn't something people had to spare. The best option all around, was to share. But share with who? Kay, cared very much about our welfare and sent Bianca an angel. Laura lived in the village and was eager to get her foot in the stirrups. A beautiful person, we all took to her. And guess what, I got to go out again. I also got stable time and turmeric for my arthritis. But hey what's this.

Drawn to Darcy, Laura rode him too. Like a ball, they bounced over the school jumps and jammed off up the gallops. Laura clicked with Darcy, and nicknamed him, pocket rocket. Yes, he was fit and happy and could move faster than muck off a shovel. That was the beautiful thing about Darcy. He didn't play up with Gina, on the contrary each step consisted of careful, caution. Aware of any rider's capabilities, he would always accommodate them. Summer took its time arriving, but by May we were rug free in the field. Excited to get out, Estrella tried to climb over her door. Upright, two hooves hanging like light bulbs, Bianca went snow white. Fortunately, the latch could still be reached. Door weighted down from flying forward, Bianca eased her legs along its ridge. Bingo, they were back on the ground. What would she do with her?

A delivery of summer shavings made a nice change. All white, I sniffed my bed. I loved the feel of them, even better the taste. Boil sweet sucking them, I swallowed to many. It hurt, I needed to lie down. Luckily, Laura was around and wouldn't let me. Instead, she took me outside and forced me to move. I didn't want to. Muscles contracting, I felt a need to collapse. I could hear Estrella calling, and for the first time ever, felt stressed by it. Not because of the concern, but because I couldn't answer. Ingesting, painful air, calling out would only aggravate me. By the time Bianca arrived, I was feeling real tired. Gloomily, I followed her back into my stable. Down in the dumps, my depression got the better of me and onto my knees

I went. Bianca tugged me up, breathed apprehension and took me back outside. There, I begrudgingly let her hands run over my belly and flanks. For the first time ever, I raised a leg to her. She shied away, I felt guilty. I could hear her thoughts racing. I followed her back into our block. Tied to my hay net, she placed her hands on my back and began to focus on the pain. A gentle fluttering of enthusiastic energy, I began to relax. Slowly, driving vitality into my soul, she inched her way towards the tender spots. I felt weird and floaty. An hour passed, the glum lifted, and I stopped pulling painful faces. Two hours, and my knots untied themselves. By the third I was bright enough to eat. Hot bran and Bute mixed, I started to scoff. Slowly, but surely the tangles straightened out. Bingo, my belly felt better, and I could sleep. Life had given me another go, for this I was grateful. Sleep came easy, even nicer, knowing that Estrella was watching over me.

A depreciation of leather, dry seat, squeaky middle, Darcy's saddle neither looked or sounded supple. The saddle fitter confirmed a broken tree and told Bianca to bin it. And so, the lucky lad got a new one. Tack wasn't something we had lots of. Make do, that was us. But, broken measures, brought new necessities. The school holidays arrived and with it, a friend of Gina's came. Poppy took to me, like a duck does water and rode me every time in the school. And to Bianca's surprise just kept coming. Alongside the attention Laura offered, we were, very lucky. It was Autumn that brought aggravation. Insects in abundance, Poor Estrella, would come in and grind her neck furiously on the door frame. Tail tight on the wall, she did the same to that. Sweet itch, the midges had invaded her neck, and nested like bugs in burrows. In the hope they'd have nowhere to live, Bianca clipped her main off completely. But it didn't stop or cure it. A massage every other day, she got through more shampoo and supplements than any animal I'd known. Still, the damned sweet itch persisted. Piriton, eased but didn't cure it. A mixture of brewer's yeast, seaweed, garlic and olive oil were all added to her food. Yet, still, they survived, causing her terrible misery. I never thought I'd say it, but I welcomed the cooler climate, for it brought relief to Estrella. Equally it was the onset of another winter. Wondering who'd want to stay and help, Bianca began to fret. For sure she'd not cope alone. A phone call offered options. Someone had passed her number on to a wealthy lady looking for a companion. And guess what, the someone, had suggested, I might be suitable. Now wait a minute, I've just got Estrella back and made friends with Poppy. Though rich, the lady lived the other side of the country. Hailstones and hiccups, I'd never be seen again. Cold on the horizon, I could see the turmoil in Bianca's face. Like me, she was getting old and had other responsibilities too. If she couldn't cope with us, weren't good homes all she'd ever aspired to find? Strong, she'd moved mountains for us, witnessed how happy we were together and seen skeletons become champions. I liked Poppy, and her pedantic ways very much, couldn't she come more often? A proposal in mind, Bianca called her parents. And so, with the help of Laura, the plan to loan me, but let me stay with my friends went ahead. I will never forget the lovely look Poppy brought me, or what she whispered.

"Just because they're rich, it doesn't mean they would have looked after you."

The weather in England was cold, but dry. So much so, that we'd been allowed to stay out. Chilly, but ok, we enjoyed the togetherness, but as the sugar in the grass evaporated so did our energies. Less than half my age, Darcy became bored and wanted to play. He pushed me, teased and ran at me. It's strange how an extra few years can change ones, perception of life. It wasn't that I didn't want to frolic, cavort or run around. I just had less energy than ever before. I don't think the old bones I lived in, helped my enthusiasm. Engulfed in his youth, Darcy would sneak back, and grab hold of my buckles. Caught between his teeth, he tugged and pulled until I had a migraine. Thankfully, Laura arrived and brought him in first. Pain, migrating upon wispy straw, sleep eventually found me. In the land of nod, I dreamt of home, my tree and paddock, but most of all, my vertical muck heap. How I'd loved that bottom layer, its nooks and crannies, shrubs and secret avenues. I'd even avenged the fire through them. I heard his whistle, tea time, Jed, shook the grain maraca style. Ears up, heels high, Estrella, flew, followed me up the heap. Obedient, and with flapping nostrils, we ate. I stirred to the howling winds, momentarily, opening my eyes. Uninviting, the dark was bitter. I eavesdropped, yes, Estrella was snoring. Back in my misty bubble, I was again under my pine. Sunshine belting down on my back, I smiled in my sleep. Oh, how I'd loved, my little house on the prairie. October brought the first frosts with it. Bianca put a rug on me. But the English Weather changed its mind faster than rabbits could feed. The first rains quickly created, what I called a bog bomb. I hated this because it sat around my ankles and seeped into my bones. I wasn't in the mood to box, but Darcy was. Antagonistic, Darcy would keep tugging until I rose to the match he wanted. It wasn't anything new, we'd play fought for years, but now in my twenty seventh year, I was feeling tired. Protective, Estrella got into a habit of chasing him away before he got close enough to tug. The same age, but twice his size, he was no match for her. But, antagonise her, he did. He wasn't horrid, he just wanted to play with his old buddie. Attacking the body but not the mind, old age is unusually odd, unfair and unjust.

Lotte made her peace with Estrella, and I had a field day watching them. School lights on and the nights were spiced up. Magical moments in the making, I was tied out front to watch. Jumps up, confidence gained, boy, could she pop them. Joined by Laura and Darcy, the fun and laughter lifted everything it touched, all of us glowed. It also unleashed the masses of energy in little legs, leaving him good on a Saturday for Gina. But work, whisked Lotte away and again we were a helping hand short. A family in the making, Poppy, brought, Daisy for the day. Together they brushed Estrella, who loved the attention, treats and plaits. A ride around the field, and Estrella accepted her kind mannerism. Riding school ditched, Daisy came on a more regular basis. Estrella was a challenge but responded to the right people. She seemed to like Daisy. Age is a terrible thing for it brings insecurities to even the best of us. Hard to believe what I'd been blessed with, I began to fret I wouldn't be able to keep up with my youthful friends. This, both Bianca and Laura noticed. Careful consideration given, Laura came up with a solution. A place I could possibly retire too, it was off road, quiet and closer to home. Dogs allowed, a river running around its perimeter, all I needed was a drawbridge. Mentally I was strong, but some days my physical state was a lot less. But, the youth around me kept the spark alive. And so, it was that we moved. And with Darcy, on went our spare straw. Stacked four up and two across, they were high enough for Darcy to nibble on. But, Darcy had other ideas. Raising his front legs, he reared onto the straw and spun his neck to see where I was. Luckily, Laura was behind in her car. Shock, put aside, she kept her eyes on him, as well as the road. Darcy delivered, the trailer returned. I didn't mind going in, Estrella at my side and we got going. Only two stables free, we went next door to Darcy and shared like in the old days. Big too, they were. So much so, it took three bales of straw to fill just half of it. Hay, it was plentiful and unlike the mouthfuls I gorged, Estrella, nice, nibbled, hers.

The metal bars took me back to France, a flashback of the abattoir, I shook it off. It wasn't France, life was good, had got us this far. A sensitive soul, Estrella was nervous. Didn't like change and took time to settle. Content, I stared at her. Balanced upon her beautiful leg stilts, she was an elegant mare. Retire? No, not me. So long as I have life in my legs, I won't be left behind. Billy appeared with Bianca. I hadn't seen her for a bit, but as always, she came with a beaming smile. How she'd loved the rides around the font and through the villages. Snuffling for opportunities she had the nose of a blood hound. Young, fast and free, batteries in her legs, Billy had kept up. Leaning over the door frame, Estrella greeted her. It was a pleasant sight. I didn't realise the ceiling was part Perspex until beneath it that night. Glittering, the stars shone upon us. Took me back to my youth and the twinkling streaks that had shimmered upon me and my mother. While Estrella slept, one of the webs came to life. Unlike the spider I was born with, this one was settled, relaxed and able to roam without feeling frightened. We didn't know it was Christmas. Not, until we woke up to our stockings. Our names embroidered on each one, it over spilt with treats. These, we were truly grateful of. Our first day out on the land was awesome. Bucking like hares, we breathed every new odour out there. Plentiful, the grass was emerald green. Gathering breath, I admired the river running along our field. Wide and alive, it housed dozens of swans and ducks. Poised and pretty, Darcy loved his new habitat as much as me. Gazing from him to Estrella and back again, I quietly smiled to myself. How far he'd come since the riding school. The fear and frown gone, his coat shone, and I don't think I'd ever seen him so bright in winter. Polished crystals, his eyes were stunning, serious, clever and content. But, most of all, happy. Through Bianca, I had found all my friends, and I think through us, she'd found her besties, too. I often wonder how many other 'new forest,' ponies have been to Spain and back again? I like to think he's the only one. Fit for a king, he was my little pony. Estrella embraced the land with empathy. Rolling like a marble, her legs swivelled, punched the air and reached sideways. Being stubborn and only physically strong, she would never have coped with what I did. Man would simply have broken her soul and permanently punished her. But through perseverance and kindness, she was soft and safe. Kind to the children. Floating on the rides, taking all in her stride, she was a remarkable mare. The black foal who'd grown into a stunning white swan, she was my best friend, she was our shooting star.

My life was tragic, but through Kindness, is now magic

I share with my friends, for alone is not nice

I've learnt to trust, and dance on ice

I've even kissed a human, once or twice

It's, taken time, but I now know, that some, can be nice

I am old and grey, but I have to say,

I do love life, and my sweet meadow hay!

L000064817

Together in Christ

Following the Northern Saints
Compiled by John Woodside

R. C. Diocese of Aberdeen

First published in Scotland in 2016

by

R.C. Diocese of Aberdeen
3 Queen's Cross
Aberdeen
AB15 4XU

www.dioceseofaberdeen.org
R.C. Diocese of Aberdeen Charitable Trust,
a registered Scottish Charity, No SC005122

ISBN: 978-0-9955604-0-6

Cover design by John Woodside:
Celtic pattern by Helen Love; carvings by Harry W. Bain

Printed and bound by Geerings Print Ltd, Ashford, Kent

Contents

Acknowledgements

Thanks are due to a number of people for helping to make this publication possible. They have generously given their time and labour, as acknowledged below.

For permission to use Collects for St Mary MacKillop, St Ninian: ©2010, International Commission on English in the Liturgy Corporation. All rights reserved; from the National and Diocesan Calendars: ©The Bishops' Conference of Scotland. All rights reserved; for the Collect translation for St Sunniva: Fr Marcelin Rediu, Molde Parish Church, Norway. For proof checking, Bishop Emeritus Peter Moran. For general editing and translation of Collects from the Aberdeen Breviary, Eileen Grant.

Thanks also to those who have granted permission to use their photographs of places associated with our local saints: Scottish Church History Society, all ©SCHR: St Manire's stone (9665); St Medan's Chapel (546); St Congan's Church (853); St Fittick's Church (729); Andrew Yool: St Brendan window, Birnie Kirk; Ron Smith: St Machar's Cathedral; St John Ogilvie statue; Ronny Lansley: Balnakiel Church; Fear Liath Mor: St Nathalan's church, Tullich; Ian Forbes, Blairs Museum: St Maelrubha's bell; Sigrid Towrie: St Rognvald; "KiwiBetsy" (megalithic.co.uk): St Fumac's Well; Mother Mary, Unst: St Sunniva icon; Cowan Watson: Nine Maidens; Andrew Forde: St Nathalan, Cowie; Marc Calhoun: St Tredwells' chapel; St Mary's, Inverness: St Mary MacKillop window; Thor Lanesskog: St Olaf altar frontal; Eileen Grant: St Colman's, Portmahomack; Mortlach Church; Inverness.

The following photographers have made their work available, licensed for reuse under the Creative Commons Licence: Ray Oaks: St Erchard's, Kincardine O'Neil; Dave Connor: Fortrose Cathedral; Sylvia Duckworth: Strath of Kildonan; Martyn Gorman: St Adamnan's Chapel, Nether Leask; Guillaume Piolle: Eilean Donan Castle; "Stevekeiretsu": St Magnus' Cathedral; Bill Reid: Kineddar Kirk; "Flaxton": St Fergus; Chris Dyos: St Duthac shrine; Andrew Forde: St Nathalan, Cowie. Copyright on all other photographs belongs to the author.

i

Preface

"Can you tell me who are the local saints here? Wherever I live, I like to know the local saints and ask their prayers." That question of a friend remained in my mind. It has led me, years later, to approach Deacon John Woodside and ask him to gather together these portraits of the lives and legends of the Saints associated with our Diocese. Here they are: reaching from Shetland and Orkney to Applecross and Deeside, forming a kind of heavenly network, another geography. I am most grateful to Deacon John for presenting their stories in such an informed and accessible way.

In a sense, this is a companion volume to Ron Smith's recent work on Our Lady of Aberdeen and her well-known statue.

We do not want to be a people or a place that has lost its memory or its culture. The Gospel of Christ has long touched our land and its history. It has left its mark in place-names and dedications, holy places and artefacts. It has shaped the hidden landscapes of hearts. It is actively cherished by the many different Christian communities, rural and urban, that are alive today. Saints are those on whom the person of Christ has had a particularly intense and transformative impact. They are still living members of the Body of Christ. It can only enrich us to "know who they are and ask their prayers". As a Preface of the Mass says so well, "By their way of life, You offer us an example, by communion with them, You give us companionship, by their intercession, sure support."

May this book at once interest, intrigue and inspire. "Encouraged by so great a cloud of witnesses, may we run as victors in the race before us and win with them the imperishable crown of glory, through Christ our Lord" (*Roman Missal, Preface I of Saints*).

Bishop Hugh Gilbert OSB
St Moluag's Day, 25 June 2016

Introduction

This new compilation of saints' lives draws from the legends of those early Christians who lived their faith by evangelizing what is now Northern Scotland, much of which forms what is now the Diocese of Aberdeen. Numerous holy men and women were popularly acclaimed saints in the early middle ages without the canonisation process that the Church now operates, and it is to some of these pre-reformation saints that we turn for inspiration in the post-modern secular Scottish society of our time.

This book is a "primer" that hopefully will enthuse you and will allow you to be drawn deeper into the fabric of Scotland's rich Christian spiritual heritage, and to explore further the beauty of God's creation that abounds in our countryside, villages and towns.

Much of what is now the diocese of Aberdeen was formerly the mainland geographical area occupied by the northern Picts who formed a society with some similarity to their Gaelic and British neighbours. These people usually lived in small rural farming communities located either adjacent to rivers or to the seashore (the super-highways of that period). There were some larger settlements around the major forts or religious establishments, and we know that there was regular trade not only within Pictland and the bordering Celtic areas, but also across the surrounding seas.

The mission to the northern Picts traditionally was initiated by the followers of St Ninian whose evangelizing successes began in Galloway before breaking out in all directions, particularly northwards along the eastern seaboard. The Venerable Bede reports Ninian's mission with the southern Picts but omits the evangelizing work of Ninian's followers as they moved northwards proclaiming the Gospel and establishing small Christian communities, before continuing to the next area where they would proclaim the Word of God.[1]

---

[1] Bede, *Ecclesiastical History of the English People* (Penguin Classics, London)

1

Recent historical and archaeological research into the Northern Picts is helping to turn legend into fact. Could the remains of the Pictish Monastery discovered at Portmahomack provide crucial evidence to confirm an early evangelization launched by Ninian's followers northwards across the firth from Aberdour in Buchan,[2] then continuing from what is now modern Ross-shire, to establish small Christian communities along the east coast to Caithness and Sutherland (or even to Orkney and Shetland), before returning down the coast via Inverness, to Burghead, and back to their primitive Buchan monastery?

Many scholars continue to debate the "real" Ninian and his missionary activities. For our purpose, however, we are most grateful for those early Christians who, from the late 4th century onwards, initially brought the Gospel to such isolated communities in the most difficult of circumstances. St Columba and his followers are often cited as the "prime evangelizers of Scotland"; the truth, however, is that they were re-evangelizing in the footsteps of those saints who preceded them by as much as a century or more beforehand.

As throughout other Christian lands, the cult of Saints was of great importance in Pictland. Although the Pictish rulers and their successors may have patronised the great saints of the Church such as Mary, Peter, Andrew, and other Apostles, many of the lesser, more obscure saints were of significant importance to the people who established great devotion to them over a long period. Some of the Saints in this book, such as Drostan, Donnan, Erchard, Garnait and Talorcan, deserve to be better known for their contributions to the establishment of Christianity in Scotland.

This compilation relates stories and legends about some of the holy men and women who crossed the North of Scotland over more than a thousand years. Again, a combination of several hagiographies may have been confusingly woven into an individual saint, or have undergone a makeover from Pictish to

---

[2] Martin Carver, *Portmahomack, Monastery of the Picts* (University Press, Edinburgh, 2010)

Gaelic Celt, female to male and vice-versa, but these were real people who made the Christian life accessible and inspired many others to follow in their footsteps.

In compiling such a book, it is necessary to decide whom to include or omit. The saints of central and lowland Scotland, who also had a significant part in the medieval evangelization of their country, are excluded for another occasion. Elsewhere, there is much material on our national saints Andrew and Margaret, that can be accessed through most literary media.

There is a recent resurgence of pilgrimages to holy places throughout Scotland, being regularly followed by both civil and Church groups. [3] In these uncertain economic times, these pilgrimages bring multiple benefits for the hospitality and tourist trade as more routes come on-stream. Curious enquirers seek to know more about Christianity, ancient and modern, and discover history that has not been accessible until this century. The modern phenomenon of genealogy drives many to learn more about their roots and antecedents, aided and abetted by modern technology and improved access to historical records. Although, since the Reformation, many saintly legends may seem to have vanished in the mists of time, there is a renewed interest in saintly role models whose examples have taken on some relevance for today's society that sees the dissolution of families and communities. The saints are part of our Christian inheritance that only makes sense by placing them in the context and culture of their time.

It is hoped that this short book will inspire you to do some saint searching of your own and discover the Christian genes that inform the history of several peoples who would eventually unite to become the Scottish Nation. The history of Christianity in Scotland continues to develop to this day, and if you want, you too can make a valuable contribution. I invite you to embrace the short prayer included for each saint, and make it your own.

Deacon John Woodside, Banff 2016

---

[3] http://www.sprf.org.uk & http://celticpilgrimage.weebly.com

Saint Ninian
Bishop, 5th century

 It is pleasing to tell that St Ninian has regained some popularity since the visit of Pope Benedict to Scotland a few years ago. There is a growing number of books and articles about different aspects of his life, but sadly, there is little or no new evidence available about this holy man of God or meaningful interaction with the primary sources. There are, however, questions, interpretations and arguments continually raised by academics about the "real" identity and life of this proto-evangelist of our nation – his date and origins, his role and achievements, his means, and the area covered by his mission and ministry.

What archaeologists have found in the earliest phases of site excavation at Whithorn, was not a church building per se, but evidence of early Christian practices; sophisticated trading contacts reaching as far as Gaul and Tunisia; literacy, knowledge of the liturgy and an élite material culture, similar to that found in both monastic and other high status secular settlements. They also found evidence of centuries of continued occupation and of Christian practice, plus a breadth of cultures, languages, artistic styles and technologies, all woven together, as other missionaries or invaders appropriated the famous shrine.

Archaeologists and historians continue to debate the findings on the site and around its sister site at Kirkmadrine in the nearby Rhins of Galloway where early burial stones, post-dating the Latinus stone,[4] are now considered to indicate an early monastery. Whithorn looks more like a secular site, possibly a royal one, with evidence of the first Christian converts' burials and lavish funeral rites. More investigation is required and Whithorn will remain at

---

[4] c.450, Scotland's oldest Christian monument, now in Whithorn Museum

the centre of debate about the nature of post-Roman society and culture in Britain, the nature and spread of Christianity, craft and trade, relations between Britain and Ireland, and between secular and ecclesiastical society.[5]

If we are to rely on the "traditional narrative" of Ninian's *Life* by Aelred (believed to have been written in the 12th century), containing almost everything that is in Bede, and the 8th century *Miracula Nynie Episcopi*, then we find statements about both the fixed date for the life of Ninian and the construction of his monastery Candida Casa.

The purpose of both the *Miracula* (as its title shows) and Aelred's *Life* are not to provide all the facts of Ninian's life, but to emphasize Ninian's holiness through his miracles. Bede's account may be based on "facts" reported to him, but Clancy opines that this account is a concise later addition to Bede's original text.

This suits Bede's purpose implicitly by comparing "a type of ecclesiastical organization he disliked with one of which he completely approved", resulting in many contentious and unproven points.[6]

The story that follows, therefore, draws from the "traditional narrative" and other various sources, doing so with a conscious knowledge of some of the difficulties indicated by numerous academics and experts on our subject.[7] It is said that Ninian, a Briton, was born around 360, and his father was a British chieftain who had converted to Christianity. As the young Ninian had a strong desire to study Christianity, he travelled to Rome to further his learning. The Pope of the time welcomed Ninian and arranged that Church tradition, dogmas and doctrines were available for him to study.

---

[5] http://www.whithorn.com/

[6] T. O. Clancy, "The Real Saint Ninian" (Edinburgh: Innes Review vol.52, no. 1, Spring 2001)

[7] A. Boyle, "Saint Ninian: Some Outstanding Problems" (Innes Review 19, 1968), pp. 57-70

After a period of some fifteen years in Rome, Ninian was ordained to the priesthood and episcopate by Pope St Siricius and sent back to evangelize in his native country, establishing a small monastic community in the region now called Galloway before setting out to evangelize other areas of the country. He was the first missionary bishop residing in Scotland for whom there is any record.

Although Bede acknowledges Ninian's mission to the Southern Picts who inhabited the old Roman province of Valentia south of the Forth, others consider that the early missionary activity in the Eastern and Northern reaches of Scotland was initiated by Ninian and his small band of evangelists, thereby preparing the way for the advent of Columba's later re-evangelization of the country. The most influential and successful were St Drostan and his "Three", more of whom in another chapter.

We may accept that Ninian's recollection of the churches that he had seen during his travels on mainland Europe had inspired him to build something more substantial than the simple buildings that he found in Galloway.

It may also be possible that through his contacts made in Europe, he arranged for masons from Gaul to complete the first stone church in Britain, called Candida Casa, "White House", on the Isle of Whithorn peninsula.

Ninian laboured long and hard and was more than seventy years of age when he died, and was buried at the church that he had built and dedicated to St Martin. Later the church was renamed after Ninian and became renowned for pilgrimages from Scotland, Ireland and England. Thereafter, many churches in Scotland were built and dedicated to St Ninian, and a pre-reformation memorial altar was endowed by the Scottish nation in the Carmelite Church at Bruges.

Some suggest that the majority of places named after Ninian date from some centuries later when his cult gained popularity, or when it was pitted against Columba's increasingly popular cult, particularly in the 8th to 12th centuries.[8] Clancy opines that despite the over-optimistic work of W. Douglas Simpson earlier in the 20th century, there is still not a single church dedication to Ninian that can be shown to be earlier than the twelfth century.[9] It is still possible, however, that Ninian and his followers' evangelization endeavours touched many parts of Scotland from St Ninian's Isle in Shetland, to Northern and Southern Pictland, and the Isle of Whithorn in Galloway.

During the 19th century, whilst some restoration work was being carried out at a church in Turriff, Aberdeenshire, workers discovered a piece of an old fresco with a portrait of St Ninian. Unfortunately, the fresco was not preserved and has been lost forever. Further west, the old Burgh of Nairn was placed under Ninian's patronage, and many holy wells from Galloway to Orkney bear his name.

The site of the chapel on St Ninian's Isle, Shetland, was excavated in the late 1950s and in 2000/2001. The dedication to Ninian, however, is not thought to be contemporary with the founding of the chapel.

Evidence of traces of a wall has been found beneath it so we know it is not the earliest chapel on the site. A treasure trove was buried under a cross-marked slab close to the altar, consisting of many different items of silver that included bowls, weaponry and jewellery, considered to be either a familial or an ecclesiastical hoard. The collection is now in the National Museum of Scotland, but replicas can be seen in the Shetland Museum.

The graveyard adjacent to the chapel reveals a continuity of pre-Christian and Christian burials. Excavation found a group of babies, aligned east-west and with tiny crosses at their heads, buried under empty cists, and these may represent the point at which Christian practices were being introduced, with pre-

---

[8] E. S. Towill, *The Saints of Scotland* (Edinburgh: St Andrew Press, 1983) p.203
[9] T. O .Clancy, "The real St Ninian" (Innes Review 52, no. 1, Spring 2001) pp.1-28

Christian tradition still lingering on. Other early Christian-Pictish finds include corner-posts from stone shrines and stones with crosses carved onto them.

Ninian's feast, traditionally held on 16th September, is celebrated throughout Scotland.

Prayer (from the Revised Daily Missal):

O God, who by the teaching of your Bishop St Ninian
turned the Picts and Britons to the knowledge of your faith,
grant in your mercy, that, as by his learned teaching
we are penetrated with the light of truth,
so by his intercession we may obtain the joys of eternal life.
Through our Lord Jesus Christ, your Son,
who lives and reigns with you in the unity of the Holy Spirit,
one God, for ever and ever. Amen.

St Ternan
Bishop, 5th Century

According to the Aberdeen Breviary, St Ternan was born of noble parents in the Mearns area, possibly at Arbuthnott, and it associates him with St Palladius, the traditionally acclaimed missionary of that area who is said to have been led to Ternan by an angel, so that he could baptize and raise him in the Christian faith. Palladius' saintly influence upon Ternan led the young man to embrace the clerical state. Having heard of Pope Gregory, Ternan travelled to Rome where the Pope received him "with honour", and after seven years of being "subject to his discipline in word and deed", Ternan was consecrated bishop to return to his Pictish homeland to proclaim the Gospel. At the end of his missionary endeavours, Ternan was buried at the place now called Banchory-Ternan, where his cult was upheld beyond the medieval era, and an annual fair and festival were held in his memory.

There are two legends concerning artefacts belonging to St Ternan. The first concerns a bell called "the Ronecht", presented to him by Pope Gregory and reputed to have followed Ternan miraculously all the way to the Mearns. The holy bell was preserved at Banchory-Ternan until the Reformation, and was distinguished by being placed in the custody of an hereditary keeper, as was not uncommon in the case of other sacred relics. This bell was considered by some to have been identified with an ancient bronze bell that was dug up in 1863 when they were laying the line near the old railway station at Banchory. The bell now hangs in Banchory Ternan East Church.

In the Aberdeen Breviary there is a short paragraph which tells the following story. One springtime, St Machar asked St Ternan to send him some corn seed, but not having any, Ternan returned to Machar sacks full of sand. Seeing Ternan's great faith, Machar sowed the sand as he would for natural seed, and was rewarded by

9

a bumper harvest through the holy bishops' merits. As with many similar stories, an accurate chronology was not always adhered to!

There is also a story that for more than a thousand years after his death, St Ternan's head was secured in a metal case adorned with gold and silver, and was an object of veneration as the skin remained intact on the saint's skull at the place where he had been anointed at his Episcopal consecration.

Also at Banchory could once be found the St Matthew volume of his four Books of the Gospels that was enclosed in a gold and silver adorned metal case. In addition, there was a reliquary containing the saint's relics allegedly held in the treasury of the Church of Aberdeen – sadly, both were lost at some time during the post-Reformation period.

The churches at Slains, in Aberdeenshire, Upper Banchory and Arbuthnott in the Mearns, were dedicated to St Ternan. He is also remembered in Uist and Benbecula; and churches at Taransay in Harris, and at Findon, in the Mearns, were named after the saint. There were also holy wells commemorating him at Findon and at Slains.

St Ternan's feast day is given as June 12th.

Prayer (from the Aberdeen Breviary):

Defend us, O Lord, by your protection: and through the intercession of Saint Ternan, your confessor and bishop, guard us from all spiritual wickedness. Through Christ our Lord. Amen.

St Erchard (aka. Irchard, Yrchard or Merchard)
Bishop, 5th century

Here we encounter a Pictish saint with a plethora of names, and a hagiography that could be confused with several better known saints of his era, and we hear one of many stories about a bell. Somehow his legend has survived and it deserves to be heard once again.

It is said that St Erchard was born to pagan parents at the Pictish settlement whose remains may still be seen on the hillside above Tolmauds, a few miles to the north of Kincardine O'Neil, known by the locals as "Kinker" (between Banchory and Ballater). The Aberdeen Breviary tells us that from his childhood years he began a holy life that included fasting, vigils and prayers whilst detesting the manners and vices of evil and wicked men. In his early youth, Erchard embraced the Christian Faith, and as a student was mentored by St Ternan at Banchory (*banchor* is a term used to denote a Christian seat of learning and instruction), and was subsequently ordained priest by his mentor, collaborating in his future missionary labours and becoming one of Ternan's greatest disciples.

Erchard's story may be of major significance in the primary evangelization of Alba – this almost overlooked and unknown saint whom we will call Erchard, surely may be ranked equally with the early Pictish missionaries Nathalan, Ternan and Drostan. Erchard's mission to spread the Christian Faith, encouraged by Ternan, also followed in the footsteps of his predecessor St Ninian, travelling to the Great Glen, known in ancient times as the "Valley of the Saints", which is the supposed route taken by Ninian on his return to Whithorn. Erchard's missionary work was mainly amongst the Picts and must have been a major influence on the primary evangelization of the Pictish nation; and perhaps his prior evangelizing achievements were the reason why Columba found it relatively easy to be a catalyst in the conversion of the High King Brude when the two met a century later at Craig Phadrig near

Inverness. The fact that Erchard, like Ternan, Drostan and Nathalan, was a Pict himself and understood the language was a major advantage and added greatly to his ability to proclaim and explain the Gospel.

Local legend tells us that Erchard, with two of his companions on his mission northwards, journeyed via the *muinntir* (community) at Clova (close to Lumsden) to that at Dunbeath in Strathglass (Caithness). Whilst in Strathglass he discovered three bright new bells buried in the earth at the foot of a certain tree and resolved to end his wanderings and found his new church at the place where the bell rang of its own accord for the third time. Taking one for himself, he gave the others to his fellow-missionaries, bidding each to erect a church on the spot where his bell should ring of its own accord for the third time; and agreeing to do likewise with regard to his own bell. One of those companions founded a church at Glenconvinth, in Strathglass, the other at Broadford, Isle of Skye. Erchard eventually arrived at Glenmoriston on the banks of Loch Ness and here the bell rang for the first time at *Suidh Mhercheird*, St Merchard's Seat. The second time it rang at *Fuaran Mhercheird*, St Merchard's Well at Ballintombuie, Glenmoriston, where a spring of excellent quality water still bears his name. The bell rang for a third time at a spot beside the river Moriston, known afterwards as *Clachan Mhercheird*, St Merchard's Church.

A bell locally associated with the saint lay preserved there for centuries on a tombstone in the burying-ground at *Clachan Mhercheird*, and although the church fell into decay in the early seventeenth century, the bell remained in the churchyard, resting on a narrow pointed spar of granite. Whilst the spar remains in situ, the bell was removed by some strangers visiting around 1873 and has never been returned.

So here is another "bell legend" about a bell with various miraculous properties that included: curing the sick if they touched it in faith; the bell finding its way back if removed from the Clachan; the bell ringing of its own accord when a funeral was approaching the graveyard; and finally, if cast on the water, the bell would float on the surface.

Like his predecessors Ninian and Ternan, Erchard journeyed to Rome where Pope St Gregory, on hearing of Erchard's sanctity, consecrated him as bishop. Returning to Alba (Scotland) with the permission and blessing of the Pope, he ended his days in Aberdeenshire after a prolonged illness. At the spot where the cart that was carrying his body to burial was miraculously stopped, he was laid to rest and a church was erected in his memory at the place we know today as Kincardine-O'Neil.

An annual fair was formerly held there on St Erchard's feast and throughout the octave. Another of the saint's churches was in Glenmoriston with an ancient burial ground adjoining it, with a few stones of the old building still scattered around. His feast day may be celebrated on August 24th.

Prayer (from the Aberdeen Breviary):

Almighty and merciful God, who by the faith of your bishop Erchard did free the Picts from the enslavement of the pagans, grant to all who seek him devoutly to be freed from all deceit of enemies and from everlasting damnation. Through Christ our Lord. Amen.

St Devenick
Confessor, 6th century

Tradition (and the Aberdeen Breviary) relates that Devenick was a contemporary of St Machar, and preached the Gospel mainly in Caithness where he subsequently died. Forbes reckons that Devenick is from the Columban period[10], but Knight thinks that he flourished in the fifth century.[11] The legend of this saint, whose name is not in any of the Irish lists, is found in the Aberdeen Breviary as follows[12]:

"When the blessed fathers Columba and Mauricius (Machar) were preaching in Scotland, Devinicus, a very old man, also flourished. He divided the work of the ministry between himself and Mauricius, going to the Provincia Cathinorum (Caithness) while Mauricius went to the Picts. Saint Mauricius said, 'Now again we shall be joined. Even in the celestial life shall we forever be joined together, and rejoice with Christ. But one thing I desire, that as death is at hand, when my time comes, let my body be brought to this place and be buried here.'

"The saint agreed, and Devinicus went to the Cathini, preaching the Word. At length Devinicus came to die, and told them to take his body to some of the churches of Mauricius, mindful of his old engagement. And this was done. The following night Saint Mauricius saw angels descending on the church where the holy body lay, and said, 'A guest Cometh, to whom we must pay honour'; but on coming they found not the body, for they who carried it, wishing to rest, had borne it to a

---

[10] A. P. Forbes, *Kalendars of Scottish Saints* (Douglas, Edinburgh 1872)
[11] G.A.F. Knight, *Archaeological light on the Early Christianity of Scotland* (London, 1933)
[12] Aberdeen Breviary

place called Crostan[13]. There they held vigil, and then brought it to a place called Banquhory Devynik, where a church was raised in his honour."

After Devinick's death in Caithness, his body was brought south to the outskirts of Aberdeen to an area now known as Banchory-Devenick in accordance with his continually expressed desire to rest in the district of St Machar, for whom he had the greatest respect and admiration during his life. Below is an extract of old poetry that tells how his followers are believed to have complied with Devenick's burial request:

"Then devoutly they bore the corpse
To a place called Banchory;
And there solemnly with honour
They prepared for it a tomb.
Over him there they built a church
Where God yet does not cease to work
Through his prayers, many miracles,
To sick and hurt folk giving healing.
Men call that place where he lay
Banchory-Devenick to this day."

The *banchor* (school or seat of learning) with which Devenick is associated is well known and, very surprisingly, was situated not very far from another founded by St Ternan slightly higher up the Dee valley. Although the fact that two such *banchors* were located close together was unusual, it was evidence that Northern Pictland was the powerhouse and source of Christian evangelization in the early medieval period. In addition, there were other major Christian missionary communities concentrated in and around the areas at Methlick, Kynõr (near Huntly), Mortlach, Aberdour, Deer,

---

[13] Is it possible that this is a spelling error, and that Devenick's body on its way for burial from Caithness crossed the Moray Firth near the place of Drostan at Old Aberdour, before conveying it onwards?

Turriff, Clova, Newtonmore, and Dunbeath (Strathglass). Archibald Scott in *The Pictish Nation*, written in 1917, lists 26 local Pictish centres at the beginning of the eighth century, of which eight were in the north-east of Scotland. Plainly, this part of the country was in the vanguard of Christian mission, with many areas having received the Gospel 150 years before St Columba's birth!

In the cathedral church of St Machar in Aberdeen, there was an altar dedicated to St Devenick, and he was titular of one of the possessions of the cathedral, the church of Methlick on the River Ythan, another spring nearby with a holy miraculous well bearing his name. A fair in that parish and another held at Milton of Glenesk, Forfarshire (now called Angus), known as "Saint Denick's", contain the name in a shortened form and were held in November. Although a post-reformation church was built in 1642 at Banchory-Devenick, it was said to be on the site of an even earlier church of St Devenick, who is thought to be buried on or near the site.

St Devenick's Feast is on November 13th.

Prayer (from the Aberdeen Breviary):

O Lord, God, and Saviour of all, be near to our prayers, and at the intercession for us of Saint Devenick, your confessor, cleanse the guilt of our sins, that we may be able to enjoy everlasting glory. Through Christ our Lord. Amen.

Saint Columba
Abbot, c.521-597

In St Columba, when the myths and legends are sifted, we discover a real saint, a holy man of God and of His people. Like most saints of the Celtic era, there is a great deal of myth which needs to be searched to find the "real" Columba, even though there exists much information found in various Irish Annals, Adomnán's *Vita Columbae*, [14] Bede's *Ecclesiastical History of the English People*, [15] and the Middle Irish *Life of Colum Cille.*

Columba, the evangelist of the north-western region of Scotland was born at Garten, Donegal, in Ireland around AD521, into the Cenel Conaill clan where both parents were of "royal" lineage. It seems that the young Columba was destined for the Church from a young age and was sent to study under St Finnio, a British missionary, and in the schools of Moville, Clonard, and Glasnevin, in the course of time being ordained priest.

As a young man, he founded his first monastery at Derry; this was to be the precursor of the many foundations which he energetically established in Ireland and Scotland. Early in the 560s, Columba was caught up in some type of controversy, resulting in his temporary excommunication (lifted shortly thereafter), and his exile with twelve companions across the Irish sea to the island of Iona which was gifted to him by the king of Dal Riata, Conall mac Comgaill. [16]

Iona quickly became the epicentre from which Christianity

---

[14] Adomnán, *Life of St Columba*, http://www.fordham.edu/halsall/basis/columba-e.asp

[15] Bede, *Ecclesiastical History of the English People,* rev. edn (London: Penguin, 1990)

[16] Alan Macquarrie ed., *Legends of Scottish Saints* (Dublin: 4 Courts Press, 2012), p.344

was diffused throughout the country northwest of the Grampians, and it is said that these missionaries penetrated even as far north as Orkney and Shetland. Adomnán credits the Iona mission with the conversion of the northern Picts, including King Bridei at Inverness, but this may have been more a diplomatic mission to facilitate safe passage for Columba's evangelists, rather than a direct attempt to evangelize the Picts who were generally hostile to the Gaels. Perhaps this dialogue was only possible because Columba was a Christian rather than a Gaelic prince, and because the Picts had been previously evangelized and therefore had a friendly disposition towards the Christian faith?

For some 34 years, Columba and his helpers were so successful in their evangelizing efforts that monasteries, churches and centres of learning sprang up in the northwest highlands of Scotland, both on the adjacent islands and on the mainland.

Some modern scholarship suggests that Christianity reached Pictland many years before Columba's mission through the evangelizing efforts of St Ninian's followers, who travelled up the east coast of Scotland, crossing the firth from Buchan to Ross.

These men moved into the northern extremities before travelling via Inverness to Fortrui (the Pictish capital, opined to be around Burghead in Moray). The so-called Columban monasteries and communities along the Moray Firth may possibly be attributed to St Colm of Buchan, one of "The Drostan Three".[17]

Columba was called to his heavenly reward on Sunday, 9th June 597, and according to Adomnán, died in the monastery church, kneeling before the altar and surrounded by his monastic brothers. His body was initially buried on Iona, but afterwards was removed to Ireland to be enshrined beside Sts Patrick and Bridget in the Cathedral of Down. Sadly, soldiers later burnt the cathedral and the relics were lost forever.

Columba was renowned as a man of singular purity of mind, with boundless love for souls, a warm personality, and a gentle

---

[17] D. H. Farmer, *The Oxford Dictionary of Saints* (Oxford: University Press), p.116

nature that drew men irresistibly to God.

There must have been, however, another side to this holy man, who was unafraid to carry out the most difficult diplomatic missions in order to secure the means for his evangelizing endeavours – his biographers are quick to draw attention to those numerous works that were furthered by Divine assistance and intervention.

Among the saints of Scotland he holds a foremost rank, although in reality other men and women may have completed all the initial evangelization of the Picts which facilitated the remarkable success attributed to the Columban mission.

There are many stories, miracles and legends attributed to St Columba, and he is greatly admired throughout Scotland, with all the mainstream Christian denominations admitting that he continues to be an inspiration in our times.

The churches dedicated to him throughout Scotland are too numerous to mention, and it is said that "he blessed three hundred wells which were constant", some of which may still be found at Alvah and Portsoy (Banffshire), Birse (Aberdeenshire), Invermoriston (Invernesshire), Carlaverock (Angus), Cambusnethan (Lanarkshire), Alness (Ross-shire), Kirkholm (Galloway), and on the islands of Eigg, Iona and the Garvellachs (south of Oban),. His feast is celebrated in Scotland on 9th June.

Prayer (from the Liturgical Calendar of Scotland):

Pour into our hearts, O Lord, we pray,
a longing for heavenly glory,
and grant that we may come,
bearing in our hands sheaves of justice,
to where the holy Abbot Saint Columba shines with you.
Through our Lord Jesus Christ, your Son,
who lives and reigns with you and the Holy Spirit,
one God, for ever and ever. Amen.

Saint Drostan
Abbot and Hermit, c. 6th century

My interest in the cult of St Drostan began when I relocated to Banffshire, and discovered that the area had witnessed a major Christian mission during the Pictish era, perhaps before the advent of St Columba.

In common with life-stories of many Celtic saints, there is one common legend concerning Drostan, and several other unsubstantiated "stories". The first, and most popular version, is from the story added in Gaelic around the late 11th or early 12th century to the margins of several pages in the 10th century *Book of Deer*.[18] These additions briefly relate to the origin of the Columban monastery at Deer on the land granted to Columba by the Pictish ruler of the time (possibly named Bede), given to Drostan by Columba before his departure.[19]

As Bede initially gave land on the coast at Aberdour to Drostan when he began his missionary activities in the region, it may not be so strange that the monastic settlement returned to the care of Drostan. This most popular version from the *Book of Deer* has been retold thereafter, with some embellishment, in the medieval Aberdeen Breviary.[20]

Dom Michael Barrett's biography of Drostan is similar to that of Forbes with some supplementary details. He recounts that Drostan was descended from the line of King Aidan of Dalriada, friend of St Columba, and for that reason was sent to Ireland for his education and religious formation by the saint.

On completion of his studies, Drostan then returned to Pictland to live as a hermit at Glenesk prior to moving to Iona,

---

[18] See K. Jackson, *The Gaelic Notes in the Book of Deer* (Cambridge: Cambridge University Press, 2008)
[19] Forbes, *Kalendars*
[20] Macquarrie, *Legends* pp.328, 346,348, 353-4,368.

where he entered the monastery under Columba's rule, before accompanying Columba on his mission to the Picts.

Barrett goes on to state that Drostan preached the Gospel in and around Glen Urquhart which in pre-reformation days was called Saint Drostan's, Urquhart, where a plot of ground, said to have been cultivated by the saint when he lived there as its apostle, was known as Saint Drostan's Croft. The saint's cross was preserved at St Ninian's chapel in the Glen, and the custodian of the relic had the use of the croft as reward for his services. According to Barrett, Drostan died in his monastery of Deer and was buried at Aberdour where "miracles were wrought at his tomb".[21]

The Victorian author, Archibald Scott, was convinced that Drostan was one of St Ninian's twelve disciples whose mission was to evangelize the Pictish Nation in an area that ran along the coast from Moray to Buchan, and northwards across the sea to Ross and Caithness. Scott asserts that Drostan was a Briton and his father was prince of Demetia, now part of South Wales.

Although Drostan's exact dates are unknown, Scott reminds us that the Buchan authorities gave Drostan's date as c. 500, and *A View of the Diocese of Aberdeen* gave the date of his co-worker, St Fergus, as "the beginning of the sixth age", i.e. 520.[22] There is no extant record, however, as to which British or Pictish school Drostan was trained at prior to his mission in Pictland.

What can be considered authentic is that Drostan landed on the shore around Aberdour, established a community with his group of missionaries, and later moved inland, settling at Deer under the sanction of Bede, then Pictish ruler of Buchan, who had initially been hostile to the saint's settlement. Scott writes that some centuries later during the Gaelic ascendency in Pictland, the names of Drostan, Colm, and Fergus were removed from their proper historical setting, and were woven into legends intended to

---

[21] Dom Michael Barrett, *A Calendar of Scottish Saints* ((Fort Augustus: Abbey Press, 1919), pp.106-108

[22] *A View of the Diocese of Aberdeen* (Aberdeen: Spalding Club 1843)

create a belief in the superiority of the Gaelic mission in Scotland.

The absorption of both the people and the property from the old Pictish Church into the Columban and post-Columban missions took place, with Scott claiming that the Gaelic entry in the Book of Deer boldly transforms St Colm to Columba (Columcille), as leader of the mission into Pictland, with Drostan the Briton as a subordinate to him.[23]

In the *Trustus cona thriur* ("Drostan with his Three"), Drostan is referred to by Angus the Culdee as contemporary with St Finbar (early 6th century), referring specifically to St Drust, Trust, or Drostan, of Deer, with his three disciples named as Sts Colm (or Colman), Medan, and Fergus.

Macquarrie suggests that Drostan's name may be of Pictish origin, and is sympathetic towards the assertion that Drostan was another Pictish saint who was "demoted" around this period. It is interesting to relate that the Aberdeen Breviary mentions Drostan's association with Columba (but not with Colm or Fergus), and attributes a miracle of restoring the blind priest Symon's sight.[24]

St Drostan and his missionaries also founded many churches south of the Moray Firth, bringing many outlying Pictish tribes under the influence of the Gospel. This included the following ancient Church-sites as representative of Drostan's foundations:

Aberdour in Buchan; Insch in the Garioch; at Rothiemay on the River Deveron; at Aberlour and Alvie on the River Spey; and at Glen Urquhart, where Sts Ninian and Erchard had reputedly previously prepared a way for the Church.

Across the Moray Firth from Buchan, St Drostan and his co-missionaries founded churches in Caithness at the following sites: Kirk o' Tear (the Caithness pronunciation of "Deer"); the Church of Canisbay; Drostan's Church-site at Brabstermire; St Drostan's (Trothan's) at Castletown of Olrig; a Church-site and churchyard at Westerdale on the Thurso river; and St Trostan's at Westfield.

---

[23] A.B. Scott, *The Pictish Nation* (Edinburgh: T. N. Foulis, 1918) pp.132-137

[24] Macquarrie, *Legends,* pp.353-4

Skene points to the canon of Celtic Church history, to remind us that the early Celts gave to a church the name of its actual founder. Therefore the affiliation of ancient church-sites to these men is a guarantee, apart from any records, of personal work at the site in a bygone era. It is acknowledged that whilst Drostan and "his three" were extending the Church in the northern parts of Pictland, other Britons and certain Irish Picts were maintaining a mission in the Brito-Pictish border districts.[25]

The recently published *Legends of Scottish Saints (In the Aberdeen Breviary)*, edited by Alan Macquarrie, indicates that although the Aberdeen Breviary associates Dalquongle (perhaps Dercongal near Dumfries), Glenesk and Aberdour with Drostan, and refers to Drostan's affiliation with his hermitage at Glenesk and tomb at Aberdour, surprisingly neither Deer, nor the foundation of its abbey, nor its Book, are mentioned. Macquarrie draws attention to the mention of the fairs held at Old Deer and Rothiemay on 14th December, and the relics of Drostan's crucifix being located formerly at the parish church in Urquhart.[26]

Is it possible, as Scott claims, that we have another case of an established Pictish saint and evangelizer, who pre-dates the Columban evangelization, being re-designated as a follower of Columba at a later period? Macquarrie boldly states that "there may have been a conscious Gaelicisation of the church in Pictland, perhaps about the 10th century, with native Pictish churchmen being 'rebranded' for political reasons."[27]

Each year St Drostan's Fairs were held at Rothiemay, Aberlour (for 3 days) and Old Deer (for 8 days). Many pre-reformation churches throughout the area formerly known as Pictland were attributed to Drostan but surprisingly there is only one dedication to him in the Diocese of Aberdeen, which he shares with Our Lady, at Fraserburgh.

---

[25] Skene's *Celtic Scotland* (Edinburgh: D. Douglas 1886), book ii. ch. vi. p. 232.
[26] Macquarrie, *Legends*, pp.353-354
[27] Macquarrie, *Legends*, p xxix

In this so-called "post-Christian era", there is a need for positive Church role models who can inspire Christians boldly to evangelize a hostile and secular society with Gospel values. Much will be gained by further research into the life and times of St Drostan whose story deserves to be told so that he may regain his rightful place in history as one of the most dedicated missionaries of the Pictish era, preparing the way for those who were to follow him north of the Grampians.

The Feast of St Drostan is an optional diocesan memorial for 12th July.

Prayer (from the Aberdeen Diocesan Calendar):

Lord our God,
you chose Saint Drostan
to sow the good seed of your word
in the hearts of our forebears.
Grant to us, at his intercession,
an ever greater harvest of faith,
that we may come at last to share in your glory,
Through Christ our Lord. Amen

Saint Brendan (Brandon)
Abbot, 486-577

As with many Celtic saints, there are a few historical facts interspersed among the many legends of St Brendan but the stories often had a more inspirational purpose, and need to be re-told in our time.

St Brendan (or Brandon) "the Navigator" was born near Tralee in Ireland, and as a youth, became the disciple of St Jarlath of Tuam. As a young man he crossed the Irish sea to spend some years studying in the Abbey of Llancarfan, in Glamorganshire, where it is said that he baptized Machutus (better known as St Malo), who is reputed to be the evangelizer of the Celts in Brittany.

Brendan founded several monasteries when he returned to Ireland. Clonfert, on the river Shannon, became the largest and most important of them, and it is said that there were as many as three thousand monks in his various monastic foundations in both Ireland and Scotland. It is thought that his Scottish foundations were on the islands of Bute and Tiree, but his many dedications suggest that devotion to him in Scotland was more widespread.

The old church at Boyndie dedicated to the saint, with the nearby Brandon's Haven, both located in Banffshire, and the old church at Birnie near Elgin, in Moray, are all found within the diocese of Aberdeen. The earliest church in continuous use in the district, parts dating from the 12th century, Birnie is thought to have been the seat or *cathedra* of the Bishop of Moray. The seat was moved to Kinneddar, Lossiemouth, before Elgin Cathedral was founded in 1224.

Brendan's name will always be associated with his legendary seafaring skills related in the romantic narratives of the *Navigatio Sancti Brendani Abbatis*. An Irish monk probably composed these in the 9/10th century, telling of Brendan's westward voyages and incredible exploits.[28]

---

[28] Macquarrie, *Legends*, p.334

In the early 20th century, Barrett said that it was beyond doubt that Brendan and his followers sailed to undiscovered regions on their missionary voyages and they possibly discovered America.[29] It was not until 1976-7, however, that a group of seven men led by the author Tim Severin in a large replica of Brendan's boat, sailed from Galway via the West Coast of Scotland, following the saint's route across the Atlantic via Iceland and Greenland to the American coast.[30]

The feast of St Brendan may be celebrated on 16th May but is not included in the Liturgical Calendars for Scotland or for the Diocese of Aberdeen.

Prayer (from the Aberdeen Breviary):
Almighty and everlasting God, graciously have mercy on your servants invoking your most holy name: and at the intercession of St Brendan, your confessor and abbot, confirm your mercy upon us in good actions. Through Christ Our Lord. Amen.

---

[29] Barrett, *Calendar*, pp.79-80
[30] T. Severin, *The Brendan Voyage* (London, Gill & Macmillan, 2005)

Saint Kessog/Kessoch/Mackessog
Bishop, Confessor and Martyr, 560

The Aberdeen Breviary indicates that Kessog was born in Munster of Irish noble stock, and although his legend probably predates this publication, it is somewhat surprising that there is no mention of him in the Irish Annals or Martyrologies.

Although there is no record of him arriving in Scotland, tradition has it that Kessog's missionary work was first performed in and around the area of Lennox (East Dunbartonshire). Around 510, however, he later retreated to *Innis a' Mhanaich* (Monk's Island) in Loch Lomond where he founded a monastery. The legend continues that sometime later he was murdered near Bandry by brigands or mercenaries on the druid New Year, March 25, near an ancient druid site. This site was marked by a cairn to which pilgrims added stones as they arrived, and it is related that in the 18th century, during road building operations at Bandry, south of Luss, an ancient statue of a man dressed in bishop's robes was found.[31]

Another version of Kessog's story says that being martyred in a foreign country, and his body being conveyed to Scotland for burial, the herbs with which it was surrounded took root and grew where he was laid to rest; hence the name Luss (herbs) was given to the spot, and was afterwards extended to the parish. The place of his burial is called Carnmacheasaig where there was a memorial cairn until 1796.

Luss parish has a rather obscure history but there is early evidence of Christianity with two incised cross-slabs with the shape, size and position of the burial enclosure pointing in the

---

[31] http://www.helensburgh-heritage.co.uk/index.php?option=com_content&view=article&id=472:the-story-of-st-kessog-of-luss&catid=91:religion-&Itemid=492

same direction within the churchyard.[32] The original church at Luss had the privilege of sanctuary granted by King Robert Bruce in 1313, which extended for three miles round it, so that no one could be molested within that boundary for any cause. In olden times, the Scots army adopted the saint's name as a battle cry and sometimes he is represented as the patron of soldiers, wearing a kind of military dress. It is also reputed that Bruce considered Kessog to be the true patron saint of Scotland and, as such, carried relics of the saint at the Battle of Bannockburn.

There was also a church dedicated to Kessog at Auchterarder, with fairs held annually on his feast-day at Auchterarder, Callander and Comrie, Perthshire. Not far from Callander is a conical mound bearing his name.

Another two places are dedicated to this saint near Inverness, one of which can be found at South Kessock, where people travelling north of Inverness had the choice on their journey either of taking the Kessock Ferry (run by Dominicans) across the Beauly Firth to North Kessock on the Black Isle, or of making a land detour via Beauly. In 1982 a new bridge was built across the Firth that by-passed both Inverness and Beauly. Another regular pilgrim route was via the Cromarty to Nigg crossing, en route to St Duthac's Shrine in Tain.

St Kessog's feast day was celebrated on March 10th.

Prayer (from the Aberdeen Breviary):

O God, who caused Saint Kessog, your confessor and bishop, to come to the fullness of your grace, grant us, we pray, forgiveness of our sins, and by his intervention to be freed from all the disturbances and dangers of this world. Through Christ Our Lord. Amen

---

[32] Macquarrie, *Legends*, p.375

Saint Machar
Bishop, 6th century

What little is known about St Machar is surrounded by historical legend and myth, with only a few facts and scant evidence being available from the Aberdeen Breviary and *The Fifth Life of Columba*.[33]

Machar was said to have been the son of Fiachna, an Irish chieftain, and to have been baptized by St Colman. As a youth, he became a follower of St Columba and accompanied him to Iona with eleven other disciples. Some years later, he became a bishop, and Columba sent him with twelve others to bring the Gospel to the pagan Picts of Strathdon in the north east of Scotland. Tradition tells that Columba instructed Machar to found a church at the place where a river's windings formed the shape of a bishop's pastoral staff. Finding such a place by the river Don, at the spot now known as Old Aberdeen, Machar founded a humble church that rose to become the magnificent cathedral that now bears his name.

The cathedral, standing within its own village, is one of the few medieval cathedrals in Scotland to survive the Reformation. Parts of it have survived almost unaltered over the ages, although the choir and chancel have been lost, the chancel in 1560 and the choir almost a century later when Cromwell's troops removed stones from it and from the ruined bishop's palace. Today only the nave and aisles of the earlier building remain.

In Old Aberdeen, not far from the church gateway, can also be found St Machar's or Chanonry Well, from which in a bygone era (possibly 18th century), the water was drawn for baptisms held in the cathedral. In Balnagowan Wood, near Aboyne, there is a St

---

[33] Towill, *The Saints of Scotland*, p.147

Machar's Well next to a stone bearing a carved cross. At Corgarff, in Strathdon, there is another spring known as "Tobar Mhachar" (the well of St Machar) which was renowned for its miraculous properties. There is a popular story about a priest, who, in time of famine, drew from this spring three fine salmon that provided food until supplies came from elsewhere.[34]

Also in Aberdeenshire at Kildrummie, there was a place named after the saint – "Macker's Haugh".

In addition to the St Machar's cathedral in Old Aberdeen, there are two parishes in Aberdeenshire, formerly linked, known as New and Old Machar, respectively. Macquarrie suggests that it is from here that the stories about Machar derive in part from genuine traditions in the area, one suggestion being that the saint's name came from the area – the Gaelic *machair* denoting a fertile sandy plain near the sea.[35] To this day a great deal of mystery surrounds the monk who founded the church that still bears his name.

St Machar's feast is celebrated on 13th November and features in the current Calendar for the Diocese of Aberdeen as an Obligatory Memorial.

Prayer (from the Aberdeen Diocesan Calendar):

Lord God,
You sent Saint Machar
to minister to your people as their shepherd.
Help us to follow his example
that, in the midst of present trials,
we may keep a lively faith
in the sure hope of enjoying future glory.
Through Christ our Lord. Amen.

---

[34] Barrett, *Calendar*, p.163
[35] Macquarrie *Legends*, p.381

Saint Moluag or Lughaidh
Bishop and Confessor, d.592

According to the Irish annals, St Moluag was born in Ireland and although little is known about his early family life or education, he became a member of the monastic community in the renowned abbey of Bangor. It was there that his vocation was nurtured under the direction of St Comgall, and it is said that after leaving his native land to preach to the pagans of northern Scotland, he founded more than one hundred monasteries. Depending upon which story one believes, Moluag was either friend or adversary of St Columba. A traditional tale says that a rock on which Moluag stood detached itself from the Irish coast and carried him across the sea into Loch Linnhe, landing on the island of Lismore. There, he converted the islanders to Christianity and established a centre for evangelism, before moving on to mainland Ross-shire where he founded another centre at Rosemarkie on the shores of the Moray Firth to evangelize the Highlands, creating Christian communities, dedicated to the Mother of God, as he moved among the Picts.

According to tradition, Moluag lived to extreme old age, and died at Rosemarkie in 592, near the place where later the Church would erect a great rose-pink stone slab upon which was carved a Christian cross amongst Pictish emblems. It is said by some that he was buried at this spot, but if so, his relics must have been afterwards translated to the cathedral on Lismore. Nowadays, when visiting the parish church there, one can see how the choir, along with the original doorways, piscina and sedilia of the medieval cathedral at Clachan have been restored and are in use, with the buttresses and two external doorways visible.[36]

Prior to the Reformation there was much devotion shown towards Moluag in both Scotland and Ireland, with many places and churches dedicated to him, including those at Clatt and

---

[36] Macquarrie, *Legends*, pp. 395-398

31

Tarland, Aberdeenshire; Mortlach in Banffshire; Alyth, Perthshire; Kilmuir on Skye; and on Mull, Raasay, Tiree, Pabay, Lewis and other islands. An ancient burial ground at Auchterawe, near Fort Augustus, styled Kilmalomaig, is called after this saint.

In some of the dedications his name appears in various forms as the original Celtic name Lughaidh (pronounced *Lua*) became changed by the addition of the title of honour *mo*, as a prefix, and the endearing suffix *ag*. At Clatt a "Saint Mallock's Fair" was held annually for eight days, and at Tarland, the "Luoch Fair".

In 1010, Malcolm II founded an abbey at Mortlach in thanksgiving for a victory obtained over the Danes after the Scots had invoked the aid of Our Lady and St Moluag. Some of the saint's relics were preserved there and his holy well was located nearby.

For centuries St Moluag's "Bachuil Mòr" (blackthorn staff) was in the care of its hereditary custodians, the Livingstones of Lismore. For a time, it was held by the Duke of Argyll, but was returned to the care of the Livingstones, in the person of the Baron of Bachuil. It is known that Moluag's abbatial bell was in existence up to the 16th century but disappeared during the Reformation. An ancient bell, however, discovered in 1814 at Kilmichael-Glassary, Argyllshire, was thought to be the lost treasure and is now preserved in the National Museum in Edinburgh. Moluag's story deserves to be re-told in the hope that this great evangelizing missionary may once again take his rightful place among the proto-evangelists of Scotland. The feast of St Moluag may be celebrated on June 25th.

Prayer (from the Aberdeen Breviary):

O God, merciful by nature and compassionate by disposition, graciously listen to the prayers of those who pray to you: that you deign to pour forth your grace upon us through the intervention of your bishop Saint Moluag, and that after we have obtained forgiveness from our sins we may come to eternal rest. Through Christ our Lord. Amen.

Saint Medan/Modan
c. 6th century

Once again, a virtually unknown saint is included in this compilation. One tradition concerning St Drostan says that three companions accompanied him on his early missionary journeys among the Picts, one of whom was known as Medan.

There are several place names in the north east of Scotland linked with his name, and the old church of Filorth/Philorth (now Fraserburgh), Aberdeenshire, was dedicated to this saint who was a bishop in great favour with King Conran (AD 503).[37] St Medan or Modan is still regarded as the patron saint of Fraserburgh and his name is found in various places throughout the town.

The Aberdeen Breviary gives two offices for a saint of this name, one for November 14th and the other for February 4th, where he is described as "*abbot* and confessor. The Martyrology of Aberdeen says he was honoured "apud Falkirk", where his arm was long kept.[38] Forbes, however, suggests that to this saint we must attribute Auchmedden, in the parish of Aberdour, near Philorth, and Pitmedden, in the parish of Udny, also in Aberdeenshire.

At Freswick, Canisbay in Cathness, stood St Modan's or Maddan's chapel, not far from chapels dedicated to St Drostan at Ackergill and Brabster. The present parish church of Canisbay is the most northerly church in mainland Scotland and was the original burial place of Jan de Groot, after whom nearby John o' Groats was named.

There is also reference to Medan found at Fintray, where his relics were said to have been preserved and where his feast was in former times celebrated on February 4th. Forbes wrote that the minister possessed a silver cup belonging to the parish, bearing the

---

[37] *A View of the Diocese of Aberdeen*
[38] Hector Boece, History of Scotland, trans. John Bellenden , vol. ii. (ed. 1821), p. 58

date of 1632, said by tradition to have been formed of the beaten silver which had once wrapped the head of St Medan, the titular saint of the parish. He recorded also that "in the days of popish superstition, it was wont to be carried through the parish in procession, for the purpose of bringing down rain, or clearing up the weather".[39]

In the years to come, thanks to continuing progress in research and archaeological projects, perhaps the missionary journeys of St Drostan and his Three will be unravelled and revealed for the sake of what some believe to be our post-Christian society in great need of Christian role models.

St Medan's feast may have been celebrated on either March 1st or November 14th.

Prayer (from the Aberdeen Breviary for November 14th):

Almighty and everlasting God, look graciously upon this day of festival, and may your Church always rejoice in its celebration, through the intercession of Saint Medan, your bishop and confessor: that you may bring to perfection the prayers of all those who believe in you. Through Christ our Lord. Amen.

---

[39] Forbes *Kalendars,* pp. 402-3

Saint Fumac
c. 6th century?

When researching the lives of our saints, one of the main challenges is to try and locate a primary, or at least a secondary, source or hagiography. When Fumac's name was suggested for this compilation, there was little evidence found concerning this "local" saint who previously had been specially venerated in Banffshire where he was the patron of Botriphnie or "Fumac Kirk" near Keith. According to Forbes, however, there are traces of his cult also in Caithness.[40] One of the old almanacs refers to a "Saint Fumac's fair at Dinet", and at Chapel of Dine, in Watten, both in Caithness.[41]

According to local tradition, it is said that St Fumac bathed every morning, summer and winter, in a deep spring, and by way of penance went round the bounds of the parish on his knees praying that its residents would be spared from the plague. Water from the spring finds its way eventually into the River Isla which flows through Keith. The stone-lined well is still accessible, near the Drummuir stop on the Keith to Dufftown railway.

Until two centuries ago, the wooden image of the saint was carefully kept in the parish of Botriphnie, and an old woman who acted as its custodian washed it with all due solemnity in nearby St Fumac's Well annually on his feast day on the 3rd of May.[42] The practice was possibly associated with prayer for plentiful rain for the fields. This well was renowned for its healing properties, and according to an eighteenth century manuscript, the image of the saint was preserved until 1847 when too much rain fell and a flood of the River Isla swept it away to Banff, where the parish minister,

---

[40] MS *Account of Scottish Bishops in the Library at Slains Castle* (near Cruden Bay, Aberdeenshire), 1726
[41] Forbes, *Kalendars*, pp. 351-2
[42] Mackinlay 1914, 504 found in
http://saintsplaces.gla.ac.uk/place.php?id=1317322789

considering it to be idolatrous, zealously burnt it.[43]

There was also a 5 1/2 feet high cross-bearing slab that stood in Botriphnie cemetery until around 1820, when it was destroyed by a blacksmith who possibly used it as a hearthstone for his smithy. It was probably the cross beside which St Fumac's Fair was held at Botriphnie.

A modern wooden statue of the saint, carved from a tree trunk, stands today in Drummuir railway station. In 2007, Ron Smith of Keith published a small collection of short stories for children, entitled *Fumac the Good*, loosely based on the life and legend of St Fumac. Both statue and tales give an image of a traditional kindly hermit saint, well versed in the flowers and plants around him and of whom wild animals are unafraid.

St Fumac's feast is believed to have been celebrated on May 3rd and St Fumac's Fair is still celebrated each year in Drummuir on the Saturday nearest to that date.

Prayer:

Heavenly Father, by the example of Saint Fumac, we continue to pray that those affected by illness and the modern plagues of society will find their consolation in you, and be healed according to your will, through Christ Our Lord. Amen

---

[43] J. Robertson ed., *Illustrations of the Topography and Antiquities of the Shires of Aberdeen and Banff*, vol. ii (Aberdeen: Spalding Club, 1843) p. 253, note.

Saint Marnan (Marnock/Marnoch)
Bishop and Confessor, c. 7th Century

Throughout Scotland there are place names and dedications to several Sts Marnan/Marnock/Marnoch, but towards the end of the 15th century it is clear from entries in the Aberdeen Breviary that two main saint cults with these names become pre-eminent, that of Marnan at Aberchirder in Banffshire, and Marnock at Kilmarnock in Ayrshire.

As so often is the case with many of the Celtic saints, the name changes "by the addition of particles expressive of reverence".[44] The original form of the name was a contraction of the Gaelic name Ernin that probably originates from the old Irish word that means "iron".

It is possible that the legends of these two saints became entwined over the centuries, and Macquarrie suggests that Marnan's cult may be an "off-shoot of a well-known Irish saint of related name", but this has not been proven.[45] For our purpose, we shall focus upon the cult of the Banffshire saint known locally as Marnan.

Very little is known of Marnan's origins, as there does not seem to have been any surviving *vita* available. From the Aberdeen Breviary, however, we learn that he was both bishop and confessor, and tradition recalls that he was a passionate preacher, labouring as a missionary in the Moray area until he died and was buried at Aberchirder in Banffshire around 625.

Located a couple of miles from Aberchirder is the village of Marnoch, named from its connection with the saint, and the area is traditionally known as the site of early monastic settlements. For centuries, St Marnan's shrine was a popular pilgrimage place, and tradition relates that his relics, then preserved at Aberchirder but

---

[44] Barrett, *Calendar*, p. 32
[45] Macquarrie *Legends*, p.390

no longer found, were miraculous, his head often carried in procession to ensure good weather.

Another legend tells that it was customary every Sunday to have lights placed around the head, which was then washed in water used by the sick to cure their illnesses. Evidence for the veneration of bodily relics of Scottish saints in any age is very rare.[46]

Although the church in which his remains were honoured no longer stands, a holy well at Aberchirder still bears his name. In bygone years, an annual village event, known as "Marnock Fair", was held on the second Tuesday in March, but like most Scottish religious festivals it has been discontinued since the Reformation.

Near Ballater in Aberdeenshire, there is a ruined church of Inchmarnock located on an island in the river Dee.[47] In addition to places in North East Scotland, traces of the cults of St Marnan/Marnock are found in many districts of Western Scotland, especially Ayrshire and Argyll.

Places and churches dedicated to the saints were often interchangeable, and later medieval sources and calendars differentiate between the two saints and their cults by ascribing different dates to the individuals: Marnan on 1st March and Marnock on 25th October. There is no entry in the current Liturgical Calendar for the Diocese of Aberdeen.

Prayer (from the Aberdeen Breviary for 1st March):

O God, who are the life of all those who believe in you: hear your servants who humbly pray to you, and grant that while we celebrate the solemnities of your confessor and bishop, Saint Marnan, we may be fervently fired with love of your name. Through Christ Our Lord. Amen.

---

[46] Macquarrie, *Legends*, p.389
[47] Towill, *The Saints of Scotland*, p.165

38

Saint Adomnán (Adamnan)
Abbot, 627-704

This saint, whose name means "wee Adam" was born in the Donegal area of Ireland c. 627 and was said to belong to the same family as St Columba. Probably more is known about this Gaelic Saint than many others, as accounts of his missionary life and death including the *Vitae Columbae,* have survived to the present day.[48] Bede, who may possibly have met Adomnán, mentioned his mission and writings in some detail in his *Ecclesiastical History of the English People.*[49]

Elected Abbot of Iona at the age of 55, Adomnán held the appointment until his death in 704. He was not only a successful and prominent churchman of his time, but was also renowned as a traveller, scholar, lawmaker and politician. As an ecclesiastical politician, Adomnán was responsible for securing the royal burials on Iona of Egfirth, King of Northumbria in 685, followed by Brude MacBile, King of the Picts, in 693.[50] In 697, he was a prominent participant at the Synod of Birr, attended by chieftains and clerics from Ireland, Dál Riata and Pictland, and was instrumental in obtaining the passing of the Cáin Adomnáin or "The Law of the Innocents". This law exempted women and other non-combatants from being compelled to serve on the battlefield and also forbade the killing at any time of women, children and clerics.

In 701, Adomnán travelled to Northumbria, to seek the release of Irish captives along with reparation for injuries committed by King Aldfrid's subjects in the Province of Meath.[51]

St Adomnán is most renowned for his life of St Columba,

---

[48] A.O. & M.O. Anderson (eds), *Adomnán of Iona, Life of Saint Columba* (London, 1995)
[49] Bede, *Ecclesiastical History,* pp. 293-297
[50] Towill, *The Saints of Scotland,* p.1
[51] Barrett, *Calendar,* p.136

which has been called by a competent judge "the most complete piece of such biography that all Europe can boast of, not only at so early a period, but throughout the whole Middle Ages".[52] He is also the author of one of the earliest European treatises on the Holy Land. Though the saint died at Iona, his relics were carried to Ireland, but were restored at some point to Iona, as they were being venerated there in 1520.

So why has Adomnán of Iona been included in this booklet and where are the connections with the Diocese of Aberdeen? He was one of the most popular of the Scottish saints, and many churches were dedicated to him, his influence spreading also to the North.

Few names have passed through such various transformations in the course of ages as that of Adomnán, and he is known under the forms of Aunan, Arnty, Eunan, Ounan, Teunan (St Eunan), Skeulan, Eonan, Ewen, and even Arnold.

The chief Adomnán attributions in the Diocese were at Aboyne and Forvie in Aberdeenshire; Abriachan in Inverness-shire; and at Forglen (The Teunan Kirk) in Banffshire. At Aboyne there were places known as the "Skeulan Tree" and "Skeulan Well", and Damsey (Adamnan's Isle) in Orkney, takes its name from this saint.

Barrett tells us that at "Firth-on-the-Spey", part of the pre-reformation Diocese of Moray, there was a very ancient bronze bell, long kept on a windowsill of the old church.[53] Tradition relates that when moved it produced a sound similar to the words "Tom Eunan, Tom Eunan" until it was restored to its original locus, which stood on the hill bearing that name: Tom Eódhnain, near Loch Insh, Kingussie, south of Inverness. The Insh church is dedicated to St Adamnan and the bell still hangs in an alcove. Also in the little church is a modern window engraved with a copy of the St John's Cross on Iona.

---

[52] John Pinkerton, *Vitae sanctorum scotiae* (1789)
[53] Barrett, *Calendar,* p.137

St Adomnán's feast may be celebrated on 23rd September, but it does not feature in the current Liturgical Calendar for the Diocese of Aberdeen.

Prayer (from the Aberdeen Breviary):

O God, who has made this day joyful in honour of Saint Adomnán, your confessor and abbot: grant us, we pray, that through his intercession and merits we may rejoice before the presence of your divine majesty in eternal glory. Through Christ Our Lord. Amen.

Saint Maelrubha
Abbot, 642-722)

St Maelrubha, through his mission as an influential evangelizer and monk, provides a historical link between the modern dioceses of Aberdeen and Argyll and the Isles. Like many a Celtic saint, the story of his life is somewhat complex, confusing and lacking irrefutable historical evidence, but is interesting nonetheless.

According to tradition, Maelrubha was born near Derry in 642. He was related to the noble Niall of the Nine Hostages through his father Elganach, and through his maternal lineage he was of Pictish stock, thereby combining the branches of the Celts who at that time were engaged in bitter rivalry between Ireland and Alba (Scotland). Although he was of noble birth, Maelrubha became a monk as a youngster at Bangor under the rule of his kinsman, St Comgall.

Around 671, he followed the Celtic monastic tradition of *peregrinatio*, which required the practitioner to cut himself off from his homeland to travel to a distant place, to gain a deeper relationship with God in order to discern and follow His will. Maelrubha crossed the sea to Scotland and after two years of missionary work, he founded a monastery at Applecross in Wester Ross, where he was abbot for more than fifty years. He is also reputed to have founded a church on a small island in Loch Maree, both loch and island taking their names from the saint.

St Maelrubha acquired a great reputation for holiness and evangelization, throughout not only the west coast and isles of northern Scotland but also in Easter Ross and the surrounding area.

There is an old Scottish tradition, quoted by the Aberdeen Breviary, which tells of a Viking attack at "Urquhart" in Ross-shire, where for three days Maelrubha was left lying severely wounded while the angels consoled him until he died.[54] Boyle disputes his title to martyrdom, however, in his 1981 article, suggesting confusion with another martyr.[55] Another story relates how he was slain by Danes near Bettyhill, where he had a cell. More reliable sources, from contemporary Irish annals, simply record that he died at Applecross, aged 80.

Often the saint's name at these dedications varies, such as: Samareirs (St Mareirs at Forres), Summaruff (St Maruff, at Fordyce), Maree, Mulruy, Mury, and many others.

The devotion to this saint is attested by the numerous dedications of churches to his memory, and Barrett tells us that antiquarians enumerate at least twenty-one of these.[56] The principal sites were Applecross (where he was buried), Urquhart (the reputed place of his martyrdom), Forres, Fordyce, Keith, Contin, Gairloch, Loch Maree, Portree, and Arisaig.

In the early 20th century, near the church at Applecross, one could find *Maelrubha's River* and the martyr's grave called *Cladh Maree*, with the saint's seat *Suidhe Maree* located a couple of miles away. There are also various other traces of him in the place names around the neighbourhood, while many dedications formerly supposed to be in honour of Our Lady are now identified as those of St Maelrubha under the title of Maree: evidenced by the traditional Gaelic pronunciation of their respective names.

In Loch Maree, Wester Ross, there is a small island named Innis Maree on which stand the ruins of an ancient chapel and grave, and nearby is a deep well whose miraculous water was once renowned for curing mental illnesses. There was also an adjacent oak tree studded with nails, to each of which were formerly attached scraps of pilgrim's clothing.

At Balnakeil, Durness, in Sutherland, the most north-westerly site in the diocese, lie the ruins of a little church, whose

---

[54] A. Macquarrie, *The Saints of Scotland* (Edinburgh: John Donald, 1997), pp. 197, 383

[55] A. Boyle, "Notes on Scottish Saints" (Innes Review 32, Issue 2 1981) pp.72-73

[56] Barrett, *Calendar*, p.67-71

original foundation was made by St Maelrubha in 722.

Within the diocese of Aberdeen, annual fairs were held on the saint's feast day in bygone years at Forres in Moray, Fordyce in Banffshire, and Lairg in Sutherland (at the latter place under the name of Saint Murie).

The town of Keith in Banffshire was known previously as Kethmalruf, or "Keith of Maelrubha"; and at Contin in Easter Ross the ancient church was dedicated to the saint with an annual fair called Feille Maree (familiarly known as the "August Market") which was later transferred to Dingwall.

Probably the oldest Christian artefact in Blairs Museum, Aberdeen, is an ancient Celtic bell, attributed to St Maelrubha and recorded as coming originally from Applecross. It is thought to have been hung on a tree and struck to call people to prayer, rather than having a clapper for ringing.

St Maelrubha's feast was formerly observed in Scotland on 27th August, but has in recent times been celebrated on 21st April, and features in the Liturgical Calendar for the Diocese of Aberdeen, where it is observed as an Optional Memorial.

Prayer (from the Aberdeen Diocesan Calendar):

Lord,
you sent Saint Maelrubha
to preach the Gospel by word and example
to a people still in darkness.
Give us his courage and zeal
to bring the light of Christ to those around us,
that we may enjoy with them
the full vision of your glory
in the sanctuary of heaven.
Through Christ our Lord. Amen.

Saint Nathalan (Nechtan)
Bishop, died 678

Tradition relates that St Nathalan was born of Pictish nobility at Tullich, near Ballater in modern Aberdeenshire. As a young man, he was well known for his great holiness, and was "imbued by liberal studies".[57] He dedicated himself to contemplation, which he expressed by spending much time manually cultivating the land – a voluntary penitential means of subduing his passions.

There are many miracles attributed to him, and there is a story concerning the occasion when he gave away all his corn and possessions to the poor in time of famine. As there was a severe shortage of grain, he had the fields sown with sand (as directed in a divine revelation), and the people were rewarded with a plentiful harvest.

In another season, however, when his crops failed to produce as he expected, he blamed God and lost his faith. Ashamed of his behaviour, Nathalan imposed a penance on himself by locking his arm to his side and wearing a heavy chain on his leg. He threw the key into the River Dee at a place known as "The Pool of the Key" and vowed not to free himself until he had made a pilgrimage to the shrines of Sts Peter and Paul in Rome.[58] Whilst in Rome, he bought a fish for a meal and found the key in its stomach; this he took as a divine indication to discontinue his penance.

After a few more years spent in divine contemplation in Rome, Nathalan was ordained bishop by the Pope and returned to his native region in Scotland where he built several churches at his own expense in Bethelnie (in the old parish of Meldrum), Cowie,

---

[57] Macquarrie, *Legends*, p. 21
[58] Barrett, *Calendar*, p. 11

45

near Stonehaven, and also at Tullich where he had spent his early years.

Nathalan's pilgrimage to the tombs of the apostles Peter and Paul in Rome fitted within the traditional definition of pilgrimages that were "generally, journeys to holy places undertaken from motives of devotion in order to obtain supernatural help or as acts of penance or thanksgiving".[59]

St Nathalan died an old man on 8th January 678, and it is said that his body was carried in procession from Bethelnie to Tullich. At the ancient Tullich church, the top lintel of one of the doors consists of a huge slab of granite with a carved antique cross, which is thought to have been a portion of the saint's tomb.[60]

There was previously an annual holiday held on his feast day, with no work permitted, markets being held at Cowie and Oldmeldrum, called "Saint Nathalan's fair". The ancient name of Meldrum was Bothelney, a corruption of Bothnethalen, meaning "habitation of Nathalan". At the end of the 19th century, "Nauchlan's Well" could still be seen near the ruins of the old church.[61] Associated with Cowie is an old rhyme:

> "Atween the kirk and the kirk ford
> There lies Saint Nauchlan's hoard."

Nathalan became the patron saint of Deeside, and like most saints of the Celtic era, his sanctity was popularly acclaimed and not subjected to the strict canonization process of later centuries.

St Nathalan's feast is celebrated on 8th January and features in the current Liturgical Calendar for Scotland as an Optional Memorial in the Diocese of Aberdeen. It is celebrated as a Solemnity in Ballater where the Catholic church is still named for him..

---

[59] F.L. Cross, & E.A. Livingstone, (eds), *The Oxford Dictionary of the Christian Church, 3rd edn,* (Oxford: Oxford University Press, 1997), p.1288.
[60] Barrett, *Calendar,* p. 11
[61] Barrett, ibid.

Prayer (from the Aberdeen Diocesan Calendar)**:**

Loving Father,
we recall the example of your bishop, Saint Nathalan.
Grant, at his intercession,
that we may so follow him
in his love for the poor
that we may share with him
the heavenly company of your Son,
Through Christ our Lord. Amen.

Saint Boniface (Curetan)
Bishop c. 7th century

One of the most confusing and contradictory stories among the legends of saints with dedications within the diocese of Aberdeen has to that of St Boniface (or Curetan) whom the Bollandists, in a lost Utrecht manuscript, identify as "Curetan from Alba, surnamed Boniface". It is claimed that he was an Israelite from the line of Rhadia, sister to the apostles Andrew and Peter (no such scriptural evidence exists about Rhadia).[62]

Another ancient legend linked to Boniface, which is likely to be a distortion of facts, identifies him with Pope Boniface who allegedly resigned the papacy and came from Rome with a large retinue of followers to evangelize the inhabitants of Pictland. The story recounts that after baptizing Nechtan, King of the Picts, and the subsequent adoption of Christianity by his subjects, Boniface (Curetan) was given the place of baptism with all its parochia in service of his ministry (probably around the Forfar area).

It is possible that these claims were made in connection with the "Romanising" of the Pictish church under King Nechtan because Bede's testimony tells of the king adopting the Roman computation of Easter in the year 710.[63]

It has been alleged that this holy man of God preached the Gospel to the Picts and Scots, consecrated 150 bishops, ordained 1000 priests, founded 150 churches, and baptized 36,000 persons within a period of some 60 years.

During that time, Boniface built a noteworthy church dedicated to St Peter at Rosemarkie (the Catholic church now in neighbouring Fortrose is dedicated to Sts Peter and Boniface), and from there performed "apostolic deeds", that included the curing of blindness, deafness, leprosy, and driving out demons. The

---

[62] Macquarrie, *Legends*, p.331.
[63] W F Skene, *Celtic Scotland, a history of Ancient Alban.* (Edinburgh, 1886) p229-32

legend tells of him also reviving seven dead men and redeeming many captives.[64] He was later ordained bishop of the Diocese of Ross, and the cathedral, of which the South Aisle still stands (in Fortrose) and which replaced the primitive building raised by him at Rosemarkie, was subsequently named in his honour.

Alternatively, the Boniface of Fortrose's dedication may be the Boniface born in Crediton, Devon, who then worked in Europe.

The Aberdeen Breviary informs us that he died on 16th March at the age of 84, "full of grace and virtue". His feast was kept on that date.

Prayer (from the Aberdeen Breviary):

O God, who entrusted Saint Boniface, your bishop, to rule the See of St Peter the Apostle for seven years, grant, we pray, that by his merits and prayers, we may obtain the eternal help of your mercy. Through Christ our Lord. Amen.

---

[64]Macquarrie, *Legends*, p. 332.

St Donnan/Donan
Abbot and Confessor, c.7th century

Unfortunately, much of the medieval Life of Donnan is lost, and what little we know of him is limited to the brief comments in such ancient martyrologies as Tallaght, Donegal and Oengus, and the Aberdeen Breviary (although there is no mention of his martyrdom here). The place and date of his birth are not known but he was possibly contemporary with St Columba; and it is presumed he was Irish and crossed to Galloway when he was a young adult. Rev. Archibald Black Scott asserts that St Donnan headed a very large mission into Scotland that was quite independent of Iona; and although this mission came from Ireland, there are indications that the head and members were not Dalriadic Scots.[65]

Scott also states that owing to the differences of language, and the unfriendly relationship between the Dalriads and the Northern Picts, it is evident that Donnan's mission was not carried out from Iona. On the contrary, the names, traditions, character, and chronology of certain churches of the group indicate that they originated from St Donnan, who sent his Missionaries from his *muinntir* (monastic community) on the Ulligh, or Helmsdale River, near modern Kildonan in Sutherland. In this area, there are believed to have been eight churches founded by St Donnan. For example, Fordyce in Banffshire and Strathmore in Caithness are separated by the whole breadth of the Moray Firth, but churches were founded in each place by monks of St Donnan's *muinntir* – Fordyce by Talorcan, and Strathmore by Ciaran.[66]

By plotting places bearing his name on the map, one can discern a logical route of missionary progression northwards, and although the only St Donnan's east of the Great Glen is at Auchterless in Aberdeenshire, it has been suggested that he had a

---

[65] Published in the Transactions of the Scottish Ecclesiological Society, vol i, part iii. Rev. Archibald Black Scott, DD. Aberdeen. 1906.
[66] Martyrology of Tallaght

special connection with this local church as his "bachail" or staff was kept there until the Reformation.

There is a story that tells how St Donnan initially visited Iona to ask St Columba, to be his *annam cara* ("soul friend"), but Columba declined, claiming to have seen "the red cloak of martyrdom around him" and telling Donnan he was destined for sainthood. It is interesting to note that this is a most unusual prophecy as there is no previous indication, or record, of red martyrdom in the Christian mission to either the Gaelic, or Pictish areas.

Donnan evangelized the Isle of Eigg after travelling throughout north-west Pictland and finally established a *muinntir* on the fertile sloping land near Poll nam Partan on the south-east side of Eigg.[67]

According to some of the Irish annals, Donnan was martyred together with fifty-two monks of his community during Mass on Easter Sunday in 617, when they were murdered by invading Norsemen. The Martyrology of Donegal states that "he was beheaded and fifty-two of the monks with him" while that of Oengus suggests that the building was set on fire and they all perished in the flames. The Martyrology of Tallaght goes on to name each of the monks who were martyred. The traditional year of the massacre was 617 or 618.

In 2012, an archaeological dig on the island of Eigg unearthed the remains of St Donnan's monastery. The dig at Kildonnan Graveyard on the south-east side of the island succeeded in identifying the likely oval sub-circular enclosure and ditch belonging to Donnan's original 7th century monastic settlement. In addition, Pictish pottery and the remains of other 7th century activity from the same period were found in the graveyard. Professor John Hunter, a forensic archaeologist who led the excavation from the University of Birmingham, thought that area had been a special place for worship and burial throughout time,

---

[67] Towill, *Saints of Scotland*

dating back some 4,000 years.[68] A moving epitaph to this saint is found in a traditional song from the Western Isles:

> "Early gives the sun greeting to Donnan,
> Early sings the bird the greatness of Donnan,
> Early grows the grass on the grave of Donnan,
> The warm eye of Christ on the grave,
> The stars of the heavens on the grave.
> No harm, no harm to Donnan's dust."[69]

Surely now is the time for the mission of St Donnan and his monks to be more prominent in the story of Christianity in Scotland, and for them to be recognised as proto-martyrs of the Scottish Church.

His Feast may be celebrated on 17th April.

Prayer (from the Aberdeen Breviary):

Almighty and everlasting God, because we lift up our souls to you, forget the failings of our youth, we pray, at the intercession of Saint Donnan, your confessor and abbot: and mercifully deign to pardon us if we negligently go astray. Amen.

---

[68] Article in *Scotsman* Newspaper by Alistair Munro, 14 August 2012
[69] McLeod, K.(ed). Songs of the Hebrides, and other Celtic songs from the Highlands of Scotland. London: Boosey & Co, 1909. Vol.2.

St Talorcan (Talarican, Talorgan, or Tarquin)
Confessor and Bishop, Patron of Fordyce, c. 7th century

Once again, we encounter a saint with a variety of names but we can relate him to one particular hagiography. In his introduction to his superb *Legends of Scottish Saints*, Allan Macquarrie asserts that there are examples of certainly (or probably) Pictish saints who are identified as Irish, or of continental origin, in the Aberdeen Breviary. There is no doubt whatsoever that there was a conscious Gaelicisation of the Church around the 10th century, with churchmen in Pictland being rebranded as Gaels, and Talorcan seems to have suffered this fate. Accordingly, the Aberdeen Breviary claims that he is of Irish noble stock and is one of the Irish missionaries to Scotland, although there is no mention of him in the Irish calendars. Clearly, however, his name is of Pictish origin. He spent most of his fruitful ministry in the mission fields of Northern Pictland, leading by example and preaching, and it is related that there were many healings of diseases and miracles through the merits of this holy man.

Like other saints of this age, Talorcan was said to have been "decorated with Episcopal insignia with great mysteries" by St Gregory for the conversion of unbelieving peoples. Talorcan was indeed a most holy man whose life "was in accordance with the sacrament of atonement, and who presented daily sacrifices to almighty God". Although by today's standards his life could be regarded as one of stern discipline, he was certainly regarded as possessing desirable personal qualities that attracted people of his time.

One of the most eye-catching villages in Banffshire is Fordyce (near Banff), and in its centre, just a short distance north of Fordyce Castle, are found the remains of one of the most fascinating ruined churches you are likely to encounter anywhere in Scotland. It is dedicated to the area's first bishop, Talorcan, who established an early church here towards the end of the sixth century, and his memory is preserved both in the dedication of the

53

church and in the name of St Tarquin's Well, a healing well whose traces can still be seen beside a nearby burn. It is said that after his death, St Talorcan's Day was celebrated here on 30th October each year where a fair was held on his feast and during the octave. Sadly such feast days and fairs are held no more.

In addition to his association with the church in Fordyce, Talorcan's reputation is shown by the numerous dedications in his name: from the large district of Kiltarlity in Inverness-shire that takes its name from the saint, and in which Beauly Priory was situated; across westwards to the church and burial-ground known as Ceilltarraglan that once existed on the plain above the rocks to the north of Loch Portree in the Isle of Skye; and possibly beyond to the island of Taransay in the Outer Hebrides where we find *Eaglais Tarain*, or Church of Tarran, where women were laid to rest. Tarran may be an alternative name for Talorcan but the Aberdeen Breviary associates it also with Ternan. Names often differ, depending on location.

The feast of St Talorcan may today be celebrated on 30th October.

Prayer (from the Aberdeen Breviary):

Almighty and everlasting God, fill our hearts, we pray, through the intercession and merits of Saint Talorcan, your confessor and bishop, with unquenchable love for you, which the floods of our sin can never overcome in us. Through Christ our Lord. Amen.

Saint Fiacre (Fittick/Fotin)
Abbot, 7th century

It is somewhat difficult to know where to start when relating the life of St Fiacre (or Fittick). Some say that he was born near Kilkenny into a noble Irish family around 590, where a hermitage and holy well frequented by pilgrims into the 19th century was named after him. Others suggest that he may have been born a son of the Dalriadan King Eugene IV, and raised on Iona. What is certain is that he went to France, and Scottish tradition suggests he was sent back by the Bishop of Meaux to the North of Scotland to bring Christianity to the Picts. On his journey home, Fiacre was swept overboard from his ship during a storm and was washed ashore at Nigg Bay, near Aberdeen, where he refreshed himself from a well, which took his name, and built a church. It has been suggested that Fiacre was a missionary for a time in Scotland before ending his days at Breuil, near Meaux, in France, where he became famous for miracles both before and after his death.

The Breviary of Aberdeen contains much of the office for St Fiacre's feast; however, it adds no specific details of his legend in Scotland but is mainly concerned with his monastic foundation in Meaux. Macquarrie strongly disagrees with Forbes that the dedication at Torry (Nigg) was to St Fiacre of Meaux. The Martyrology of Aberdeen on 23 December has the following: *Sancti Fotini episcopi et martyris apud Neyg Sancti Andree diocesis* ("of St Photinus, bishop and martyr at Nigg in the Diocese of St Andrews"). Macquarrie, however, suggests that the original commemoration of St Fittick's church was to neither Fiacre nor Photinus (1st century Bishop of Lyons), and that possibly the original Fittick was in fact a local Pictish saint who has been misidentified with a continental saint and "depictified".[70]

If evidence is needed of the saint's residence in the neighbourhood of Nigg on the opposite bank of the Dee from

---

[70] Macquarrie, *Legends*, p.410

Aberdeen at some time in his life, for centuries there was a clear spring and remains of a well nearby on Balnagask Headland, now lost to coastal erosion. This holy well's healing powers were renowned and frequented, especially on the first Sunday of May. Though the well survived the ravages of the Reformation, it was felt necessary to impose severe penalties on those who believed in its efficacy, as we read in the 1630 records of the Kirk Session of Aberdeen – "Margrat Davidson, spous to Andro Adam, fined £5 for sending her child to be washed at St Fiackre's Well and leaving an offering."[71] One can still visit the burial ground and roofless ruins of the church, rebuilt in 1242 and again in the early 18th century, dedicated to St Fittick.

The church of Nigg was within the diocese of St Andrews. It was bestowed by King William the Lion on the abbey of Arbroath at the time of its foundation. Under the designation of "Nyg ultra le moneth" ("beyond the Mounth", i.e. the Grampian Mountains), the rebuilt church was consecrated by Bishop David de Bernham on 30th July 1242. One of the caves along the coast of the parish has received the name of Holy Man's Cove from a tradition that it was occupied by a hermit, but there does not seem any reason to regard its inmate as the founder of the ancient church.

In addition to his cult at Nigg, there are some traces where his name is found in various forms. It has been conjectured that St Figgat's Stone in Inverallan Churchyard, outside Grantown-on-Spey, is called after him. It bears an antique cross with a stem about fifteen inches long incised on both sides, and is alternatively styled the Priest's Stone. If St Fiacre's name was attached to it, then he was probably associated with the now vanished church whose foundations were dug up many years ago. It is also alleged that St Fiacre may have had a chapel in Fortingall parish, Perthshire, where there are two names that a Mr Charles Stewart considers to be reminiscent of him. These are Linne-a-Fhiachre, i.e. St Fiacre's Pool, on Allt-Odhar, and Clach-ma-luchaig, a large

---

[71] William Robbie, *Aberdeen: Its Traditions and History* (D. Wyllie, Aberdeen 1893), p. 119.

St Ninian's Isle, Shetland

St Erchard's Church, Kincardine O'Neil

St Drostan's Well, Aberdour, near Banff

St Brendan,
Birnie Kirk,
near Elgin

Looking
towards
Kessock from
Inverness.

St Machar's Cathedral,
Aberdeen

St Moluag's, Mortlach,
Dufftown

St Medan's Chapel, Philorth, Fraserburgh

St Fumac's well, Drummuir

St Marnan's chair, Old Marnoch Church, near Aberchirder

St Maelrubha's Church, Balnakiel, Durness

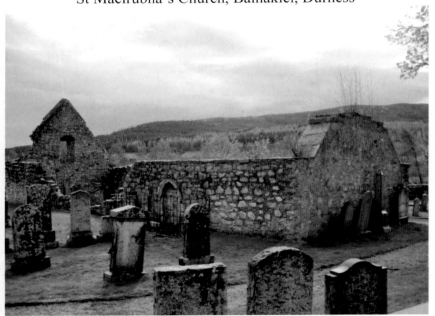

St Nathalan's, Tullich, near Ballater

St Nathalan's, Cowie, near Stonehaven

Fortrose Cathedral

St Adamnan's Chapel, Nether Leask, near Ellon

Strath of Kildonan

St Talorcan's, Fordyce

St Fittick's, Nigg, Aberdeen

St Colm's well, Portsoy

St Colman's, Portmahomack, Easter Ross

St Tredwell's (Triduana) Chapel, Papa Westray, Orkney

St Congan's Church, Turriff, Aberdeenshire

Fergus, formerly in parish
church, Wick

St Manire's stone,
Rhynabaich, Crathie

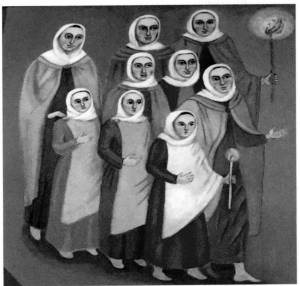

The Nine Maidens, Mural, St Mary's Cathedral, Aberdeen

Kinneddar Kirk, Lossiemouth

St Sunniva, St Sunniva Hermitage, Unst, Shetland

St Olaf altar frontal, Nidaros Cathedral, Trondheim, Norway

Fearn Collegiate Church, Tain

Shrine of St Duthac, Tain

Eilean Donan Castle, Loch Duich, Dornie

St Magnus' Cathedral, Kirkwall, Orkney

Dornoch Cathedral

St Gilbert window,
Dornoch Cathedral

St John Ogilvie,
St Thomas', Keith

St Mary MacKillop
window, St Mary's,
Inverness.

boulder situated at Balnald Beg, not far from the pool. Regarding the latter, Mr Stewart says, "My idea is that the real name is Clach-mo-Futtack. The Celtic name of Fiacre is Futtack, which with the usual honorific *mo* before it becomes Mofuttack. There is one other circumstance which connects Fiacre with Fortingall, and which naturally accounts for his having found his way there, that his tutor, St Conan, is commemorated in the parish of Fortingall at Kilchonan in Rannoch."[72]

Though we may never know who the true St Fittick was, someone of that name, however, created a lasting impression on the people of Nigg (Torry), Aberdeen, and Meaux in France, and his memory lives on in places bearing his name. His feast day is given as August 30th.

Prayer (from the Aberdeen Breviary):

O Lord, graciously bestow your mercy upon us, through the intercession of Saint Fiacre, your confessor: and through his support be favourable towards us sinners. Through Christ our Lord. Amen.

---

[72] J. M. Mackinlay, *Ancient Church Dedications in Scotland*, pp.332-335 (Douglas, Edinburgh, 1914)

St Colmán
Bishop, 676

Colmán is one of a group of saints, named Colmán, Colm, or Colmoc, whose names were prevalent in Ireland, Scotland and England, and it is probably true that this has led to much confusion concerning their cults, lives and deaths, resulting in much difficulty in knowing the truth concerning each saint as found in the various calendars on different dates. There are more than 130 saints bearing this name mentioned in Irish ecclesiastical records alone, and it is quite conceivable that their hagiographies have become intermixed.

A feast day for Colmán is noted in the Aberdeen Breviary as 18th February and in the Martyrology of Tallaght St Colmán of Moray is celebrated (one of the very few Pictish saints explicitly linked to Scotland). Macquarrie opines that it is possible that Colmán of Lindisfarne and Colmán of Moray are one and the same, as the Martyrology of Tallaght's Colmán indicates the existence of a cult in the north of Scotland for Colmán of Lindisfarne. It still does not explain, however, why the commemoration date falls on 18th February unless there is some significance in it falling the day after that of St Finnan who was Colmán of Lindisfarne's predecessor in that See.

Here, therefore, we refer to the Colmán who is the monk of Iona, chosen to succeed St Finnan as the third Bishop of Lindisfarne during a period of much controversy on our islands as to the correct calculation of Easter. The Roman system of computation was adopted gradually throughout the Church in the 6th century; however, the Church in Celtic areas was very reluctant to change the ancient method. This resulted in situations when the Church in Ireland and Britain was celebrating Easter, whilst elsewhere Lent was still being observed.

To bring about uniformity a synod was held at Whitby to allow advocates of both systems the opportunity of stating their views and presenting their case. When St Wilfrid produced convincing arguments for the acceptance of the Roman computation, it was agreed for that computation to become the norm for the Church throughout the land. It took many years, however, before the reform was completely implemented. St Colmán found so much difficulty in bringing himself to give up the old computation that he resigned his See, after ruling it for three years only, and with those of the Lindisfarne monks who held the same views he retired to Iona.

It is said that Colmán later founded a church in honour of St Aidan at Tarbet in Easter Ross; this was afterwards, however, called by his own name. The *Martyrology of Aberdeen* states that Colmán was *sepultus dyocesi Rossensi aput Terbert*, "buried in the Diocese of Ross at Tarbet", perhaps at the early Pictish monastery at Portmahomack (between the Dornoch and Moray Firths) , which contains in its name a version of the name Colmán.[73]

In another version, there is some evidence that Colmán spent some years in Scotland and that, after a short stay at Iona, he returned to Ireland and founded a monastery at Innisbofinn, an island off the west coast, initially populating it with the monks who had accompanied him from Lindisfarne. It is there that he also had transferred most of St Aidan's relics. After this, a new foundation was made in Mayo for English monks only, known as "Mayo of the Saxons". The saint oversaw both monasteries until his death at Innisbofinn, where he was buried.

St Colmán's feast may be held on February 18th.

Prayer (from the Aberdeen Breviary):

Almighty God, grant us, we pray, constant perseverance in your holy service: and with the gentle intercession of your holy bishop and confessor Saint Colmán near us, may we be able to serve you worthily in glory. Through Christ our Lord. Amen.

---

[73] Macquarrie, *Legends*, p. 337

St Triduana
Abbess and Virgin, 4th - 8th century

St Triduana is something of a rarity when we look at the hagiography of saints in Scotland, and even more so when we investigate those who had a connection with the modern diocese of Aberdeen – there are very few women saints from our country on record for any period or place.

According to legend, after arriving from Colossae in Greece with St Rule (in the 4th century) or with St Boniface (in the 8th century), she settled to a life of prayer in a hermitage at Rescobie (Angus) with her companions. The Aberdeen Breviary tells us that she came to the unwelcome attention of Nechtan, a Pictish king who sent a message saying that he desired "the sight of her most distinguished eyes". To rid herself of his importunities, as the legend relates, Triduana bravely plucked out her beautiful eyes, her chief attraction, and sent them to her admirer. Thereafter she was associated with curing eye disorders.

It is known that Triduana was revered in various parts of Scotland, and like other saints, her name has undergone changes in the different places as to be almost unrecognisable, being found under the various forms of Traddles, Tredwell, Tradwell, Trallew, and Trallen.

The Norse version of her name was Trøllhaena and as such she features in the *Orkneyinga Saga*. When William the Lion was king of Scotland, Earl Harald came to Scrabster (1201-2) where Bishop John of Caithness had his residence. Bishop John had refused to exact from the people an annual levy of one penny for every inhabited house – this house tax Harald had assigned to papal funds ("Peter's Pence"). Accordingly, Harald took his revenge on the Bishop, ordering him to be blinded and his tongue to be cut out. The Saga writer relates that during the torture John prayed "to the holy virgin Trøllhaena", and that later he "was brought" to her "resting place" where he regained his sight and speech. The description "resting place", led to general acceptance of Bishop John having journeyed from Scrabster to Restalrig in Edinburgh. [74]

It is, therefore, interesting to consider the tradition of a chapel to Triduana having existed in ancient times at Ballachly, roughly twenty miles from Scrabster. Now, visitors to the site at Ballachly find an overgrown burial ground in the midst of an extensive moor but close to an oasis of well cultivated farmland and a farm steading. Beside Loch Stemster there is a group of ancient standing stones with a gate leading to rough tracks to Ballachly farm, and nearby the walled and tree shaded Ballachly burial ground. Here stood the chapel of Triduana in medieval Caithness. Part of the adjoining land was known in ancient times as *Croit Trølla*, the croft of St Trøllhaena. Could it possibly be that this Caithness shrine possessed, as was common practice in medieval times, a relic, a bone of St Triduana, and so would have qualified for the description "a resting place" of the saint? If only the writer of the *Orkneyinga Saga* had named "the resting place of the holy Trøllhaena" to which Bishop John of Caithness went "to mend" his "ene". [75]

Among the saint's other dedications there is a chapel in the parish of Loth; a short distance north of Brora is Kintradwell, and near the island of Papa Westray in Orkney is St Tredwell's Loch, where the sick would wash in its curative waters. On a small peninsula on the east side of the loch there are the ruins of a small building known as St Tredwell's Chapel. We know also that relics of this saint were previously honoured at the cathedral in Aberdeen, and her tomb at Restalrig on the outskirts of Edinburgh was a favourite place of pilgrimage before the Reformation. Sadly, her tomb was desecrated and destroyed around 1560.

At Restalrig, in 1907, an octagonal building covered with a mound of earth on which trees had rooted (thought to have been a

---

[74] Joseph Anderson, ed. *Orkneyinga Saga* (Orkney: Edmonston & Douglas 1873: reprint 1973), ch. CXV.

[75] S. Cowper, "St Triduana in Caithness" ,
http://www.caithness.org/atoz/churches/ballachly/index.htm

Chapter House in the Catholic era) was discovered full of earth and rubbish, after having served as a burial place. When cleared, a beautiful little Gothic chapel with groined roof supported by a central pillar had evidently been raised over the miraculous well of St Triduana, so much scoffed at by 16th century satirists. Covered steps led down to the water within the chapel, which must have formed an upper storey above the well. Perhaps this was "Triduana's Aisle", alluded to in ancient documents. The building has been restored after its original form, being regarded not only as a valuable monument of antiquity but also a place to be visited, and maybe in years to come it will be restored as a place of holy pilgrimage.

St Triduana's feast was celebrated on October 8th.

Prayer (from the Aberdeen Breviary):

O God, who make your faithful people glad in the glorious solemnity of Saint Triduana: cause us, we pray, through her merits to be worthy of the joys of both lives [on earth and in heaven]. Though Christ our Lord. Amen.

Saint Comgan (Congan/Coan/Cowan)
Abbot and Confessor, 8th century

Yet again we have a saint of many names (and also varying cults) who by tradition was born in Ireland, the son of a Prince of Leinster, Cellach Cualann, and a brother of the holy recluse, Kentigerna. Comgan was raised to be a future leader and warrior and, on succeeding his father, he ruled his people "as a true Christian prince should do", [76] with fairness and justice. This caused violent opposition from the neighbouring chiefs and within a couple of years he left Ireland, forsaking the trappings of royalty to become "douloi Christi", one of the servants of Christ, settling in Lochalsh, Inverness-shire, where he was able to communicate with the locals in Gaelic. He is reputed to have brought with him his sister, Kentigerna, and her son, Fillan, who also contributed to his ministry around Kilchoan. This was not very far from Maelrubha's missionary centre in Applecross, and the area was certainly full of Christian activity around this time.

Tradition has it that Comgan moved to Turriff in Aberdeenshire where he founded a Christian settlement around 735 and became abbot, building his chapel and hospital on the site where the present Scottish Episcopal parish church of St Congan is located. Some Pictish stones were found nearby which are thought to have been originally from the old church walls. Comgan lived many years as a monk in great austerity, dying an old man at Turriff, and St Fillan had the body taken for burial among the Scots and Irish nobility on Iona.

Records indicate that the Earl of Buchan founded a hospital dedicated to St Congan in 1272, consisting of a collegiate establishment for a warden, six chaplains, and the maintenance of thirteen poor husbandmen of Buchan; King Robert the Bruce later added to its endowment. Parts of the remains of this institution are

---

[76] Barrett, *Calendar*, p. 147

known locally as "The Abbey Lands", and the town of Turriff held an annual fair called "Cowan Fair" on his feast-day.

St Fillan built a church in his uncle's honour at Lochalsh, and other dedications to Comgan can be found in the north and west of Scotland including Kilchowan in Kiltearn (Ross and Cromarty); Kilchoan or Kilcongan on the island of Seil; St Coan in Strath (Skye); Kilchoan in Ardnamurchan, the most westerly village on the Scottish mainland; and in Knoydart, the Kilchoan Estate where there is a very ancient ruined church dedicated to St Comgan in this westernmost Scottish village.

St Comgan's feast may be celebrated on 13th October.

Prayer (from the Aberdeen Breviary):

O God, who adorned the pious shepherd Saint Comgan, your confessor and abbot, with shining miracles: grant, we pray, that supported by his merits and protection we may be worthy to reach eternal joys. Through Christ our Lord. Amen.

Saint Fergus
Bishop, d. c.730

Although the Aberdeen Diocesan Calendar includes St Fergus, it is disappointing to tell that the Diocese does not have a parish dedicated to this saint, whom some scholars consider as one of the earliest and foremost evangelizers of North East Scotland.

Fergus is a Pictish name and, not surprisingly, the areas covered by dedications to him seem to coincide almost exactly where the great Pictish stones are located.

This saint was obviously held in high esteem, and the number of dedications to him in this area and beyond may indicate that his primary mission territory stretched from the Tay to Caithness. Could this be the same Fergus who evangelized the Buchan area that shows indications of the cult of three other Pictish saints – Drostan, Medan and Colm –known collectively as "Drostan and his Three"; an early sixth century missionary group to the Northern Picts?[77]

Several writers comment that the account of these saints in the *Book of Deer* is probably one of many medieval attempts to emphasise the importance of Iona, Columba and the Gaelic influence on parts of Scotland that by race and culture were most certainly Pictish, and that had received the Gospel in the first wave of Christian evangelization several generations beforehand.

Another story is that, although a Pict by nationality, Fergus was a bishop in Ireland for many years, who wanted to evangelize his own land, settling in Strathearn where he founded three churches that he dedicated to St Patrick.

He then evangelized Caithness (and was recognised as the patron of Wick), and after some time he travelled to Buchan, where he built a church at Lungley or Langley, a place afterwards known as St Fergus (near Peterhead). [78] He finally moved to

[77] Towill, *The Saints of Scotland*, pp.86-87
[78] Macquarrie, *Legends,* p.358

Glamis where he founded another church, where he subsequently died and was buried.[79]

Some authors think that during his time in Ireland, Fergus may be identified as the same person as "a Pictish Bishop of Ireland" who attended the church council at Rome in 721 called by Pope Gregory II.

Macquarrie, however, opines that this may be another case of a Pict being "Hibernicised", like a number of other certainly, or probably, Pictish saints in the Aberdeen Breviary.[80]

Several dedications to this saint were found in the northern and eastern parts of Scotland including the churches at Wick and Halkirk, in Caithness; Dyce and St Fergus, in Aberdeenshire; Dalarossie, a parish on the upper river Findhorn; and his well, called "Fergan Well" located at Kirkmichael in Banffshire (famous for its miraculous cures of skin diseases).

There were also annual fairs held at Glamis on his feast-day (known as "Fergusmas") that continued for five days, and another fair at Wick – sadly our country now has very few fairs dedicated to our saints. In addition, all traces of relics belonging to St Fergus have been lost.

His head was venerated in the Abbey of Scone, where James IV provided a silver reliquary for it; his arm was preserved at the old cathedral in Aberdeen; his pastoral staff (said to calm storms on that coast) was long treasured at St Fergus in Buchan; these have also disappeared.

Barrett tells also of an ancient image of St Fergus that existed at Wick until 1613, when a local minister, who was subsequently drowned by the indignant town inhabitants for his action, destroyed it.[81]

All these bear witness to the devotion borne towards St Fergus in a bygone era, and today the feast of St Fergus is included in the Liturgical Calendar of Scotland 18th November as an optional

---

[79] M. Barrett, *Calendar*, p.171

[80] Macquarrie, *Legends,* p.358

[81] Barrett, *Calendar*, p.171

memorial in the Diocese of Aberdeen on 18th November. It is celebrated as a Solemnity in Wick.

Prayer (from the Aberdeen Diocesan Calendar):

Almighty and eternal God,
inspire us by the prayer and example
of Saint Fergus, your bishop:
that, being steadfast in faith
and fruitful in good works,
we may obtain your gift of everlasting life.
Through Christ our Lord. Amen

The Nine Maidens
8th century

The Nine Maidens are unique in Scottish hagiology by virtue of their being sisters, but occasionally we find maidens or virgins associated in groups. In the legend of St Boniface we learn of two virgins Crescentia and Triduana, who were included amongst a certain number of bishops and other clerical attendants; and in one of the legends of St Regulus reference is made to three virgins from Collossae – Triduana, Potentia, and Cineria. The Aberdeen Breviary also relates that St Brigid brought nine virgins with her when she came from Ireland to Abernethy, Scotland, where she was said to have built a "basilica".[82]

Tradition relates that during the lifetime of their father (St Donald) the maidens devoted their youth to the Religious Life, and lived with him in strict seclusion in the Glen of Ogilvy, before entering a convent when he died. The fame of the Maidens certainly spread beyond the county of Angus into areas that are located now in the Diocese of Aberdeen.

Although the church of Drumblade, near Huntly, had St Hilary as its patron, located on the lands of Chapelton in the same parish, was a chapel standing on a knoll with a cemetery dedicated to the Nine Maidens. At the foot of the knoll is a spring known as the Chapel Well. In a charter of 1624, conveying the Chapel Croft, the chapel on Chapelton is called "Ninemadinchapell". The foundations of the building and the gravestones in the churchyard were removed to build a farm steading.[83]

In Logie wood, about three miles from the church of Auchendoir, is a spring known as the Nine Maidens' Well. The parish church was dedicated to St Mary, but there may have been a chapel dedicated to the Nine Maidens near their spring, though

---

[82] Macquarrie, *Legends*, p13

[83] James Macdonald ed., *The Place-Names of West Aberdeenshire,* s.v. 'Chapelton' (Aberdeen: Spalding Club 1899)

definite evidence has not been found.[84]

There is limited information about the individual identities and lives of the maidens; however, St Mayota/Mayoc and her sisters Sts Fincana/Findchán and Findoc/Fyndoca merit a mention in the *Aberdeen Breviary* in which spiritual blessings are sought through the intercession of Blessed Mayota the Virgin.[85]

This saint is probably better known as Mayoc, as the parish of Drumoak by the River Dee is not only dedicated to her but also named after her – Drumoak signifying the ridge of St Maok or Mayoca. An alternative name for the parish was Dalmaik, and an article in the *Old Statistical Account of Scotland* says that "In this part of the country it is almost always called *Dalmaik*. The church and manse are situated by the river Dee, near a well which has still the name of *Saint Maik's Well*."[86] Before the Reformation, the patron saint's feast was celebrated with due solemnity in Drumoak church, when her virtues were fittingly made known to the parishioners.[87]

Unsurprisingly, St Fincana poses more of a problem as there is difference of opinion as to her festival day, with both 21st August and 13th October assigned to a saint of that name; some suggest that there were two Fincanas: one from the sixth century and another from the eighth.[88] Under 13th October in the *Martyrology of Donegal*, is found the name Findsech or Finnsech, Virgin of Sliabh Guaire in Gailenga, which slightly resembles that of Fincana. Located at Echt, not very far from Drumoak, there was a church dedicated to St Fincana where her feast was commemorated on 13th October.

St Findoc, venerated at one time in the Diocese of Dunblane, shares a feast day with her sister St Fincana on 13th October. A chapel dedicated to her was located on an island in Loch Awe and

---

[84] J. M. Mackinlay, "Traces of the Cultus of the Nine Maidens in Scotland".

[85] Macquarrie, *Legends*, pp.10-15, 363, 391-92

[86] Vol. iii (1790), p. 315.

[87] J. F.Mackinlay, *Traces of the Cultus of the Nine Maidens* (Aberdeen: Proceedings of the Society of Antiquaries of Scotland, 1906) p.264

[88] Collections, Aberd. and Banff, p. 636.

Barrett mentions a chapel dedicated to St Fyndoca at Findo Gask, near Dunning, in Perthshire, where a fair was once held for the octave of her feast.[89]

To conclude, it is interesting to tell that the Story of the Nine Maidens and their father had made a deep impression on the imagination of people of North East Scotland, as indicated by a salutation made in quite modern times to a Buchan farmer who had nine daughters: "James, James, good luck to you! You are as rich as Saint Donevald."[90] They are now immortalised in the murals in St Mary's Cathedral, Aberdeen, as the *Nine MacDonald Maidens*.

A feast day for the Nine Maidens is given as July 18th.

Prayer (from the Office of St Mayoc in the Aberdeen Breviary):

O God, who show forth your almighty power most to sinners by pitying them, multiply your mercy upon us, and through the intercession of St Mayoc [and her holy virgin sisters], mercifully permit us to obtain the grace of your forgiveness. Through Christ our Lord. Amen.

(or from the Office of Sts Findchán and Findoc):

Lord Jesus Christ, author of virginity, preserve the chastity of our mind and body: and through the intercession and merits of your holy virgins Findoc and Findchán, may we be joined to their holy fellowship in heaven. Amen.

---

[89] Barrett, *Calendar,* p. 148
[90] J. B. Pratt, *Buchan* (Turriff, Scotland: Heritage Press 1981), p. 206

Saint Manir/Manire/Manirus
Bishop and Confessor, 824

Again we find an obscure Pictish saint with perhaps multiple identities. There is modest information on Manir available from primary sources, so much of what follows may be a braid woven of legend, tradition, conjecture, supposition, and fact.

The Aberdeen Breviary relates that his mission was to the pagans in and around Deeside and was especially honoured not only at Crathie, Ballater, but also at Balvenie, Braemar, places linked by mountainous passes.[91] The Martyrology of Aberdeen names him bishop, and the Aberdeen Breviary account mentions in Matins Lesson 2 that much idolatry and superstition remained after the Catholic faith was received by the Scots, "because of the difference of language of that race, among whom teachers of Christ were less learned and expert in preaching and teaching".[92] After the ascendancy of the "Gaelic church" in Scotland, it became common practice to undermine the success of the early Pictish evangelizers at every opportunity. Manir is credited as being very skilled in both tongues, i.e., Pictish and Gaelic, which is not unsurprising for a bishop of that period, as he may have spent some time training with the Church in Ireland. Of even more use to him would have been his reputed mastery of the many different dialects spoken at the time.

According to one Norwegian source, St Manir (sometimes spelled Manire, Monire, Miniar or Niniar) was born around 700 in Scotland and is said to have been one of Drostan's successors at Deer, with a foundation in that district near Aberdour, but no evidence of the saint can be found at this location.[93] There is, however, some evidence that his missionary foundation was located at Rhynabaich, a knoll two miles east-north-east of the

---

[91] Macquarrie, *Legends*, p.387
[92] Macquarrie, *Legends*, p7.
[93] http://www.katolsk.no/biografier/historisk/maniskott

North Deeside Road near Crathie in Upper Deeside, in modern Aberdeenshire. A solitary standing-stone is all that remains of Manir's establishment, but local place-names such as "allt eaglais" (the burn of the church); "creag eaglais", (the hill of the church); "pollmanire" (the pool of Manire) – a deep salmon pool on the river Dee almost opposite Balmoral Castle – recall the activities of this almost forgotten saint who died in 824. Like the majority of saints of this period in Northern Pictland, although perhaps suffering some persecution, Manir did not gain a martyr's crown. He is believed to have been buried in his church at Crathie, and was especially venerated in Crathie and Balvenie on either 18th or 19th December.

Interestingly, Mackinlay states that, "The church or chapel of St Manires (or Chapel Majore, according to Alexander), who flourished in the 6th century, stood on a knoll between Lebhal and Rhynabaich (near Crathie, Upper Deeside), surrounded by a burial ground used within living memory for unbaptized children."[94] There is a standing stone which, it has been suggested by A.I. Maconnachie, may have been used as a reading desk for the chapel and was said to be the remains of a stone circle. Alexander Keith, writing in 1732, mentions "The Chappel of Hermites at Miacras or Micras" as being extant.[95]

It has been said that Manir was the last of the Pictish missionary saints evangelizing on Deeside, but could it be possible that there were two saints with similar names? In addition to the saint whose brief hagiography is above, could there be another St Manir, a 6th century successor to Drostan of Deer, who evangelized in Northern Pictland, including Balvenie and near Aberdour?

Does the little known legacy of Manir remain and have some influence in our country and its people? Crathie may well have

---

[94] J. M. Mackinlay *Ancient Church Dedications in Scotland*, (Douglas, Edinburgh 1914), p.321.
[95] Spalding Club 1847-69: A I McConnachie 1898; J Stirton 1925; W M Alexander 1952.

been a place of Christian worship since the 9th century when a church was founded on the banks of the River Dee, possibly by St Manir. A later church, dedicated to St Manire, was build in the 13th century and later still, in the early 18th century. Crathie Kirk continues to be the church where the Royal Family worship when they reside at Balmoral Castle. I wonder if they know Manir's story?

St Manir's feast may be celebrated on December 18th.

Prayer (from the Aberdeen Breviary):

To you, O Lord, we humbly pray that through the intervention of Saint Manir, your confessor and bishop, we may be able to rest with him and to live forever in heaven with you, who are the way, the truth and the life. Through Christ our Lord. Amen.

Saint Gartnait (Gerardine/Gernadius)
Confessor, d. c.934

When entering the town of Lossiemouth from the eastern approach, there is a Presbyterian church dedicated to St Gerardine situated at the top of the Stotfield hill that dominates the landscape stretching from Seatown to Branderburgh. The saint's name, derived from Gernadius which is the Latinisation of the Pictish name Gartnait, is no longer popular in Scotland. There are very few dedications to the saint throughout the nation and no parish dedicated to him in the modern diocese of Aberdeen or its predecessors.

The saint's original dedication at Kinneddar, near Drainie, was where traditionally he founded his monastery "in the same parish of Drainie where he associated himself with many fellow-soldiers in Christ, and built a church under the direction of angels" [96] Archaeological excavations have found a large quantity of Pictish and early Christian sculpture, including portions of a tomb-shrine, in the area. The Bishops of Moray once resided in nearby Kinneddar Castle.

Gartnait is described as leaving his monastery to seek the life of a hermit, and in corroboration of the tradition, a cave with an ancient Gothic doorway and window-opening, known as "Gerardine's Cave", was located intact for many centuries on the cliff known as "Holyman's Head", before being demolished in the early 19th century by a drunken sailor.

The whole cliff face, including the cave, was quarried from 1870 onwards. Sadly, there is also no remaining trace of the spring of water known traditionally as "Gerardine's Well" from which the anchorite reputedly drank all those years ago.

Tradition also tells that on stormy nights, the saint would pace the beach below his cell, lantern in hand, to warn off vessels from the dangerous rocks. This is commemorated in the old

---

[96] Barrett, *Calendar*, pp.161-162

Lossiemouth Burgh seal bearing the motto *Per noctem lux* ("light through the night") and a representation of the saint with his lantern. It is also the motto of the local school.

The Aberdeen Breviary provided six lessons and a prayer for Gartnait, claiming that this saint was of Irish nationality, but Macquarrie suggests that Gartnait was another Pictish saint whose ethnicity was altered or suppressed in the 10/11th century when Pictish churchmen were "rebranded" as Irish or Scots as part of the Gaelicisation of the Church in Scotland.[97]

Sadly, the legend of St Gartnait, monk and hermit, whose feast is on the 8th November, has been forgotten in the annals of time and is largely unknown to Christians of our era.

Prayer: (from the Aberdeen Breviary):

Almighty God, may your confessor Saint Gartnait obtain your glory for us: that we may be forever joyful standing before you with him in the light of eternal blessedness. Through Christ our Lord. Amen.

---

[97] Macquarrie, *Legends*, p.365

Saint Sunniva
10/11th Century

Elsewhere in this compilation, you will find reference to Scandinavian saints Magnus, Olaf, and Rognvald, but why should the Irish Saint Sunniva be included here as there is neither parish nor church building dedicated to her in the North of Scotland? Perhaps Sunniva may be regarded as the cement between the early evangelization efforts of the Pictish church in Orkney and Shetland, the Irish mission (via Iona), and the establishment of Christianity in Norway? The legend of the saintly Sunniva traverses the super sea-highway from Ireland to Norway, from West to East (unlike her male Viking counterparts who travel East-West), conceivably landing ashore on both Orkney and Shetland where there are traditional dedications to her sanctity. It may be of some interest that both the Roman Catholic and Orthodox Churches revere her as a saint.

Over the years, it has come to be generally accepted that Orkney and Shetland were evangelized by the early Christian missionaries when they were part of the Pictish dominions at the turn of the 7th century. Whether this was an initial evangelization, or a re-evangelization by the Columban monks from Iona is not certain. When the Norwegian settlers arrived on the islands some two centuries later, they found an established Christian church mainly with monks of Pictish origin. Although the new settlers would have been pagans, there is a suggestion that individual groups became Christian long before the conversion of Earl Sigurd on the orders of King Olaf Tryggvason in 995.[98]

An abbreviated legend of St Sunniva, as it was recorded in the Middle Ages, is presented here for your delectation. Around the time of Håkon Jarl (about 970–995), a Chieftain died in the West

---

[98] Ronald G Cant, "The Church in Orkney and Shetland and its relations with Norway and Scotland in the Middle Ages", in *Northern Scotland*, Volume 1 (First Series) Issue 1, Page 1-18, ISSN 0306-5278 Available Online Oct 2014

of Ireland, and was succeeded by his daughter Sunniva, reputed to be a beautiful and wise Christian queen, who sought advice and help from friends and subjects alike in the rule of her large territory. Her reputation attracted the attention of a group of pagan Vikings who came to propose marriage, but Sunniva had already decided to serve God alone and to lead a pure life in his honour, and had no ambition to marry any man, heathen or otherwise. This refusal led to the Vikings wreaking havoc on her realm, and many of her subjects suggested that she, with them also, should flee the country. Faithful to the Celtic Christian tradition of *peregrinatio*, they launched out into the deep in their ships, with neither sails, nor oars, nor rudder, nor any attire, weapons or armour. Sunniva placed both her own life, and the lives of her fellow voyagers, into God's hands, praying that He should navigate, and steer their way according to His will. For some time they seemed to drift on the ocean until they were finally brought to the islands on the coast of Norway, south of Stad.

Sunniva and her companions landed ashore at Selja, and remained there for a long time, serving God and one another with great love and by leading a frugal life. When the local inhabitants discovered that there were strangers on the islands, who they thought were rustlers intent on stealing their sheep, they enlisted the assistance of Håkon Jarl. Håkon Jarl responded by raising an army, and travelling to the islands ready for battle. It is said that when Sunniva and her Christian community saw the army approaching, and fearing that they were about to be attacked, they fled into their caves and prayed that Almighty God would give their souls eternal and blissful peace in Paradise. The story further tells of huge rocks falling down in front of the caves in which they had taken refuge, and the collapse of the cave roofs resulting in the deaths of the holy men and women, granting them eternal salvation as a reward for their service on earth. After Håkon Jarl had died, and Olaf Tryggvason (995-1000) had taken the throne in Norway, there were tales of strange occurrences on Selja, with a beautiful light often seen shining there. In response, Olaf, Bishop Sigurd and many men travelled to the island where they found Sunniva's uncorrupted body, as if she had just died. In 1170, her body was moved to Bergen where she rested "in a large and beautiful shrine, on the high altar of the church".[99] During the Reformation the shrine was moved to the nearby Benedictine monastery but was lost when the monastery was destroyed in 1536.

It has been claimed that the Irish princess St Sunniva is a product of the medieval imagination and never existed, and yet, Sunniva *is* real, like many other saintly legends, in the sense that she is a religious ideal not only for the people of the Middle Ages, but also for many people of our time. The communication of this ideal is the most important part of the saint's cult for the medieval church, and a story never loses in the telling, especially during a period where all books had to be written out by hand; yet, written texts could change and be adapted for a particular purpose when they were copied. This is especially true for hagiographies that were often adapted for prayerful recital in churches and monasteries. Events or details that a scribe learned from an oral source could be added to embellish the story, or shortened to emphasis the moral more clearly. Similarly, the legend of St Sunniva and the holy men and women of Selja has been passed down to us in several versions, both in Latin and in old Norse, yet despite differences in language, structure, style and content, the many versions are still closely related. Only a few medieval manuscripts have survived in Norway with the oldest versions in Old Norse as a part of the Olaf Tryggvason saga from c.1190, with a later account in the *Flateyjarbók*, an Icelandic manuscript from c.1390.[100]

An obscure phenomenon of the Celtic ecclesiastical world is found on the remote Atlantic fringes of Scotland, including the Northern and Western Isles, and Iceland, where place names containing the word *papar* (priests or monks) occur. It has been

---

[99] Else Mundals, trans. "The Legend of Sunniva", in *Flateyjarbók* (*Legender frå mellomalderen*, 1995)
[100] Saint Sunniva and the Holy Shrine, Alf Tore Hommedal and Åslaug Ommundsen, Bryggens Museum, 2011

suggested that these *papars*, Christian monastic hermits, journeyed from Ireland to remote places, as far as Iceland and the Faroe Islands via the Scottish Western Isles, Orkney and Shetland, and it is highly probable that they also followed the ocean streams to the coast of Norway. An excellent project about the Papars was undertaken by some Scottish universities at the turn of the 21st century, and has helped in a better understanding of these early Christian missionaries. Detailed reports on their findings are published on the internet and make excellent informative reading.[101]

In conclusion, it is acknowledged that although there are several medieval female hagiographies similar to that of St Sunniva, none so clearly exhibits the exercise of Celtic values through the combination of *diakonia, peregrinatio, missio ad gentes*, and martyrdom. One may argue that her Christian life contained aspects of the three types of martyrdom (Green, White and Red) promoted by the so-called "Celtic" church of her era. Green martyrdom meant staying at home and living life in total subjection to Christ – this was Sunniva's original plan; White martyrdom meant leaving home and country through love of Christ – Sunniva's exile with her companions by *peregrinatio*; and finally, Red martyrdom meant dying for the Christian faith – the response to the prayers of Sunniva and her companions. The virtue and sanctity of St Sunniva's life can be an example for all Christians in the 21st century: may she pray for us. Her feast is celebrated in Norway on July 8th.

Prayer (from the Norwegian):

Almighty God, listen with grace to our humble prayers.
Let us, who commemorate your holy martyrs Sunniva and her companions, find safety under their protection and freedom from all distress. Through our Lord Jesus Christ. Amen.

---

[101] The Papar Project, http://paparproject.org.uk/ accessed June 2016

Saint Olaf or Olave
King and Martyr, 1030

Two major saints of Norway somehow have managed to make their way into the Scottish ecclesiastical consciousness. The story of St Magnus is told elsewhere in this compilation, but Olaf's inclusion may be considered by some to be somewhat tenuous as he is, after all, the patron saint of Norway and there is little to tell of his time in our country.

Olaf's feast appears in the Martyrology on July 29th, the date that his feast was celebrated in Norway and all Scandinavian countries, but in Scotland, he was honoured on 30th March. Somewhat surprisingly, rather than a liturgy of the hours for Olaf in the Aberdeen Breviary, there is only a brief celebratory note that states:

> "If the feasts of St Olaf, martyr, and Rule, abbot, occur within Passiontide or the octave of Easter, they should be transferred, St Olaf to 29 July, on which day his passion is celebrated and St Rule to the morrow of St Michael in Monte Tumba (17 October), except in churches dedicated to them."[102]

This saint's hagiography is somewhat limited to his military successes, failures and subsequent martyrdom, rather than his sanctity and meekness. Olaf was a teenager when his father Harald, King of Norway, died, and was exiled by powerful enemies within the kingdom. He embraced the life of a Viking, and was a mercenary in England and Normandy.

It is said that Olaf travelled as far south as Gibraltar, and there dreamed that he would return home and become King of Norway. In 1015, he left England to claim the royal throne of Norway, bringing with him a number of English bishops, an indication that

---

[102] Macquarrie, *Legends*, p.411

it was his intention to convert his Kingdom to Christianity, having received Christian baptism as a youngster at Rouen, Normandy.

Olaf was renowned as a highly intelligent man, sincere in his intentions, artistically gifted (a poet) and a skilled political and military strategist and in the early days everything seemed to be going his way on his return to Norway. He was the first king to rule the entire nation effectively by creating an administrative network that kept the country together. During this period, Olaf is reputed to have embarked on many missionary excursions into pagan regions, establishing permanent Christian communities by building churches and providing resident priests according to a national plan. In addition, he introduced legal systems for both state and church ("Christian law") which became a foundation for a new national legal system based on belief in the intrinsic value of the individual, the importance of mercy and a duty to protect the weak.

Unsuccessful in making alliances with the nobles who felt threatened by the growing central authority of Olaf, and because of the peasants' major discontent concerning his manner of rule, Olaf was forced again into exile, this time to stay with his brother-in-law Grand Duke Jaroslav in Kiev, a city where Christian theology, philosophy, monasteries and art flourished. In 1030, Olaf returned to Norway for a final attempt to reclaim the throne and a decisive battle was fought at Stiklestad on 29 July, where, outnumbered and overpowered by his opponents, the King was slain.

His body was smuggled away and was buried close to where Nidaros Cathedral (Lutheran since 1537) still stands, in Trondheim. Tradition says that wondrous things began to take place shortly thereafter. There were rumours about many miraculous events, including the wounded hand of Olaf's slayer being healed when a drop of the King's blood fell on it. After a year, Olaf's body was exhumed, and with the acclamation of his subjects and the local Bishop declaring him to be a holy man, he became honoured as Norway's saint, for completing the long process of bringing Christianity and liberation to Norway.

Olaf was considered to be a just and brave monarch, fervent in the propagation of the Christian religion, though not altogether free from grievous offences against the tenets of the Church, and it was his unswerving faith, devotion and practice of penance that won him the title of saint and martyr.[103]

St Olaf's efforts to spread the Gospel in the Orkney Isles, which, along with the Shetland Isles, at that time belonged to Norway, were doubtless among the causes of devotion to him found in Scotland, with several dedications to him including: St Ollow's parish and St Ollow's Bridge (in what is now Kirkwall). St Olla's Fair, at Kirkwall, lasting for fourteen days, is described in Walter Scott's *The Pirate*.

On the South-west of Girlsta, in Shetland, is the Church of St Olla at Whiteness. Additionally, he was honoured on the Island of Lewis at Gress, north of Stornoway; and at Kirk of Cruden (Aberdeenshire), where the saint's ancient chapel was said to have been founded by Canute, there was an annual fair called St Ole's Fair dedicated to him.

Prayer (from the Norwegian):

Almighty, ever-living God, you are the crown of kings and the triumph of martyrs. We know that your blessed martyr, Olaf, intercedes for us before your face. We praise your greatness in his death and we ask you to grant us the crown of life that you have promised those who love you, through Christ our Lord. Amen

---

[103] http://www.trondheim.no/content/1117700448/The-Saint-King

Saint Duthac
Bishop (died 1065)

If you explore the town of Tain today, you may perhaps be surprised to learn that for centuries there was a shrine to St Duthac which in the middle ages drew thousands of pilgrims, and frequent visits from King James IV of Scotland and his entourage. Off the main town thoroughfare can be found three medieval church buildings for exploration. The collegiate church (erected in 1487), all that remains of the 13th century Fearn Abbey, also includes the ruins of the medieval parish church within its grounds.

Near the seashore, north-east of the collegiate church, is another ruined medieval chapel with a burial enclosure which may have been the site of an earlier Christian church and burial ground.[104]

The information in the Aberdeen Breviary about St Duthac seems to comprise the only written life of the saint, and although there no dates are mentioned there, tradition suggests he was born at the beginning of the 11th century. The breviary affirms that he was born in Tain of noble Scottish blood, and was successfully educated in the Christian faith in the local area.

It further relates a story that around this time Duthac's teacher sent him to the local smithy to get some fire. The local smith, who had a bit of a devilish spirit, took a pile of burning coals from the furnace on a shovel and threw them over Duthac, who meekly caught them, and without damage to his clothes or his body, carried them back to his teacher.[105]

There is another miracle story that tells of Duthac at a feast where one of the guests fell ill and a hungry kite flew away with both the uneaten food and a gold ring. Duthac prayed and the bird returned with the stolen food and ring – the saint kept the ring but gave the bird the food.

---

[104] Macquarrie, *Legends,* p.354
[105] Macquarrie, *Legends*, pp.74-75

After further studies in Ireland, Duthac returned to Scotland where he was consecrated bishop and enthusiastically devoted himself to the pastoral care of the people in the Moray and Ross areas. Renowned for his outstanding learning and holiness, he was constantly in great demand as a confessor.

Duthac was buried in the church at Tain, and some seven years after death his body was found to be incorrupt and was removed to a more honourable shrine in the same church. As well as many miracles attributed to him during his life, it is said that many infirm and sick people were restored to full health when they visited his grave and shrine.

St Duthac's feast is celebrated on 8th March, and features in the Liturgical Calendar of Scotland as an Optional Memorial in the Diocese of Aberdeen, and as a Solemnity in Dornie.

The tradition of pilgrimage to the sites at Tain had all but ceased, although there is a most interesting exhibition and guided tour from the museum that includes a visit to the Collegiate church. There are, however, hopeful signs of a revival of this pilgrimage, with *The St Duthac's Way*, from Tain via Aberdeen to St Andrews, now being included in the Way of St Andrews;[106] and in 2015 parishioners from Beauly went on pilgrimage to Tain to join celebrations commemorating the granting of a Papal Bull to Tain in 1492 confirming the status of the Collegiate Church.

Prayer (from the Aberdeen Diocesan Calendar):

Almighty God,
you chose Saint Duthac
to be a true shepherd of your people.
Listen to his earnest prayer,
that we may attain
the goal of our earthly pilgrimage
in the eternal abode of heaven.
Through Christ our Lord. Amen.

---

[106] www.thewayofstandrews.com

Saint Magnus
Martyr, 1075-1116)

The only other pre-Reformation Catholic cathedral in Scotland, along with Glasgow Cathedral, that remains entire and which still shelters the body of a saint is that of St Magnus which is located at Kirkwall on Orkney. His nephew Rognvald built this majestic church and the saint's miraculously preserved remains and relics were moved there in 1137 from a more humble sanctuary at Christ Church on Birsay. In all probability they stay undisturbed beneath the cathedral dedicated to Magnus.

The life story of St Magnus is described in the *Orkneyinga Saga* and a *Vita* written by Master Robert in 1137. The stories tell us that Magnus was the son of Erlend, joint Earl of Orkney with his brother Paul. Magnus Barelegs, King of Norway, appointed the young Magnus to act as his personal attendant and he accompanied the King in an expedition to pillage the Western Isles. Shortly thereafter the King's forces slaughtered the armies of the Norman Earls of Chester and Shrewsbury off the Isle of Anglesey. Magnus refused to take any part in unjust warfare and remained on board his ship, praying throughout the duration of the battle.

Soon afterwards, Magnus made his escape to the court of Malcolm III, King of Scots, where he remained for some time in safety, but continued to lament the excesses of war, atoning for the victims by penance and prayer for the rest of his days.

Around 1107, on the death of Barelegs, Magnus regained his share of Orkney but fresh contests were stirred up when Haakon, son of Paul and cousin to Magnus, laid claim to the Earldom of Orkney for himself.

In order to avoid bloodshed and war, Magnus agreed to meet Haakon on the island of Egilsay to settle the dispute in an amicable manner, but instead Haakon and his force surrounded an unarmed Magnus. Magnus became aware of the treachery too late to make any defence and prepared for the ensuing outcome by a prayer vigil and reception of the Sacraments in a church. At dawn,

Magnus courageously set out to face his adversaries and met his "barbarous death with Christian fortitude".[107]

Like many medieval saints, Magnus received the title of martyr from popular acclaim rather than by the decision of any ecclesiastical authority. As demonstrated by his story, he merited the title by shedding his blood not so much in defence of the Christian Faith as on behalf of the virtues of a Christian life, whose authenticity and intensity roused the jealous anger of his enemies.

His fair was formerly held at Watten-Wester in Caithness around the time of his feast on 16th April, known in the Middle Ages as "Magnusmas". The Diocese of Aberdeen Liturgical Calendar includes it as a Solemnity on Orkney, and an Optional Memorial throughout the remainder of the diocese.

The magnificent cathedral in Kirkwall has withstood the test of time, and remains a popular attraction for locals, pilgrims and tourists alike. On several occasions during the past 30 years, groups of Roman Catholic pilgrims and other groups have been permitted to celebrate Mass in the main cathedral sanctuary – surely more than an indication that the Ecumenical Movement continues to make steady progress in Scotland. In 1996, the Orcadian poet, George Mackay Brown, who did much to keep Magnus known through poetry and prose, died; his Requiem Mass was the first funeral Mass to be held in the cathedral since the Reformation and was celebrated, most fittingly, on April 16th.

Prayer (from Aberdeen Diocesan Calendar):

Lord,
may the martyr's crown of your servant Magnus
be our inspiration and our hope:
that, acknowledging the wonders of your power,
we may constantly give place in our hearts
to the Spirit of gentleness and peace.
Through Christ our Lord. Amen

---

[107] Barrett, *Calendar*, p. 65

Saint Rognvald (Ronald) of Orkney
c.1100-1158

Elsewhere in this compilation you can find brief accounts of the lives of Orkney's two major saints, Olaf and Magnus. It seems appropriate, therefore, that the story of Rognvald, the nephew of St Magnus, is included as the concluding episode of the establishment of Christianity on the Orkney Isles by the founding of the cathedral in Kirkwall.

Around 1100, Kali Kolsson (Rognvald), was born to Kol and Gunnhild, the sister of St Magnus, in Agder, Norway. As Magnus' nephew, Kali was a legitimate claimant to the Orkney Earldom. The Sagas tell us that Kali "was of average height, well proportioned and strong limbed, and had light chestnut hair". He was a very popular man, of more than average ability, and a renowned poet who in one of his poems claims to possess nine exceptional skills, having mastered board games, runes, reading and writing, handicrafts such as metal work, carving and carpentry, skiing, archery, rowing, music and poetry.

In 1129, he was appointed Earl of Orkney and Shetland by King Sigurd I of Norway, and was given the name Rognvald, in honour of the late Earl Rognvald Brusason, whom Rognvald's mother Gunnhild thought the most able of all the Earls of Orkney. He lived in Norway as one of the King's most trusted men. A few years later, Sigurd's successor, King Harald, ratified Rognvald's claim to the Earldom.

Rognvald then assembled a fleet and set sail for Orkney to overthrow Paul Hakonsson, the existing Earl of Orkney. After battling severe storms, Rognvald's army landed on the islands, but were met with fierce resistance from Earl Paul who did not intend to surrender his earldom. Rather than wage war on his potential subjects, Rognvald's father suggested that the earldom could be settled by a method other than war. It was proposed that Rognvald should inform the Orcadians that once he became earl, he would raise the finest church as a memorial to his saintly uncle, Magnus, a man whom the islanders venerated above all. An account of the conversation is recalled within *The Orkneyinga Saga*:

> "Build a stone minster at Kirkwall more magnificent than any in Orkney, that you'll have (it) dedicated to your uncle the holy Earl Magnus and provide it with all the funds it will need to flourish. In addition, his holy relics and the episcopal seat must be moved there."[108]

While Rognvald was capturing the hearts of the Orcadian people, it was alleged that he secretly arranged for Earl Paul to be kidnapped in Rousay and exiled from the islands. The *Orkneyinga Saga* is unclear as to the fate of the dispossessed Paul but concludes that "all men know that he (Paul) never afterwards came back to the Orkneys, nor held he any rule in Scotland". In 1136, Rognvald was hailed as Jarl, and a year later, the building of St Magnus Cathedral in Kirkwall began on a prime site by the shore – which at that time came up as far as the current Kirk Green. Rognvald's extravagant construction scheme soon ran short of money, but he agreed to his father's suggestion to restore the rights of tenure to Orkney's "ødallers" (those who own land through direct inheritance) in return for a cash payment, and the success of the scheme ensured that the building work continued unhindered.

The *Orkneyinga Saga* tells us in five chapters about Earl Rognvald's impulsive pilgrimage to the Holy Land at the suggestion of his distant relative, Eindridi Ungi. It seems that the motivation for undertaking this big scale expedition was one of prestige, rather than religious belief. The earl, with Bishop William (promoter of the cult of St Magnus) and other high-born companions, set out in fifteen ships from Orkney in the late summer of 1151. After visiting Jerusalem, the pilgrims headed

---

[108] *The Orkneyinga Saga*, Chapter 68

north via Constantinople, where they were received by the emperor. Afterwards, they sailed to Apulia and from there rode on horseback to Rome, eventually arriving home in Orkney for Christmas 1153. Interestingly, the account of their stay in the Holy Land is very short, and the description of the voyage is dominated by stories of fighting and feasting in the time-honoured Viking way.

Unfortunately, Earl Rognvald never saw the completion of his cathedral. Some five years after returning, in August 1158, he was attacked and murdered with his eight man company by Thorbjorn Klerk, a former friend and counsellor of Harald, who had been outlawed by Earl Rognvald for a murder committed in Kirkwall, following a series of violent incidents. The Earl's body was conveyed to Kirkwall and buried in St Magnus Cathedral. Alleged miracles happened at both his graveside and at the stone where he died. Rognvald is reputed to have been canonized in 1192 by Celestine III, but doubts exist as to the validity of his sainthood, because no existing records confirm it. In the eighteenth century, however, St Rognvald's relics were discovered in his magnificent cathedral, set into a stone pillar opposite the one that would be found in 1919 to contain the holy remains of St Magnus. His Memorial may be kept on 20th August and he is regarded as a patron of builders and Church leaders.

Prayer (adapted from the Aberdeen Breviary):

Almighty everlasting God, who have consecrated this day to the martyrdom of St Rognvald, graciously grant that we who celebrate his passion may know his protection. Through our Lord Jesus Christ. Amen

Saint Gilbert
Bishop (died 1245)

St Gilbert of Moray was the last Scotsman to be honoured as a saint in the medieval Aberdeen Breviary. He belonged to the noble family of de Moravia (Moray), being son of William of Duffus, who owned vast tracts of land in the north of Scotland.

After some time as a priest, Gilbert was appointed by King Alexander II as Archdeacon of Moray with both secular and religious authority in an area notorious for its lawlessness. The See of Caithness became vacant when Bishop Adam was murdered at Halkirk, and subsequently Gilbert was consecrated bishop as Adam's successor. The bishop's seat was then moved south to Dornoch, safer from outlaws and invaders.

Gilbert, mainly at his own expense, extended a rather poor and insignificant church at Dornoch dedicated to St Finbarr, a 6th century Irish missionary saint. It is said that Gilbert considered it a privilege to help with his own hands in the building work and he personally oversaw the manufacture of the glass for the cathedral windows at the Sideray glass works that he founded especially for the task.

The main cathedral reflected a beautiful English-style structure, with aisles, transepts, central tower and spire. When it was completed, Gilbert then formed a Chapter, as there were as yet no canons. "He followed the model of Lincoln Cathedral and established the rite of that church in the ceremonial of the services. The dignitaries and canons were ten in number, and there were also sufficient vicars choral, or minor ecclesiastics, to enable the sacred offices to be celebrated with becoming solemnity."[109]

It has been suggested that Gilbert was associated with St Duthac of Tain and that he contributed to the latter's cult status in the pre-Reformation era. During Gilbert's episcopacy, he was renowned for his generosity and charity, providing several

---

[109] Barrett, *Calendar*, p. 58

hospices for the poor. He also had a reputation as a virtuous administrator and fine preacher, with his ascetic private life being an inspiration to all – he is reputed to have civilised Caithness.

Gilbert reputedly worked many miracles during his life and among them is recorded the restoration of a dumb man's speech by means of prayer and the sign of the cross; on another occasion when his enemies attempted to burn his books, they miraculously survived untouched.

When Gilbert died he was laid to rest in his cathedral, and a century later it was dedicated to him. Dom Michael Barrett, writing in the early 20th century, states that *"no trace of Saint Gilbert's resting-place remains except a portion of a broken statue which probably formed part of it... Gilbert's relics were greatly honoured in Catholic ages"*[110].

As the Aberdeen Breviary antiphon for St Gilbert says: *"Gilbert taught the pattern of charity to all; he shone forth then with miracles of divine power, and gave away everything he had in works of piety."*[111] His outstanding example as a spiritual and secular leader, his charitable benevolence and the application of his talents to the difficulties of his time, offer a fine model for both clergy and laity in our era.

St Gilbert's feast is on 1st April and may be celebrated in the Diocese of Aberdeen as an Optional Memorial.

Prayer (from the Aberdeen Diocesan Calendar):

Lord our God,
you charged Saint Gilbert with burning zeal
for the honour of your house.
With his merits interceding for us,
heal our weakness of body and soul and lead us to the place
where your glory dwells.
Through Christ our Lord. Amen.

---

[110] Barrett, *Calendar*, p. 59
[111] Macquarrie, *Legends*, p.99.

Saint John Ogilvie
Priest and Martyr, 1579-1615

John Ogilvie was born in 1579 on Ogilvie lands at the perimeter of the town of Keith, Banffshire. The son of Walter, baron of Drumna-Keith, whose father, James, had been Treasurer to Mary Queen of Scots, his family were "well-connected" Calvinist nobles whose Clan pedigree was deeply rooted in the Scottish Catholic tradition stretching back to William, King of Scots, and Queen Margaret (later acclaimed a saint).

In 1592 his father James sent his son abroad as a youth to mainland Europe to learn and absorb the benefits of French Calvinism. Mainland Europe was a hotbed of religious controversies which the young John soon encountered in his travels through France, Germany and Italy. On return to France, a period of prayer, meditation and spiritual guidance ensued with the help of Fr Cornelius van den Steen, known also as Cornelius a Lapide. John was subsequently received into the Catholic Church at the Scots College in Louvain/Douai (which is now in Belgium).

Financial difficulties at the Scots College resulted in the dispersal of some students, and in 1598 John with the assistance of a Papal bursary, re-located to the Jesuit College at Olmutz in Bohemia. After more study and prayer, he began his novitiate with the Society of Jesus on 5th November 1599 at Brunn in Bohemia-Moravia (Czech Republic), and later in Graz, Austria. From this time onwards, he was educated in science and the liberal arts, and underwent a rigorous spiritual and human formation, taking his vows as a member of the Society in 1601. He remained there until 1606, studying philosophy and teaching grammar in the lower school before a further teaching period in Vienna. He returned to Olmutz for more studies prior to his ordination at Paris in 1610, before relocation to Rouen.

During this period, John heard about the plight and extreme difficulties of Catholics in his homeland, resulting in the conviction that his future priestly mission was to be at the service of Scottish Catholics. It took some three years of repeated pleading with his superiors, during which time he was refused twice, before he was permitted to return to Scotland. John was fully aware of the many dangers that his "clandestine" mission would face in and around Edinburgh, Glasgow and Renfrew.

His activities soon attracted unwelcome attention. The former presbyterian, Archbishop Spottiswoode, was at this time enforcing the religious policies of King James VI/I, and it was not long before information was passed to the authorities by a "Roman Catholic convert" concerning Fr Ogilvie's missionary activities and celebration of the Sacraments in their midst. Swiftly arrested and put in jail, John was tortured, using the method of "the boot", together with sleep deprivation and starvation in an unsuccessful attempt to break down his resistance and obtain a full confession of his "crimes". Consistently maintaining his loyalty to the king in temporal matters, he refused, even at the insistence of King James himself, to substitute crown for Pope in spiritual matters, while at the same time keeping strict silence concerning the names and whereabouts of other Catholics in Scotland.

Fr John was tried for treason at the Tolbooth, Glasgow Cross, on 10th March 1615. In response to the charges, he affirmed that he would "die in defence of the King's civil authority, but he could not obey him on spiritual matters". Within two hours, the jury found him guilty, and condemned him to death that afternoon by hanging and then quartering.

He spent three hours in prayer before the sheriff came to escort him to the place of his public execution. Holding his rosary, John mounted the scaffold and prayed briefly as the hangman tied his hands, led him up the ladder and pushed him off. John did not die instantly, so the hangman pulled his legs downwards to end his ordeal. Some discontented onlookers whispered against the injustice of the trial and execution, and instead of the body being quartered, it was hastily removed for secret burial in a criminal's plot on the outskirts of Glasgow.

Revered by the Jesuit Society and throughout the Church, the martyred John Ogilvie became a *cause célèbre* throughout Europe.

Finally, in 1929, the Church declared him "Blessed". In October 1975, after five years of intensive medical investigations, and checking of all medical records and examinations by the Church in Scotland and in Rome, it was officially confirmed that there was no natural explanation for the recovery from terminal illness for Mr John Fagan, member of a parish dedicated to Blessed John Ogilvie in Glasgow's Easterhouse area, and the Congregation of the Causes of Saints in Rome accepted that a miracle had taken place. It was in May, 1976, that approval came for the Blessed John Ogilvie to be declared Scotland's first post-reformation Saint and martyr. The prayerful petitions offered by thousands of dedicated Scots, including this writer, for John's canonization, were answered, and his feast is celebrated on 10th March.

The National Shrine of St John Ogilvie is in the Jesuit Church of St Aloysius in Glasgow but there is also a shrine in St Thomas' in Keith which is well worth a visit. In 2015, on 4th July, to celebrate the 400th anniversary of his martyrdom, the National Pilgrimage was held in Keith where, despite the unseasonably inclement weather, over one thousand pilgrims from all over Scotland attended an open air Mass.

Prayer (from the Revised Daily Missal):

Almighty everlasting God, who made your Martyr St John Ogilvie
an invincible defender of the Catholic Faith,
grant, through his intercession,
that each day we may increase in faith, hope and charity.
Through our Lord Jesus Christ, your Son. Amen.

Saint Mary of the Cross MacKillop
Patron of Australia 1842–1909

It may seem somewhat strange to include Mary MacKillop in a compilation of almost exclusively pre-Reformation saints whose mission was exercised in an area of Scotland that is now part of the Roman Catholic Diocese of Aberdeen. Although Mary is an Australian 20th century saint, her parents migrated to Australia from Roy Bridge and Fort William in the modern diocese of Argyll and the Isles, and we learn that there are also several connections with the Diocese of Aberdeen. Mary's father Alexander, as a young man, aspired to a priestly vocation and was educated for several years at St Mary's College, Blairs, Aberdeenshire (then in Kincardineshire), which from 1829 was the national seminary for Scotland. On completion of his time at Blairs, he continued his priestly studies and training at the Scots College in Rome, but decided not to pursue a clerical vocation and left the college before ordination. Alexander arrived in Australia in 1838, met Mary's mother, Flora, in Melbourne in 1840, and married her that same year. Mary was the eldest of eight children, and although the family were never wealthy, she was educated both at home and at private schools. In 1860, Mary obtained the position of governess and included local poor children in her education class, and two years later, she moved to Portland, Victoria, and opened her own boarding school.

In 1866, at the invitation of Fr Woods who was seriously concerned about the lack of education in the State of South Australia, Mary and her two sisters moved to Penola and opened a Catholic school. Around this time, Mary made a declaration of her dedication to God and began wearing black, and by 1867 became the first sister and mother superior of the newly formed community of the Sisters of Saint Joseph of the Sacred Heart, taking the religious name Sister Mary of the Cross. She then moved to Adelaide to found a convent and a new school at the request of the local bishop. Fr Woods and Mary developed a rule for the new religious community, with an emphasis on poverty, a dependence on divine providence, no ownership of personal belongings, a firm faith that God would provide and a willingness to go where needed.

The local Bishop approved the rule, and by late 1867 an additional ten religious sisters had joined the community, and by 1871, the Congregation had grown to 130 sisters who were working in more than 40 schools and charitable institutions across the states of South Australia and Queensland.

Sr Mary travelled to Rome in 1873 to seek formal approval from Pope Pius IX for the religious congregation and its Rule. The authorities in Rome, however, granted only a temporary approval whilst making some changes to the Rule, including a declaration that the Superior General and her council were the authorities in charge of the community. This trial basis lasted until Sr Mary returned to Australia in January 1875, after an absence of nearly two years, bringing with her the official approval from Rome for her sisters and the work they did, materials for her school and books for the convent library. It was during this interim period 1873-1874 that Sr Mary travelled widely in Europe to observe educational methods, arriving in Scotland in October 1873.

During her visit to Scotland, she wrote several letters to her congregation, and stories of her travels were compiled in a recent book by Sr Patricia Keane, Co-ordinatior of the Mary MacKillop Centre in Adelaide.[112] We know that Mary began her journey into the present Diocese of Aberdeen by sailing on a steamer from Fort William along the Caledonian Canal en route to visit her cousin, Dean Coll MacDonald, who was based at Fort Augustus. During this short boat trip, Mary encountered Fr Alexander Forbes whom she had met two months previously whilst on pilgrimage to Paray-le-Monial in France. They had a long happy conversation upon the wonderful ways of Providence that resulted in Forbes seeing to

---

[112] Patricia M. Keane RSJ, *Blessed Mary MacKillop. The Scottish Connection. Her Journey through Scotland October 1873-January 1874* (N.S.W. Australia: Sisters of St Joseph of the Sacred Heart 2007)

Mary's needs and expenses. On learning of her onward itinerary he invited her to visit his parish at Nairn to tell him more about her Congregation's mission in Australia.

Mary disembarked at Fort Augustus and stayed in the parish for three days, though, unfortunately, no record exists of her activity during this time. From Keane's book, we learn that Mary would have probably travelled around this rural parish area before being accompanied by Fr MacDonald to meet Fr Alexander Bissett, the neighbouring parish priest at Stratherrick, which is located on the southern bank of Loch Ness, some ten miles by road from Fort Augustus. From her letter to the Sisters, it is evident that Mary enjoyed her visit and the company of Fr Bissett: "Father Coll left me under the care of the best and nicest priest that I had yet met since I left Rome – the one, perhaps, who of all others gave my soul the help and encouragement so sadly needed. I need not say that I left Stratherrick with regret." Rather than Mary returning south to Fort Augustus, it is probable that Fr Bissett accompanied Mary to the nearby ferry stop Foyers, where she could continue her journey northwards to Inverness.[113]

Frs MacDonald and Bissett had written letters of introduction on behalf of Mary, that were sent to Fr William Dawson, the parish priest of St Mary's, Inverness, who welcomed Mary when the ferry arrived at Inverness. Dawson was reputed to be "of a kindly and amiable disposition, who won the respect of Catholic and Protestant alike".

Overlooking the banks of the River Ness and adjacent to the parish church, stands the convent building, occupied at that time by Franciscan Sisters, where Mary spent two days with the community in what were somewhat cramped and uncomfortable conditions. Mary made no mention of this when she commented in a letter that "it was so nice to feel myself once more inside a convent and away from the incessant chatter of the world." In the same letter, Mary mentions her experiences with the clergy, writing "The priests in Scotland are so good and so highly

---

[113] Keane, *Scottish Connection*, p.23

respected. In the parts where I have been, they are much respected even by the Ministers of other denominations with whom they keep on most friendly terms and are always allowed the lead in most things."[114]

After her short stay in Inverness, Mary travelled by train to Nairn thanks to the generosity of Fr Dawson who had purchased a first class ticket for her journey, and instructed a friend to see to her comfort. Mary made her way to meet Fr Forbes whom she had previously met on the Great Pilgrimage and Caledonian ferry. She spent "a happy day and night" at his house, commenting that his church was "so sweetly clean and all so perfect ... whilst in their houses and manner of living, they (the clergy) were so poor and simple but so clean."[115]

On the 16th December, Sr Mary set out on the journey by train to Aberdeen, again travelling first class, thanks to the generosity of Fr Forbes. Unfortunately, she became stranded at Keith Junction and had to spend the night in the waiting room at Keith station before her onward journey the following morning at 6:00am. Arriving at Aberdeen around 9.00am on the 17th December, Mary enjoyed the hospitality of the Franciscan sisters at their convent in the city, and took an opportunity to visit some nuns of another community who had the care of a large orphanage in the city. This must surely have been the newly founded accommodation for the elderly poor and destitute and deserted children established by the Sisters of Nazareth at Clarence Street (now Claremont Street), Aberdeen. Construction of the central section had begun in 1871 and the building was finally opened as "Nazareth House" in 1877.

Before leaving for Edinburgh on 18th December, Mary met with Bishop John MacDonald who had been consecrated vicar apostolic for the Northern District at Aberdeen in 1869. This concluded the saint's visit to the present-day Diocese of Aberdeen and she spent a further month in Edinburgh before her eventual return to Australia in January 1875.

---

[114] Keane, *Scottish Connection*, p.24
[115] Keane, *Scottish Connection*, p.25

St Mary of the Cross MacKillop died on 8 August 1909 in the Josephite convent in North Sydney. Cardinal Moran, the Archbishop of Sydney, said "I consider this day to have assisted at the deathbed of a Saint." The process for her canonization was begun in 1925, with Mary being beatified in 1995 by Pope John Paul II, with her canonization announced by Pope Benedict XVI on 19 February 2010 and subsequently taking place on 17 October 2010. This made her the first Australian saint recognised by the Catholic Church. She holds a special place for the Church in Scotland, particularly at Roy Bridge where there is a shrine at St Margaret's church, and at St Mary's church in Inverness where in 2013 a new stained glass window was unveiled in her memory. Her feast day is on August 8th.

Prayer (from the Revised Australian Missal):

O God, source of all goodness,
who have shown us in Saint Mary
a woman of faith living by the power of the Cross,
teach us, we pray, by her example
to live the gospel in changing times
and to respect and defend
the human dignity of all in our land.
Through our Lord.

(or for Mass at Places of Pilgrimage associated with her):

O God, who called Saint Mary MacKillop
to seek your Kingdom in this world
through the pursuit of perfect charity,
grant us through her intercession
to advance with joyful spirit
along the way of love.
Through our Lord Jesus Christ. Amen.

Calendar of Saints

January 8	St Nathalan*[116]
February 18	St Colmán*
March 1	St Marnan/Marnock
March 8	St Duthac*
March 10	St John Ogilvie
March 10	St Kessog
March 16	St Boniface/Curitan
March 30	St Olaf
April 1	St Gilbert*
April 16	St Magnus*
April 17	St Donnan
April 21	St Maelrubha*
May 3	St Fumac
May 16	St Brandon/Brendan*
June 9	St Columba
June 12	St Ternan
June 25	St Moluag*
July 8	St Sunniva
July 12	St Drostan*
July 18 (Dec. 23)	The Nine Maidens/St Mayoc
August 8	St Mary MacKillop
August 20	St Rognvald
August 24	St Erchard
August 30	St Fiacre/Fittick
September 16	St Ninian*
September 23	St Adomnán*
October 8	St Triduana
October 13	St Comgan*
October 30	St Talorcan*
November 8	St Gartnait/Gerardine*
November 13	St Machar*
November 13	St Devenick
November 14	St Medan
November 18	St Fergus*
December 18	St Manir

---

[116] Feasts of Saints marked * were restored to the Calendar by Leo XIII in 1898.

Bibliography

A View of the Diocese of Aberdeen (Aberdeen: Spalding Club 1843)

Aberdeen Diocesan Calendar (1978; rev. 2011)

Adomnán, *Life of St Columba*
http://www.fordham.edu/halsall/basis/columba-e.asp

Anderson, A.O, & M.O. (eds), Adomnán of Iona, Life of Saint Columba (London, 1995)

Anderson, Joseph ed. *Orkneyinga Saga* (Orkney: Edmonston & Douglas 1873: reprint 1973

Attwater, D. *Dictionary of Saints* (London: Penguin 1983)

Barrett, M., *A Calendar of Scottish Saints* (Fort Augustus: Abbey Press, 1919)

Bede, *Ecclesiastical History of the English People,* rev. edn (London: Penguin, 1990)

Black, A.B., *The Pictish Nation. Its People and Its Church* (Edinburgh: T. N. Foulis, 1918)

Boece, Hector, *Scotorum Historia*, trans. John Bellenden , (vol. ii. ed. 1821

Boyle, A., *Saint Ninian: Some Outstanding Problems* (Innes Review 19, 1968, pp. 57-70)

Boyle, A. "Notes on Scottish Saints" (Innes Review 32, Issue 2 1981)

Brooke, D., *Wild Men and Holy Places* (Edinburgh: Canongate Press, 1994)

Cameron, N.M., Wright, D.F., Lachman D. C., Meek D. E., et al, *Dictionary of Scottish Church History & Theology* (Edinburgh: T&T Clark, 1993)

Cant, Roger G., "The Church in Orkney and Shetland and its relations with Norway and Scotland in the Middle Ages", in *Northern Scotland*, Volume 1 (1st Series, Issue 1), p. 1-18.

Carver, M., *Portmahomack. Monastery of the Picts* (Edinburgh: Edinburgh University Press, 2008)

Clancy, T.O.," The Real Saint Ninian" (Edinburgh U. P.: Innes Review vol. 52, no. 1, Spring 2001)

Cowper, S., "St Triduana in Caithness",
http://www.caithness.org/atoz/churches/ballachly/index.htm

Crammond, W., *Annals of Banff* (Aberdeen: Milne & Hutchison, 1891)

Cross, F.L & Livingstone, E.A. (eds), *The Oxford Dictionary of the Christian Church*, 3rd edn. (Oxford: Oxford University Press, 1997)

Donaldson, C., *Martin of Tours. The Shaping of Celtic Spirituality* (Norwich: Canterbury, 1997)

Dowden, J., *The Celtic Church in Scotland* (London: SPCK, 1894)

Farmer, D. H., *The Oxford Dictionary of Saints* (Oxford: University Press)

Forbes, A.P., *Kalendars of Scottish Saints* (Edinburgh: 1842)

Hommedal, Alf Tore & Ommundsen, Åslaug, Saint Sunniva and the Holy Shrine (Bryggens Museum, 2011)

Jackson, K., *The Gaelic Notes in the Book of Deer* (Cambridge: Cambridge University Press, 2008)

Keane, Patricia M. RSJ, Blessed Mary MacKillop. *The Scottish Connection. Her Journey through Scotland October 1873-January 1874* (N.S.W. Australia: Sisters of St Joseph of the Sacred Heart 2007)

Knight, G.A.F., *Archaeological light on the Early Christianity of Scotland* (Edinburgh University Press 1933)

Macdonald, James ed., *The Place-Names of West Aberdeenshire* (Aberdeen: Spalding Club 1899)

J. M. Mackinlay *Ancient Church Dedications in Scotland*, (Edinburgh: Douglas 1914)

J. F.Mackinlay, J. F., *Traces of the Cultus of the Nine Maidens* (Aberdeen: Proceedings of the Society of Antiquaries of Scotland, 1906)

McLeod, K.(ed). *Songs of the Hebrides, and other Celtic songs from the Highlands of Scotland* (London: Boosey & Co, 1909. Vol.2.

Macquarrie, A., *Legends of Scottish Saints* (Dublin: 4 Courts Press, 2012)

Macquarrie, A., *The Saints of Scotland* (Edinburgh: John Donald, 1997)

MacQueen, J., *Saint Nynia,* (Edinburgh: John Donald, 2005)

McLeod, N. K., *Churches of Buchan* (Aberdeen: Milne, 1899)

Meek, D. E., *The Quest for Celtic Christianity,* 2010 edn, (Edinburgh: Handel Press, 2010)

Moran, P. F., *Irish Saints in Great Britain* (Dublin: Gill, 1879)

Mundals, Else, trans."The Legend of Sunniva", in *Flateyjarbók* (*Legender frå mellomalderen*, 1995)

Munro, Alistair, Article in *Scotsman* Newspaper (14 August 2012)

Pinkerton, John, *Vitae sanctorum scotiae* (1789)

Pratt, J.B., *Buchan* (Turriff, Scotland: Heritage Press 1981)

Ritson, J., *Annals of Caledonia,* Vols. 1 & 2 (Edinburgh: Ballantyne, 1828)

Robbie, William, *Aberdeen: Its Traditions and History* (Aberdeen: D. Wyllie 1893)

Robertson, J. ed., *Illustrations of the Topography and Antiquities of the Shires of Aberdeen and Banff*, vol. ii (Aberdeen: Spalding Club, 1843)

Scott, A.B., *The Pictish Nation* (Edinburgh: T. N. Foulis, 1918)

Scott, A. B., *Transactions of the Scottish Ecclesiological Society*, vol i, part iii. (Aberdeen. 1906)

Severin, T., *The Brendan Voyage* (London: Gill & Macmillan, 2005)

Skene, W. F., *Celtic Scotland. A History of Ancient Alban*, (Edinburgh: David Douglas, 1886)

Skene, W. F., *Chronicles of the Picts, Chronicles of the Scots* (Edinburgh: 1867)

Smith, Ron, *St. John Ogilvie. The story of Scotland's only post-reformation saint* (Keith: Ron Smith 2015); *Our Lady of Aberdeen* (Keith, 2013); *Fumac the Good* (Keith, 2007)

Towill, E.S., *The Saints of Scotland* (Edinburgh: St Andrew Press, 1983)

103

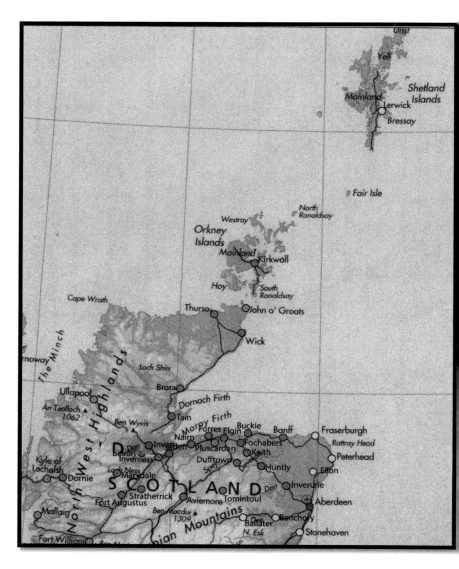

Catholic Diocese of Aberdeen showing Mass Centres